Law, Governance and Technology Series

Volume 63

The *Law, Governance and Technology Series* is intended to attract manuscripts arising from an interdisciplinary approach in law, artificial intelligence and information technologies. The idea is to bridge the gap between research in IT law and IT-applications for lawyers developing a unifying techno-legal perspective. The series will welcome proposals that have a fairly specific focus on problems or projects that will lead to innovative research charting the course for new interdisciplinary developments in law, legal theory, and law and society research as well as in computer technologies, artificial intelligence and cognitive sciences. In broad strokes, manuscripts for this series may be mainly located in the fields of the Internet law (data protection, intellectual property, Internet rights, etc.), Computational models of the legal contents and legal reasoning, Legal Information Retrieval, Electronic Data Discovery, Collaborative Tools (e.g. Online Dispute Resolution platforms), Metadata and XML Technologies (for Semantic Web Services), Technologies in Courtrooms and Judicial Offices (E-Court), Technologies for Governments and Administrations (E-Government), Legal Multimedia, and Legal Electronic Institutions (Multi-Agent Systems and Artificial Societies).

Kasper Drazewski

Copyright as a Constraint on Creating Technological Value

Springer

Kasper Drazewski
BEUC - The European Consumer Organisation
Brussels, Belgium

ISSN 2352-1902 ISSN 2352-1910 (electronic)
Law, Governance and Technology Series
ISBN 978-3-031-51275-9 ISBN 978-3-031-51276-6 (eBook)
https://doi.org/10.1007/978-3-031-51276-6

This work was supported by European University Institute
The present book is based on and represents the Author's own academic research and findings, and any opinions and observations expressed herein are his own. In no way can this book be understood to represent, summarise or paraphrase the views or positions of the European University Institute or BEUC—The European Consumer Organisation.

This Springer imprint is published by the registered company Springer Nature Switzerland AG
The registered company address is: Gewerbestrasse 11, 6330 Cham, Switzerland

Paper in this product is recyclable.

Contents

Chapter 1
Introduction: Legislating for the Digital Reality: A Moving Target

> Researchers want to use every technological tool available, and they want to develop new ones. However, the law can block valuable new technologies, like text and data mining, simply because those technologies were not imagined when the law was formed.–Hargreaves (2011)

1.1 The Divide

In this day and age, it has become difficult to speak of technical development without repeating any of the circulating clichés. It has become customary to mention it in the context of recent years as being accelerated, unprecedented, even racing; the same goes for buzz words such as the 'digital reality', 'digital age', 'digital revolution', 'age of communication', etc. I am certainly just as guilty of their use in this work for they are more than just empty slogans; if anything, I see them as an attempt at reasoning with, and defining the nature and dynamics of a relatively new period in human history brought about by the penetration of our lives by computing devices and high-speed connectivity. Whether the technological shift can indeed be said to represent actual progress is in itself a matter for debate; it could be said, to paraphrase Michael Crichton, with all the vacuum cleaners, washer-dryers, trash compactors it still takes just as long to clean the house as it did in the 1930s.[1] Be it or not progress indeed, some three decades ago humanity entered a new era, one that

[1] The reference is by the literary portrayal of the mathematician Ian Malcolm in the original Jurassic Park book (1990); Crichton used this character to offer his broad critique of what he saw as humanity glorifying technology and racing towards mindless scientism without spending the time to learn about itself. From the current perspective, seeing how much effort it sometimes takes to properly maintain an autonomous vacuum cleaner and get it to dock, sync and update properly, the observation seems to have stood the test of time. For the original discussion, see Crichton (1990).

K. Drazewski, *Copyright as a Constraint on Creating Technological Value*, Law, Governance and Technology Series 63,
https://doi.org/10.1007/978-3-031-51276-6_1

would certainly pose a challenge to legislation as we know it, the full extent of which we may not yet fully realize.

Looking up from the current debates on regulating AI systems or safeguarding individual agency in the digital sphere, it is notable how fast-progressing technological change will always find a way to put existing laws to a test. This is particularly true of copyright: its inherent protection against unauthorized copying is never a strict and ultimate prohibition; curtailed by the underlying necessity for balancing incentives,[2] it is applicable in predefined circumstances and safeguarded by a number of conditions. Whenever new technology that involves or allows copying hits the mass market,[3] a type of paradigm shift occurs; the world will never be the same again. Even if the new technological solution is later found to be infringing upon other parties' rights and, in the most extreme scenario, banished off the market,[4] the door has already been opened and the benefits already demonstrated; eventually, the void will be filled by another device or piece of software. This new reality following the launch of a new technology will see a number of questions arise: do all these conditions still apply – and more importantly, how? At times it will force us to question what it now means to copy; and when copying is, or should be, constituting an infringement. These questions have been asked by lawyers and rightsholders at least since the Xerox machine had become widely available. By what I feel would be the grand majority of users, they have also been utterly and completely ignored. In his 2003 paper, Christopher Jensen referenced the 1967 GSA Copying Equipment Handbook in saying that copying laws are in the same category as speeding laws: people forget that they are there.[5] In the 1980s, copying a mixtape from a friend who had recorded it off the radio never felt like a walk on the wild side of copyright; the same was true of burning audio CDs once personal CD-R burners became available, or swapping music files with people eager to share their collections in peer-to-peer networks.[6]

The dynamics of the divide between technology and the law may be seen as worrying. With the increasing availability of high-speed, multi-core processing power coupled with increased portability of devices along with the ever-increasing

---

[2] A commonly repeated theme is that one of the goals of copyright, and specifically copyright exceptions is (here in the words of the 2019 Copyright Directive) to 'achieve a fair balance between the rights and interests of authors and other rightholders, on the one hand, and of users on the other' (Directive (EU) 2019/790, Recital 6). For a discussion on how this balancing act is put to the test by innovation, see Chap. 6.

[3] Amongst the myriad of comments sparked by the court battle in *Oracle v. Google*, it has been noted that, assuming a strict interpretation, every Android user is culpable of unauthorized copying as every smartphone makes copies of its system files upon every boot; this was also true of the Java APIs of which Oracle claimed ownership. The case is broadly discussed in Chap. 4.

[4] See e.g., the case of the Brennan digital jukebox which allowed archiving one's library of CDs, discussed in Chap. 2. The Brennan device lost the battle but users simply turned elsewhere for ripping their audio CDs, usually using their personal computers and freely available software.

[5] See Jensen (2003).

[6] For a more detailed description of the broadening divide between the users and the expectations of the recording industry see Witt (2015).

speeds of network connections, it has been noted that the increasing rapidity of advances in information technologies have pushed the gap between the norms of copyright law and the economic reality almost to a breaking point.[7] While the gap in itself has been igniting the interest of scholars for some time now (e.g. in the area of clashes with the recording and film industries due to unauthorized downloading of multimedia content) and it has been argued that traditional means of resolving this conflict may only lead to its escalation,[8] the digital world of today has seen the arrival of a generation of information technology users who consume, digest, modify and create works of intellect while being, in the simplest of terms, accustomed to being able to get away with quite a lot. This has been named a social fact of the Internet: once handed new attractive tools, the general public will gladly use them to its leisure, without too much concern over the implication on the rights of other parties.[9] That is where the law will attempt to step in, to ensure that the interests of rightsholders are adequately protected while keeping a delicate balance to ensure that the incentives for the creation of new works remain in the system, by avoiding overprotection that would stifle innovation. This need to tread lightly is particularly visible in the world of software, where the differentiation between unprotectable idea and protected expression and debate over functional aspects of software have been the re-emerging issues of court battles since the early 1990s.[10] However, as the digital world races forward, we see the divide has more faces than just that of reuse of code: with the court battles waged over displaying thumbnail pictures in search results, the years-long war fought between book publishers and Google working to become the world's largest index and text search provider for printed books, we have seen a clash of the baseline understanding of copyright protection with that offered by a bold and aggressive innovator who claimed it was, at the end of the day, not hurting anyone.

1.2 More Flexibility or More Exceptions?

The Hargreaves' diagnosis which opens this discussion is but one voice in response to the inevitable question: how should one legislate for a changing environment—and whether this legislation should not embrace, at some levels, a measure of flexibility to allow is to adapt to the changing circumstances. In July 2018, the Irish *Dáil Éireann* (lower house of Parliament) passed a bill aimed at modernising

[7] Hugenholtz (2017); See also generally Hugenholtz and Senftleben (2011) and Tehranian (2007).

[8] See Jensen (2003), pp. 531–570; see also Litman (2002).

[9] Jensen (2003), p. 533, p. 537.

[10] *Computer Associates International, Inc. v. Altai, Inc.* U.S. Court of Appeals, Second Circuit (June 22, 1992) 982 F.2d 693, 23 USPQ2d 1241.

Irish copyright,[11] bringing together solutions such as a text and data mining exception for non-commercial research (a highly watered-down take on which later found its way into Directive 2019/790)[12] with an exception for education and teaching.[13] The bill was received by many commentators as a breath of fresh air, particularly in view of the turmoil surrounding the legislative process for the Directive and how solutions which could have offered a measure of flexibility to the EU copyright law were removed one after another.

As it is sometimes the case, that which is more important here did not make its way into the final bill. Referenced directly in the description of the draft (see fn. 11), the foundation for the proposed amendments had been laid in the 2013 Report of the Copyright Review Committee, prepared over the course of 2 years by the government-appointed expert group chaired by Eoin O'Dell of Trinity College in Dublin.[14] Amidst concerns of rightsholders about the Internet rendering it difficult to protect their rights, technology groups asking for more flexibility in the system and all stakeholders demanding a greater efficiency of the copyright system, the Report was commissioned to diagnose the inefficiencies of modern copyright law and offer solutions to improve the situation of each of the interest groups. The conclusions were multifaceted, to say the least: although the attention of the press had focused largely on the notion to set up a Copyright Council, copyright tracks in courts, a teaching exception and protection of EXIF data in photographs, there was one change that caught the attention of copyright lawyers: the proposed introduction of a precisely defined copyright exception for innovation.

Attempting to strike a balance between the incentives to creators provided by the perspective of their works receiving due protection and those to innovators seeking

[11] 'An Act to amend the Copyright and Related Rights Act 2000 to take account of certain recommendations for amendments to that Act contained in the Report of the Copyright Review Committee entitled 'Modernising Copyright' published by that Committee in October 2013 and also to take account of certain exceptions to copyright permitted by Directive 2001/29/EC of the European Parliament and of the Council of 22 May 2001 on the harmonisation of certain aspects of copyright and related rights in the information society; to make certain other amendments to that Act, including amendments in relation to references in that Act to education and fines; to make consequential amendments to the Courts of Justice Act 1924, the Courts (Supplemental Provisions) Act 1961, the Patents Act 1992, the Trade Marks Act 1996 and the Industrial Designs Act 2001; to make a certain amendment to the Patents Act 1992; to make amendments to the Patents Act 1992 and the Trade Marks Act 1996 in relation to references in those Acts to courts and fines; and to provide for related matters', as passed by Dáil Éireann, 5th July, 2018.

[12] Directive (EU) 2019/790 establishes a copyright exception for text and data mining limited to scientific research by research organisations and cultural heritage institutions, in so far as they already enjoy access under an open access scheme or through contractual arrangements (Article 3, Recital 14). Article 4 offers another exception allowing access to an unlimited pool of entities, although its practical utility is limited. For a discussion about the weaknesses of this approach, see Chap. 5.

[13] See the Bill of Dáil Éireann of 5th July, 2018, sections 225B.(1) and 57C.(1). The exception is conditional upon there being no licensing scheme in place that would be applicable for the use in question.

[14] See Copyright Review Committee (Ireland) (2013); see also id (2012).

leeway towards being able to build upon existing successful technological achievements, the Report took on a seemingly impossible task of defining an entirely new ontological legal category of innovation, describing it as a work that is 'substantially different' from the initial work, or constituting a 'substantial transformation' of the said work. This was coupled with the Berne Convention safeguards of not conflicting with the normal exploitation of the work and not precluding normal exploitation of the work. The detailed definition of innovation stretched across seven subsections and offered a not-unreasonable attempt at offering courts of law a statutory tool for handling future cases of new technological inventions which would to some extent be built by creative transformation of protected works.

The significantly trimmed bill indicated that the proposal for the open-ended innovation exception, as would be expected of a non-fair use jurisdiction, had gone down in flames with some of the critique revolving around the evergreen issue of incompatibility with the Berne Convention requirement of an exception being applicable in 'certain' special cases, despite this interpretation being in itself not immune to criticism.[15]

Ireland is not an isolated case where attempts have been made to reform copyright law to render it more responsive to technological change. A similar story happened earlier in Australia[16] with the government-appointed Copyright Law Review Committee[17] offering that an open-ended norm to replace the current fair-dealing solutions would offer greater flexibility in adapting to changing circumstances.[18] Despite the proposal falling through over concerns about transaction costs of the reform and compatibility with the Berne three-step test, the Australian Law Review Commission noted in 2013 that 'fair use would provide flexibility to respond to changing conditions and would assist innovation'.[19] Other examples would include the United Kingdom and the proposals laid down by the Gowers Review of Intellectual Property (2006) commissioned by the Chancellor of the Exchequer; the recommendation was for the UK to offer a reform of the Directive 2001/29/EC 'to allow for an exception for creative, transformative or derivative works, within the parameters of the Berne Three Step Test'[20] The Hargreaves Review of Intellectual Property (2011)[21] offered that the introduction of fair use would solve the greatest issue of the law being always created in retrospect and falling behind developments in technology. Similarly to Ireland, concerns were raised about the compatibility with

[15] For a detailed argument on why 'certain special cases' should not be construed to mean a *closed catalogue* of said special cases, see Hugenholtz (2017).

[16] For specific examples how attachment to circumscribed law put Australia years behind the U.S. in regard to new consumer technologies, see Makins (2015).

[17] See Copyright Law Review Committee (Australia) (1998); Part 1: Exceptions to the Exclusive Rights of Copyright Owners.

[18] The proposal was dropped over concerns of transaction costs and doubts regarding compatibility with the Berne three-step test.

[19] Australian Law Reform Commission (2013), Section 4.94.

[20] See Gowers (2006), Recommendation 11.

[21] Hargreaves (2011).

the international framework of copyright in its continental variation, most particularly the three-step test embodied in the Berne Convention.[22]

1.3 Flexibilising for Innovation: The Debate

In the European Union, the subject of flexibilising copyright has been a recurring theme for years, with the discussion on the feasibility of such a change inexorably pointing out the shortcomings of the current EU copyright framework in dealing with modern reality. With little legal headroom for transformative user-generated content (and this at the age of a majority of cultural communication shifting to social media), unlicensed use of copyrighted works in education alongside the inherent issues with accommodating the use of search engines and aggregation sites with EU law, it has been observed that not only does the current model affect progress in the sphere of culture, economy and society, but also undermines the social legitimacy of copyright law.[23]

This book seeks to identify patterns in copyright cases relating to technological innovation and, on the other hand, those of judicial reasoning when faced with new technology that puts the existing copyright system to the test. Aiming to demonstrate from a practical angle how copyright law deals with technological innovation, it brings together examples of court battles waged in the European Union and in the U.S., analysing the pathways of judicial reasoning in fringe cases and seeking to identify patterns that may hint at there being a profound convergence in that regard on both sides of the Atlantic, with the main differences resting less in the ultimate outcomes and more in the legal framework allowing judges to reach them.

Due to the nature of grassroots innovation arising among non-commercially motivated individuals, we may never see a big copyright case where the future of a technology developed in this manner would be decided. One of the points made here, however, is that this type of technological creativity should not be underestimated, despite rarely benefiting from being catered for in the law.[24] The dawn of the digital age had brought to life and been driven by networks of contributors who did not have the backing of powerful companies and multimillion innovation budgets; these were academics, nerds and enthusiasts who, in the absence of network connections, would often use the United States Postal Service and its paper envelopes that would accommodate a floppy disk to share and exchange their results. In a certain way, this work also constitutes a tribute to their efforts.

---

[22] Outside of Europe, adoption of fair use or its close resemblance has been effected in Israel, Liberia, Malaysia, the Philippines, Singapore, South Korea, Sri Lanka and Taiwan. See Band and Gerafi (2013).

[23] Hugenholtz (2017).

[24] For a discussion exploring the alleyways for integration of interests of users from a consumer law perspective, see Reyna (2020).

The subject is closely related to the theoretical debate on rules v. standards, pitting against each other the benefits arising from the clarity and predictability offered by bright-line rules, and the adaptability and flexibility that standards are deemed to offer. As famously observed by Pierre J. Schlag in 1985, this dialectic is as omnipresent in the legal discourse as it is patterned and stereotyped, with the substantive context in which it arises bearing little influence on the argumentation, which in itself suffers from 'dreary predictability' on each side.[25] In the context of technological innovation however, being a type of subject matter that typically deals with the yet unknown and undiscovered, regulation with rigid rules will always carry the risk of over- or underinclusiveness where—in the words of Lawrence Solum—it is difficult to define in advance all the circumstances which should count as exceptions to the rule.[26]

From a practical perspective, a relatable approach to exploring the theoretical aspects of the debate could draw from the convergence hypothesis offered by Frederick Schauer in 2003.[27] According to Schauer, practical application by actors entrusted with the interpretation and application of rules and standards will see their decision-making gravitate towards blurring the lines between the two and, effectively, putting an end to the distinction that underlies the debate. Examples of such behaviour—to paraphrase Schauer, refusing to accept that rules are 'infinitely precise' and standards 'infinitely vague'—are commonly found throughout the case studies discussed in this work.

A considerable law-and-economics contribution to this debate was made by Kaplow in 1992,[28] observing the higher costs of establishing (compared to later enforcement) in the case of rules, and the reverse being true for standards. However, to apply this framework to technological innovation, and the copyright dilemmas it generates, would seemingly require a prospective cost-benefit analysis involving such incalculable factors as the dominant anticipated judicial practice concerning fringe cases, social cost of the lost incentive to incumbent rightsholders, the cost and likelihood of litigation, the benefits from new technologies, but most of all, the nature, character and types of use (or re-use) of intellectual property involved in the new technological solutions which are yet to appear. In other words, a rigorous cost-benefit analysis seems not to be applicable to the subject matter discussed herein as it is not possible to anticipate the future fruit of human creation.[29] The aim of this work is thus not a quantitative analysis but rather a qualitative scrutiny of judicial practice, without striving for a clear-cut distinction between rules and standards. The

[25] Schlag (1985).

[26] Solum (2004).

[27] Schauer (2003).

[28] Kaplow (1992).

[29] As famously observed by Karl Popper: 'We cannot predict, by rational or scientific methods, the future growth of our knowledge. [...] We cannot, therefore predict the future course of human history'. See Popper (1957).

underlying ambition is to concentrate on, and draw conclusions from, existing judicial practice and the doctrinal debates emerging from case law.

The substantive focus of this work is on copyright. Despite the temptation to delve into areas which are closely related to the topics of innovation, particularly in software, the clarity of focus is prioritised here. For this reason, the presented narrative tries hard to steer clear of the tempting distractions offered by the rules for innovation of the General Data Protection Regulation and manages to escape with only a short illustrative reference to the relevant provisions of the EU's nascent AI Act where it places additional obligations on innovators. Relevant as they are, these matters must remain the subject of separate analyses.

1.4 Narrative Summary

Chapter 2 establishes a comparative framework to provide examples of how a technology-related copyright case that tests the limits of copyright protection fares under the European system, and the in the open-ended copyright reality of the United States. Beginning with a look at the history of personal audio devices allowing format shifting and creation of private copies, it shows how a home musical jukebox developed in the United Kingdom, despite its only fault being that of being capable of format-shifting Audio CDs, was pushed off the market by inflexible copyright legislation as its manufacturer could not count on a fair use defence (which, ironically, was nonetheless attempted in the proceedings that ensued). At the time of early research for Chap. 2, the analogy with the iPod that had taken the market by storm seemed an obvious one; however, today, with music being commonly streamed from online services and home music servers, it becomes clear how far ahead of its time the unfortunate device had been.

The analysis then turns to the history of court cases that surrounded the birth and early years of the Google Books project. With the potential statutory damages counted in trillions of dollars, Google had placed its bet on the fair use defence and gone all-in; a defeat would have meant not just the end of the game, but likely the end of the big gambler itself. The offered account brings forth the consecutive stages of the proceedings in the U.S. and the arguments used by both sides of the dispute, contrasted against those of the Google Books case in France and its eventual defeat due to the perfectly obvious lack of legislative headroom to give the unlicensed scanning of protected works a free pass. The Google Books court battles were chosen to be discussed here for yet another reason: years down the line, the initial fears of the project killing the market for books have all been proven unjustified. Google now offers public access to its database of millions of protected titles, scanned generally without asking consent. While the occasional concerns over its security may or may not be unfounded and the moral assessment of the project may still require a slightly flexible approach, the social, educational and market benefits of the system are now clear and widely embraced by the publishing industry.

Chapter 3 delves deeper into the mechanics of legal flexibility in the realm of copyright, analysing the wording of 'flexible' rulings to seek the underlying rationale and the tactics used to substantiate judgments. This leads to an unavoidable critique of the 'transformative use' sub-doctrine that had become all but a standard in U.S. fair use judgments, yet demonstrably sometimes used both without consideration for its meaning (e.g. where the statutory four-factor analysis would have sufficed, and the statement of the use not being 'transformative' does not necessarily match the facts of the case (*Dr Seuss v. Penguin Books*), or in circumstances which were entirely outrageous—e.g. where the unlicensed publication of an article was found to be 'transformative' given that the copyright had, in the meantime, been sold to a copyright troll company which used it for a purpose different than its publication (*Rightshaven v Jama*).

Similarly to Chap. 2, the analysis of 'flexible' judgments seeks to cover both sides of the pond. Looking into the often highly creative ways of European courts trying to deal with an inflexible legislation in innovation cases aims at offering means of comparison, but also a glimpse at similarities in the attitudes of judges, seemingly seeking to achieve the same goals of a just and fair weighing of interests, while the difference rests in the tools they are handed by the legislation. This 'ulterior motive' of judges and their responsibility will be picked up in more detail in Chap. 6; this one closes with an analysis of a famous case in the Netherlands which led up to a judgment of the CJEU where the flexible stance had been chosen in a bold way to protect the Internet from the risk of overregulation.

Chapter 4 asks the question of what it means to innovate in today's world and what necessary characteristics there are to innovation in the networked digital reality. Particular focus is offered towards the largely non-commercial ways in which networked users collaborate, often working for motivations other than those of an economic nature, as described by Yochai Benkler in his works on networked information economy.[30] These social processes are traced back to the early years of the digital revolution, the pioneer days of personal computing and the subculture that arose at the time among computer aficionados who would build upon each other's results to collaboratively create software that is still among some of the most highly regarded pieces of code today. The idealistic ethos of those pioneer years, immortalized by Richard Stallman and his Free Software Foundation established to preserve and promote collaboration and free speech in software was met with an abrupt reality check when Oracle took over the failed Sun Microsystems and decided to reap benefits from the rights to the Java programming environment, previously distributed for free to aid its proliferation as an industry standard. The $9bn case of *Oracle v. Google* that subsequently ensued saw Oracle attempting to grab a hold of a piece of Android on the premise that, in the past versions of Android, a number of programming interfaces had been reproduced in its architecture due to Google's employment of former employees of Sun. Despite being technically a clash of two industry titans, the battle of *Google v. Oracle* was much more: it has been

[30] See generally Benkler (2011); see also Benkler (2017).

commented upon as being, in fact, a confrontation of two worlds. One was that of computer nerds operating in a world constantly developing and improving upon new standards and best practices, a world where somebody proprietising a programming language or an API is unthinkable and counterproductive, and the other being simply interested in monetising a valuable asset, oblivious to the fact that it would annihilate both its market share and perspectives for future development. Indeed; Oracle admitted between the lines that it was actually a 'deep pockets' case: its interest had not been in the further evolution of Java, the APIs in question, nor building its own smartphone; all that mattered was that—in the words of Annette Hurst, lead counsel for Oracle—APIs were software and software was protected. This story, particularly in view of Google's withdrawal from its reuse of the said Java APIs in subsequent incarnations of Android, allows for the drawing of a particularly interesting parallel: software innovation, and this is particularly true of its networked variety, relies on reuse of successful solutions in the same way as evolution of living organisms relies on cumulative selection. Where one of the strands becomes disrupted and cannot be replicated further, it will die once the current generation has outlived its purpose. It has been said earlier that life will find a way: most likely it always does, eventually—just as Google rewrote the contentious bits of Android without waiting for the exonerating ruling which came as late as 2021. Still, the contentious software has thus become a different product and one that intentionally did away with the 'genetic memory' of its predecessors.

Chapter 5 places this discussion in the context of the EU policy debates about introducing copyright flexibilities alongside other means of stimulating innovation such as access rights to data in view of its increasing importance to enabling innovation in the market. The discussion opens with a look at European Commission reports dating back to the discussions surrounding the inception of today's Copyright Directive. The reasoning presented there about the need to flexibilise European copyright, favours instead reliance on the market and individual negotiations for a licencing arrangement with the rights holder. This reliance on contract as a gateway towards creative reuse of the work of others becomes a framing theme for the remainder of the discussion which offers a glance on the mechanics of the Database Directive and the weak text and data mining (TDM) exceptions of the 2019 Copyright Directive before delving into the meanders of the European Commission's reasoning that had laid the foundations for the 2022 proposal for the Regulation on Harmonised Rules on Fair Access and Use of Data, also known as the Data Act.

The Data Act is a unique policy creation in many ways. It proclaims to seek to foster innovation by creating alleyways for 'productive use' of data generated by Internet-of-Things devices like smart thermostats or connected cars. The aim of the Act as stated in the Recitals was one of fostering the development of new innovative products, stimulating innovation on aftermarkets, as well as development of entirely new services making use of data originating from products or related services. To this end, users of connected products would be given seemingly unlimited data access rights combined with the right to use such data for any lawful purpose, while benefiting from the exemption from the *sui generis* right under the Database

Directive. The only limitation is—again, seemingly—using the data to the develop a product that would affect the market for the original one. A similar limitation appeared to restrict third parties with whom users of such devices have decided to share the data generated through their operation—as long as they would develop products which are new and innovative and did not result in market substitution of the original product.

However, on closer examination a much darker picture would emerge. Clues in the fabric of the proposal seemed to suggest that the new regime to govern rights to data was intentionally devised as one close to intellectual property protection, with presupposition of exclusive rights on the part of data holders (most often device manufacturers) and the rights of users and third parties, particularly from the perspective of the declared goals of the Act, this being enabling innovation and fostering competition in the market—being severely curtailed. With regulatory solutions like a broad discretion for data holders to keep physical control over data, to monitor any interactions of users or third parties with it, then to simply deny access requests they find excessive or unfounded, to ultimately defaulting to contract as the basis of the relationships envisaged under the Act, the Commission's finalized proposal ultimately reads like a elaborate initiative aiming at creating quasi-property rights in data to strengthen the position of data holders versus any other entities who might wish to benefit from this data—including users who generated it in the first place and the third parties they might wish to share it with.

The reliance on contract as the major policy tool also means that, similarly as in regard to straightforward licencing of intellectual property, the only path for a would-be innovator would be to rely on negotiating with rights holders—which, as the chapter demonstrates, is counterproductive in projects based on spontaneous cumulative creativity.

Chapter 6 offers an attempt to characterise the dynamic between a court of law and a case where a new technological solution that has stumbled upon inflexible legislation; one that could be dubbed a legislative choke point. It asks the question whether such 'choke points' and the risks they pose differ depending on whether the copyright challenges faced by innovators are different for the big market players and the smallest ones; seemingly, the answer is largely in the negative.

The discussion then transitions towards addressing the big question: the underlying teleological rationale being the real point of convergence of judges in the U.S. and those in Europe. While it is perhaps no wonder in the United States, seeing as how the entire premise of U.S. copyright is largely utilitarian and aims to serve the ultimate goals of progress of science and useful arts, it may yet come as a surprise where it is also used as a supporting argument in European copyright cases, often powered by the wording of the InfoSoc Directive and the recent rulings of the CJEU, with national courts seemingly following suit. The analysis brings forth examples of teleological language used on both sides of the Atlantic, usually as a supporting argument, and hypothesises that the developments seen on the EU side are, in fact, a sign of judicial pragmatism where the inflexible national legislation can only be overcome by venturing beyond the letter of the law. This is argued to be the ultimate indication that in infringement cases on the cutting edge of technological progress, the role of the judges is particularly profound in ensuring that statutory law—which, by its nature, is doomed to remain a few steps behind technological progress—does not terminate efforts which otherwise would have brought considerable benefits to society at large.

It is not the aim of this work to cite or attempt to overshadow the broad and lengthy discussion among scholars on the mechanics for transplanting fair use, and transformative use for that matter, onto European soil. It does, however, strive to indicate that, despite all its shortcomings which are discussed here with considerable ambition for mercilessness, the concept of transformative use—the way it was forged by Pierre Leval in his landmark paper of 1990—remains the most fitting to manage a rapidly changing area and ensure that its development is not left ungoverned but at the same time does not suffer from being subjected to unavoidably outdated legislation. Having gone this large circle through discussing the risks of the European approach, the language of the rulings, the creativity that continental judges are forced into, having looked at how the 'poor man's innovation' has laid the foundations for the digital revolution and is still around today; lastly, having looked at how judges seem to look to the spirit of the law in fringe cases on both sides of the Atlantic (also where national law does not seem to give them enough leeway to do so comfortably) the story unavoidably comes back to where it began: to the model allowing to give new technology a free pass where it reuses existing intellectual property, but does so by treating it as a raw material for creating something entirely new and valuable, with little connection or harm to the original product; in other words, where the new use is indeed transformative.

References

Australian Law Reform Commission (2013) Copyright and the Digital Economy (ALRC Report 122). Commonwealth of Australia 2013. Available at https://www.alrc.gov.au/wp-content/uploads/2019/08/final_report_alrc_122_2nd_december_2013_.pdf. Accessed 3 Sept 2023

Band J, Gerafi J (2013) Fair use/fair dealing handbook. SSRN Electronic Journal. https://doi.org/10.2139/ssrn.2333863. https://infojustice.org/wp-content/uploads/2013/03/band-and-gerafi-2013.pdf. Accessed 3 Sept 2023

Benkler Y (2011) Growth-oriented law for the networked information economy: emphasizing freedom to operate over power to appropriate. In: Litan RE (ed) Rules for growth: promoting innovation and growth through legal reform. Ewing Marion Kauffman Foundation, Kansas City, pp 313–314

Benkler Y (2017) Law, innovation, and collaboration in networked economy and society. Ann Rev Law Soc Sci 13:231–250. https://doi.org/10.1146/annurev-lawsocsci-110316-113340

Crichton M (1990) Jurassic Park. Knopf, New York

Gowers A (2006) Gowers review of intellectual property. HMSO, Norwich, England

Hargreaves I (2011) Digital Opportunity a review of Intellectual Property and Growth. Considerati, Amsterdam, available online at https://www.gov.uk/government/publications/digital-opportunity-review-of-intellectual-property-and-growth. Accessed 3 Sept 2023

Hugenholtz PB (2017) Flexible copyright: can EU author's right accommodate fair use? In: Okediji RL (ed) Copyright law in an age of limitations and exceptions. Cambridge University Press, New York, pp 275–291

Hugenholtz PB, Senftleben M (2011) Fair use in Europe: In Search of Flexibilities. SSRN Electronic Journal. https://doi.org/10.2139/ssrn.1959554

Jensen C (2003) The more things change, the more they stay the same: copyright, digital technology, and social norms. Stanford Law Rev 56(2):531–570. Retrieved from http://www.jstor.org/stable/1229614

Kaplow L (1992) Rules versus standards: an economic analysis. Duke Law J 42:557. https://doi.org/10.2307/1372840

Litman J (2002) War stories. Benjamin N. Cardozo School of Law, Yeshiva University, Jacob Burns Institute for Advanced Legal Studies, New York

Makins A (2015) Copyright and compliance when the law can't keep up: a risk management strategy for innovation in online classrooms. THETA 2015 paper, available at https://www.semanticscholar.org/paper/Copyright-and-compliance-when-the-law-can't-keep-A-Makins/0d4ffffb717601e5f17e42e56259a2d829da0802. Accessed 3 Sept 2023

Popper KR (1957) The poverty of historicism. Beacon Press, Boston

Reyna A (2020) What place for fairness in digital content contracts? An Assessment of the Interplay between EU Copyright and Consumer Law. Nomos 2020. ISBN 978-3-8487-7814-0

Schauer F (2003) The convergence of rules and standards. N.Z. Law Rev 303

Schlag PJ (1985) Rules and Standards. UCLA Law Rev 33:379, Available at https://scholar.law.colorado.edu/articles/1034. Accessed 3 Sept 2023

Solum LB (2004) Legal Theory Lexicon 026: Rules, Standards, Principles, Catalogs and Discretion, last rev August 7, 2021, available online at http://lsolum.typepad.com/legal_theory_lexicon/2004/03/legal_theory_le_3.html. Accessed 3 Sept 2023

Tehranian J (2007) Infringement Nation: Copyright Reform and the Law/Norm Gap. Utah Law Review 2007:537; Loyola-LA Legal Studies Paper No. 2007-46; U of Utah Legal Studies Paper No. 08-20. Available at SSRN: https://ssrn.com/abstract=1029151

Witt S (2015) How music got free the end of an industry, the turn of the century, and the patient-zero of piracy. Viking, New York

Chapter 2
Welcoming Digital Innovation: Why America Seems to Get It Right

2.1 Introduction: A Word on Methodology

The recent history of intellectual property cases on both sides of the Atlantic provides numerous stories on how new technological solutions and innovative technologies have put justice systems to the test. Put crudely, innovation has, at times, the bad habit of being innovative; therefore, it does not always benefit from being legislated for in advance. This 'shortcoming' appears to be more of an issue in legal systems relying on precise rules instead of flexible standards that would leave room for interpretation by courts of law. Conversely, legal systems allowing greater discretion to judges seem to be ultimately more welcoming of new digital technologies and find it easier to deal with the challenges they present from the intellectual property perspective. As a prime example, U.S. copyright law hands the judge a flexible fair use test to apply to the individual case, weighing its unique aspects, including general considerations such as the benefit to the public, and to reach a conclusion that was not necessarily foreseeable at the time of the statutory law being drafted.

This opening chapter seeks to offer a glance at a selection of cases where the continental approach to copyright law, and copyright exceptions, failed—in terms of providing a legal environment that would allow and facilitate the introduction of a technological innovation—and then to emulate (or demonstrate, where a similar case has been decided under both systems) their course under a more flexible system, based on the applicable legislation and existing similar case law. In other words, the idea is to take the same (or highly similar) input material, then to observe how it fares under two systems of copyright law, to allow drawing conclusions by means of comparison of both outputs.

To increase reliability of the comparison, the first case subjected to analysis is from the United Kingdom. Pitting it against similar cases of the United States will allow to compare results achieved in two common law jurisdictions, with the

K. Drazewski, *Copyright as a Constraint on Creating Technological Value*, Law, Governance and Technology Series 63,
https://doi.org/10.1007/978-3-031-51276-6_2

differences resting within the respective states' approach to copyright exceptions. These will be discussed in detail in the case study that follows.

Further on, the chapter will delve into a chain of cases surrounding the Google Library Project which have been decided both in the United States and on European soil and are therefore a valuable basis for comparison.[1]

2.2 How Copyright May Hurt Innovation: The Lost Case of the Brennan JB7

2.2.1 Overview

The Advertising Standards Authority (ASA) is the advertising market regulator for the United Kingdom tasked with ensuring the advertising publications in the UK comply with relevant legislation. Its activity is financed through a levy on the advertising industry and its decisions are binding upon advertisers. Appeal via the procedure of independent review may be undertaken in the event of appearance of additional evidence not previously available in the course of the investigation, or as a result of a substantial flaw in the adjudication or investigation.[2] Sanctions for non-compliance include fines imposed by the Office of Fair Trading under the provisions of the Control of Misleading Advertisements Regulations 1988.

In March 2011, the ASA investigated an advertising campaign for the Brennan JB7, a British-made digital jukebox by 3GA Ltd., representing a new generation of a compact-size home music server available at a relatively low cost. Designed as an all-in-one integrated solution for playback of CDs, ripping them onto the internal hard drive, digitalization of analog recordings and management of the music database and featuring support for wireless USB keyboards for ease of operation, the JB7 was praised for its versatility, ease of use even for the computer-illiterate and earned wide recognition, including the 2008 Hi-Fi Choice Best Buy Award. The ASA launched its investigation to verify whether the advertising incited consumers to break the law, by means of illegally copying music without permission from the copyright owner.

In the course of the proceedings, 3GA Ltd. stated they were not aware of any owners of the player being charged for, or convicted of, infringing copyright; therefore, there could be no evidence that the ad incited consumers to break the law unless a judgment was entered against a JB7 owner. 3GA also argued that the JB7 was essentially a music player, and the creation of an electronic copy was a side feature in its operation (in contrast to a cassette recorder or CD burner, which are intended specifically to produce physical copies) and had 'no independent economic

[1] Further cases showing some of the European struggles for flexibility are discussed in Chap. 3.

[2] ASA Adjudication on 3GA Ltd., Complaint 140,713. Information on the procedure and a database of ASA rulings may be found at http://asa.org.uk/.

significance'.[3] In the proceedings, 3GA stated—rather misguidedly—that this made the case fall under the fair dealing exception to UK copyright law. 3GA admitted that the JB7, similarly to a computer, could be used for illegal activity (e.g. borrowing CDs to rip them into the electronic memory of the device) but, they claimed, so could any other household item, and there was no need to include warnings in the advertising of socks that they could be used in armed robberies. In response to the inquiry of why copyright breach warnings were not included in their advertising, 3GA argued against such inclusion, stating that '*it was not possible to summarise copyright law in such a way*' and it could actually lead consumers on to *begin* committing violations with the Brennan, e.g. by ripping borrowed CDs.

The ASA found 3GA in breach of CAP Code (Edition 12) rules 1.10 (Legality) and 3.1 and 3.3 (Misleading advertising). The verdict stated that the JB7 combined the functions of a player, storage and recording device and its advertising clearly made a selling point out of its ability to copy music off CDs, vinyls and cassettes without seeking permission of the copyright owner, thus encouraging customers to do so and misleadingly implying that it was a legal and acceptable practice. 3GA was ordered to cease its advertising in its current form and ensure that future ads '*prominently state*' the unlawful nature of such use of the device.

2.2.2 The 'Fair Dealing' Defense of 3GA

3GA's line of defense demonstrates how the company attempted to push the line of unlawful activity from what was essentially making a private copy of copyrighted material by means of space-shifting, which was disallowed under UK copyright law, to making copies of material obtained without paying the copyright holder. Hence the argument meant undoubtedly to contrast this activity with the allegedly 'truly illegal' use involving ripping of borrowed CDs using either computers or Brennan devices. Either by error or as a litigation tactic, in claiming that space-shifting one's legally purchased CD fell under the fair dealing exception, 3GA confused fair dealing (a system of exceptions provided in Sections 28 and on of UK Copyright, Designs and Patents Act 1988) with fair use as present e.g. in the copyright system of the United States. Built as a catalogue of semi-open exceptions (e.g. 'fair dealing with a work for the purpose of criticism or review', '*fair dealing with a work (other than a photograph) for the purpose of reporting current events*' [Section 30], '*fair dealing with a literary, dramatic, musical or artistic work for the purposes of research for a non-commercial purpose*'[Section 29]), fair dealing provisions allow use of copyrighted works notwithstanding the subsistence of copyright and

[3] ASA Adjudication on 3GA Ltd., archived at https://web.archive.org/web/20141230180119/http://www.asa.org.uk/Rulings/Adjudications/2011/3/3GA-Ltd/TF_ADJ_50026.aspx#.VKLofA04. For a case summary, see Waelde et al. (2016) p. 164.

acts defined therein do not infringe copyright, or may be done without infringing copyright, and in some cases still require consent of the copyright holder.

It should be stressed that, although lacking a definition of the term *fair dealing* itself and therefore left semi-open within the confines of the exceptions stated in the cited provisions, the UK fair dealing exceptions do not incorporate a flexible open-ended norm to counterbalance copyright restrictions. What is provided in its stead, is a list of specific circumscribed exclusions (research and private study, criticism, review, news reporting, incidental inclusion etc.) from the protection regime. The remaining flexibility is, therefore, left within the meaning of the '*fair dealing*' quantifier as used in the cited provisions. Case law on this matter examines aspects such as the significance of intentions and motives of the user of another's copyrighted work. As an example somehow addressing the misguided conviction of 3GA Ltd. in the Brennan case, in *Pro Sieben v Carlton Television* it was stated '*this court should not* [...] *give any encouragement to the notion that all that is required is for the user to have the sincere belief, however misguided*' that their actions fell under the relevant fair dealing exception. Also, matters of public interest as may also be considered when examining the applicability of the term *fair dealing*; such was the case of *Hubbard v Vosper* [1972] 2 QB 84 where Lafayette Ronald Hubbard, the founding father of the Church of Scientology, sought an injunction restraining breach of copyright by a former cult member, Cyril Vosper. Vosper had authored a monograph on the cult, often and liberally quoting the works of Hubbard to illustrate his points, thus providing Hubbard with grounds to sue. The court observed that '*although Mr Hubbard may possess confidential information, nevertheless, Mr Vosper has a defence of public interest. These defences are such that he should be permitted to go ahead with the publication. If what he says is true, it is only right that the dangers of this cult should be exposed. We never restrain a defendant in a libel action who says he is going to justify. So in copyright action, we ought not to restrain a defendant who has a reasonable defence of fair dealing.* [...] *The reason is because the defendant, if he is right, is entitled to publish it*[...].'[4] However, it should be stressed that, under the fair dealing scheme of exceptions, such arguments as cited above may only be made in a case where the overall qualification of the case under one of the prescribed categories of exception has already been decided as possible, and what is left to verify is whether the actions of the infringing party may be considered as indeed fair. For want of an applicable category at the time of the proceedings (i.e. a private copying exception),[5] under the

[4] *Hubbard v Vosper* [1972] 1 All ER 1023.

[5] After many years of demands from numerous circles, reforms to UK copyright rules that enable private copying, parodying and general quotation of copyrighted material were finally enacted on 1st October 2014 without providing means of 'fair compensation' for musicians, composers and rightsholders. In the following year, the new regulation was placed under judicial review on request of the British Academy of Songwriters, Composers and Authors (BASCA), Musicians' Union (MU) and UK Music. On 17 July 2015 the exception was quashed with no further interest of the UK government to revive it. See Intellectual Property Office (2015).

fair dealing copyright exception scheme, 3GA's fair dealing defence applied in the Brennan case appeared doomed from the outset.

2.2.3 *Supplying Technology as Grounds for Liability of Supplier*

Another noteworthy aspect of the Brennan case is that is drew a parallel from advertising a device that could be used to commit a violation to incitement to commit such a violation. This was not the first time that a manufacturer of technological devices with copying capability found itself under scrutiny in the UK for alleged incitement to commit violations and the matter of responsibility of the supplier of copying technologies for potential infringement committed by their users has been previously the subject of proceedings. In 1988, the electronics manufacturer Amstrad was sued by CBS Songs, acting both on behalf of itself and of other actors of the recording and entertainment industry, seeking an injunction to restrain Amstrad from selling two-cassette decks allowing direct copying of recorded material, unless technological measures were implemented to ensure that the double-decks would not be used to infringe upon copyrights. Seemingly, one of the strongest points of contention was that the machine allowed 'high-speed dubbing' allegedly meant *specifically* for speeding up and facilitating creating copies of copyrighted material. Amstrad found themselves facing a flood of allegations, including authorization of infringement, encouragement to break the law by advertising, joint infringement and common law tort (incitement to commit a tort, incitement to commit a criminal offence and negligence[6]).

The case was appealed before the House of Lords. The ruling issued by Lord Templeman found that joint infringement could only occur where the defendant had intended, procured and shared a common design for the infringement to take place, whereas procurement may be effected by inducement, incitement or persuasion. Merely by offering for sale and advertising a device which could be used for lawful and unlawful copying cannot, however, be seen as such procurement as the purchaser would only make unlawful copies because he chooses to do so and irrespective to any position Amstrad may have expressed on the matter. Amstrad '*conferred on the purchaser the power to copy but did not grant or purport to grant the right to copy*'. The case also cited *C.B.S. Inc. v. Ames Records & Tapes Ltd.* (1982) to the effect that a record library which lent out records and simultaneously

[6]The negligence was to be that of an alleged duty of care, to all owners of copyright, not to cause or permit purchasers to infringe copyright or, alternatively, that Amstrad owed a duty to take care not to facilitate by the sale of their models or by their advertisement the infringement of copyright. On a side note, this particular allegation was dismissed by Lord Templeman who stated that it is always easy to draft a proposition which is tailor-made to produce the desired result and 'since *Anns v Merton London Borough Council,* every fashionable plaintiff alleges negligence' (CBS Songs Ltd. v Amstrad Consumer Electronics Plc [1988] UKHL 15 (12 May 1988)

offered blank tapes for sale at a discount did not authorise the infringement of copyright in the records: '*Any ordinary person would, I think, assume that an authorization can only come from somebody having or purporting to have authority and that an act is not authorised by somebody who merely enables or possibly assists or even encourages another to do that act, but does not purport to have any authority which he can grant to justify the doing of the act.*'

The House of Lords cleared Amstrad of all allegations and allowed it to continue to sell its device; however, it was also observed that, in situations of new challenges arising from the proliferation of new consumer technologies, the law was not providing sufficient regulation and that it was not the power of the court to remedy the situation: '*In these proceedings the court is being asked to forbid the sale to the public of all or some selected types of tape recorder or to ensure that advertisements for tape recorders shall be censored by the court on behalf of copyright owners. The court has no power to make such orders and judges are not qualified to decide whether a restraint should be placed on the manufacture of electronic equipment or on the contents of advertising.* [. . .] *Copyright law could not envisage and now cannot cope with mass-production techniques and inventions which create a vast market for the works of a copyright owner but also provide opportunities for his rights to be infringed. Parliament could place limitations on the manufacture or sale of certain types of tape recorder and could prescribe notices and warnings to be included in advertisements. Parliament might take the view that any such restraints and prescriptions would constitute an unwarrantable interference with the development of the electronic industry and be ineffective. Parliament could legalise home copying just as the copying of sound broadcasts was expressly authorised for 'private purposes.'*'

The *Amstrad* case is a shining example of a court of law recognizing the distinction between offering and advertising a technological device which may be used both in a lawful and in an unlawful manner and incitement to unlawful use of such a device. It is, however, not representative of any general line of case law as the general consensus appears to attribute blame to those who supply the tools to commit a violation. This notwithstanding, it is also notable for clearly stating the discrepancy between the legislation and the actual situation in the market: '*Millions of breaches of the law must be committed by home copiers every year. Some home copiers may break the law in ignorance, despite extensive publicity and warning notices on records, tapes and films* [. . .] *because they estimate that the chances of detection are nonexistent. Some home copiers may consider that the entertainment and recording industry already exhibit all the characteristics of undesirable monopoly - lavish expenses, extravagant earnings and exorbitant profits - and that the blank tape is the only restraint on further increases in the prices of records. Whatever the reason for home copying* [. . .] *the beat of Sergeant Pepper and the soaring sounds of the Miserere from unlawful copies are more powerful than law-abiding instincts or twinges of conscience. A law which is treated with such contempt should be amended or repealed*'.

However seemingly reasonable the line of thought demonstrated by Lord Templeman, the Amstrad case was described as controversial and going against earlier tort cases, where anyone who assisted a tort could be found liable as an accessory.[7] It also received criticism mentioning how the supplier of the technology could assume the position of the 'malicious bystander'[8] where a person throws a knife to a villain attacking someone. In such cases, the nonexistence of a common design, procurement or conspiracy between the villain and the bystander cannot be claimed to preclude liability of the knife-supplier. It has been claimed that pragmatically, one should require that actions of the accessory have a substantial impact on the infringement[9]; it should be noted that this line of thought creates a dangerous situation to **any pioneering supplier of new technology** which, among its benefits, creates a potential for committing a violation in a new and unique manner. In such situations, the **supplier's liability could always be claimed** as without their technology, there would be no technical means of committing said violation.

As demonstrated in the much more recent Brennan case, however simplified and unnecessarily orthodox in comparison to *Amstrad*, this view on the causal link between supplying and advertising technology and the commitment of infringement—even a potential one, as pointed out by 3GA—was prominent enough for potential liability to be taken into account when marketing this type of innovations in the United Kingdom.

On 1 October 2014, the Copyright and Rights in Performances (Personal Copies for Private Use) Regulations 2014 came into force, introducing the private copying exception into UK law enabling private copying, parodying and general quotation of copyrighted material, yet without providing means of 'fair compensation' for musicians, composers and rightsholders. In the following year, the new regulation was placed under judicial review on request of the British Academy of Songwriters, Composers and Authors (BASCA), Musicians' Union (MU) and UK Music. On 17 July 2015 the exception was quashed with no further interest of the UK government in reviving it.[10]

2.2.4 Brennan Under a Fair Use Test

It has been mentioned earlier that the Brennan case would have likely met a different end under a fair use regime such as that of the United States with the written law leaving deliberately room for interpretation by the courts even despite certain

---

[7] Davies (2013), p. 431.

[8] Davies (2013), loc. cit.; on the 'malicious bystander' referencing Rogers WVH (2010), pp. 21–23, fn. 30.

[9] Davies (2013), p. 432.

[10] See Intellectual Property Office (2015). The judgment is available at http://www.bailii.org/cgi-bin/markup.cgi?doc=/ew/cases/EWHC/Admin/2015/2041.html&query=EWHC+and+2041&method=boolean#disp1. Accessed 03 September 2023.

reductions in this flexibility over the past years.[11] Such reductions can be seen as a change of policy in view of the earlier unwillingness of the Congress to shut the door on the open-ended nature of copyright exceptions; as quoted by Paul Goldstein, a former staff member of a US Senate copyright subcommittee cautioned '*not to look to Congress for help if any proposed imposition of copyright liability were to disrupt entrenched consumer habits*' as copyright holders should look to federal courts, particularly the Supreme Court, for protection against the perils brought upon them by new technologies and the actions of their users.[12] This has certainly become one of the factors which contributed to making the U.S. a particularly interesting legal environment to observe as it combines reasonably modern legislation with an open-ended fair use doctrine, yet at the same time is the arena for the most ferocious court battles between manufacturers of consumer technologies and representatives of the entertainment industry, leading to creation of case law which, to a European eye, may not always seem predictable.

Such was the case of the provisions of US Code Title 17 Sec. 1008, which states that 'no action may be brought under this title alleging infringement of copyright based on the manufacture, importation, or distribution of a digital audio recording device, a digital audio recording medium, an analog recording device, or an analog recording medium, or based on the non-commercial use by a consumer of such a device or medium for making digital musical recordings or analog musical recordings.' The term recording was then assigned a highly specific meaning in *RIAA v. Diamond Multimedia*,[13] where the manufacturer of the first portable MP3 audio player was brought under scrutiny by the Recording Industry Association of America. RIAA sought an injunction against Diamond's player on grounds that the device was non-compliant with the copy-protection requirements imposed under Audio Home Recording Act of 1992. The injunction was denied by the District Court. In appeal, the 9th Appellate Court ruled that, inter alia, music files are not 'digital music recordings' as they contain 'much more' information than merely 'sounds, and material, statements, or instructions incidental to those fixed sounds' as required by Section 1001, and that computers are not 'digital audio recording devices' on the basis that 'their 'primary purpose' is not to make digital audio copied recordings'. Thus, the requirements imposed by the Home Recording Act did not apply to the device in question. Applying this qualification to the position maintained by 3GA in its ASA proceedings, i.e. that the JB7 is not a recording device as its primary function is that of playback of music and it is unable to produce physical copies,

[11] These include the Digital Millennium Copyright Act, Pub. L. No. 105-304, 112 Stat. 2860 (1998) (codified as amended in scattered sections of 17 U.S.C. (2000)); No Electronic Theft (NET) Act, Pub. L. No. 105-147, § 2(a)–(b), 111 Stat. 2678, 2678 (1997) (codified at 17 U.S.C. §§ 101, 506); Computer Software Rental Amendments Act of 1990, Pub. L. No. 101-650, §§ 801–05, 104 Stat. 5089, 5134–37 (codified at 17 U.S.C. § 109); Record Rental Amendment of 1984, Pub. L. No. 98-450, § 2, 98 Stat. 1727, 1727 (codified at 17 U.S.C. § 109) – see Litman (2007).

[12] Goldstein (2003).

[13] *Recording Industry Association of America v. Diamond Multimedia Systems, Inc.*, 180 F.3d 1072, 51 U.S.P.Q.2d (BNA) 1115 (9th Cir. 1999).

could potentially result in the exclusion of the player from the protection allowed under Section 1008. Still, a fair use defence would remain and be likely to stand in court.

Section 107 of US Copyright code creates a vastly open-ended list of exceptions which constitute fair use of copyrighted material and a non-exhaustive list of guidelines under which the fairness of a given use is to be determined. This 'fair use test' involves looking at (1) the purpose and character of the use, including whether such use is of a commercial nature or is for non-profit educational purposes; (2) the nature of the copyrighted work; (3) the amount and substantiality of the portion used in relation to the copyrighted work as a whole; and (4) the effect of the use upon the potential market for or value of the copyrighted work.

Were one to apply a fair use defence to the Brennan case as a thought experiment, it may be reasonably expected that, irrespective of whether the court would find that Section 1008 applies, the non-commercial use of legally purchased material, along with zero influence on the potential market (since the CD was already bought be the user) would allow to conclude that there is no infringement in using the device in the manner as intended and recommended by its manufacturer. As a result, no liability of the manufacturer could be discussed due to the device being primarily intended for space-shifting of already owned recordings. This would be a conclusion very similar to that of *RIAA v. Diamond Multimedia* where the Court ultimately stated that the device in question '*merely makes copies in order to render portable, or 'space-shift' those files that already reside on a user's hard drive*' and that '*such copying is paradigmatic non-commercial personal use entirely consistent with the purposes of the* [Audio Home Recording] *Act*'. The 'space-shift' concept was an analogy to *Sony Corp. of America v. Universal City Studios* (1984) which became the foundation stone for the idea of 'time-shifting' of copyrighted television shows using a VCR being qualified as fair use under the Copyright Act, and thus not an infringement.[14] To paraphrase Judge Warren J. Ferguson who ruled against Universal in the first instance, even if the Copyright Act's exclusive rights extended to private copying and building a library, fair use would exempt private copying; and even if fair use did not apply, no acceptable theory of contributory infringement[15] could expose the producers and sellers of such devices to liability.

[14] Sony v. Universal decided matters which, according to Goldstein, should not have been decided in a win-or-lose manner in court, but instead regulated in a fine-tuned, compromise-ensuring manner in written law. See Goldstein (2003) loc. cit. This view appears to be in line with Goldstein's views as a copyright maximist (copyright optimist, as he calls it).

[15] Goldstein (2003).

2.3 Antagonizing Publishers for Science: The Google Books Litigations

I cannot imagine a definition of fair use that would not encompass the transformative uses made by Defendants' [Mass Digitization Project] and would require that I terminate this invaluable contribution to the progress of science and cultivation of the arts [...]. Judge Harold Baer—*Author's Guild* et al. *v. Hathitrust,* et al., *11 CV 6351 (HB), Opinion & order*

2.3.1 Introduction: The Timeline of Cases

This subchapter presents the chain of lawsuits surrounding the Google Library Project and the Google Books service. Despite the postulated violation being relatively simple across the board, i.e. all plaintiffs claiming their work being reproduced and used without due license, due to the cases being intertwined and overall complexity of the proceedings, in the interest of clarity they are discussed here in a timeline manner, ending with the 2015 unanimous fair use ruling by the Second Circuit[16] and the Supreme Court's denial of review in 2016.

In the meantime, Google suffered a defeat on European soil in its lawsuit brought by the La Martinière publishing group, was ordered to pay damages and cease digital reproduction of the material, with an additional penalty of EUR 10,000 a day until final removal of offending extracts of books from the database. Despite the case finding its end in a settlement years later, it remains a strong example how successful application of French copyright law by the court resulted in Google's defeat in court.[17]

2.3.2 Revolutionizing Access to Publications, But at a Price

In late 2004, the world saw the announcement of two new digital books initiatives by Google Inc. Devised as platforms for hosting and display of material supplied by rightsholders (the 'Google Print', later renamed as 'Partner Program' to avoid associations with printing out copyrighted material) and digitisation of books available in the collections of the Library of Congress, the New York Public Library and a variety of university libraries including Harvard, Stanford and Oxford ('the Library Project'). The two programs formed the foundation for Google Books: a service meant to allow free worldwide access to its proprietary database of scanned and

[16] Authors Guild v. Google Inc. (2d Cir. 2015) Docket No. 13-4829-cv, decided October 16, 2015.

[17] On a side note, in the *La Martinière* case, Google attempted a defense that it had used successfully before in France in *H&K, Andre R. v. Google,* claiming application of US law and its fair use exceptions. See Lopez-Tarruella (2012), p. 347.

optically recognised books. Optical recognition meant that researchers, librarians, scientists the world over could benefit, on a massive scale, from full text indexing of books which have never before been issued in an electronic format. From the perspective of academic researchers, librarians, even common users, the benefits of the system were massive. Being able to text-search rare and not always easily available volumes buried deep in libraries halfway around the world, coupled with instantly displayed information on the available editions and means on getting one's hands on the tangible volume, was nothing short of truly revolutionary.

Relying on the fair use doctrine, Google never asked copyright holders for permission, nor did it intend to. Some scholars pointed out that, with the transaction costs of contacting every copyright holder, assuming coverage by fair use exceptions was the only feasible way to proceed.[18] To reinforce this position, the project was never intended to provide open access to books which were readily available from publishers. Instead, full access was only enabled for books which were out of print and not covered by copyright; for the majority of volumes, however, the user would only see 'snippets' (arbitrarily selected blocks of a few sentences) surrounding the text that matched the input search criteria.[19] Despite initial claims that snippets were available only where the publishers had granted their consent, Google had in fact adopted an opt-out model.[20] Consequently, copyright holders were not queried prior to digitalization of a volume and making it available in snippet form. Ultimately, despite being of massive importance for the usability of the entire tool, the snippet view became the chief bone of contention in the lawsuits that soon followed.

2.3.3 Litigation in the United States

2.3.3.1 First Complaints. Author's Guild v. Google: 'A Wilful, Massive Copyright Infringement'

On September 20th, 2005 came the class action complaint from authors Herbert Mitgang, Betty Miles Daniel Hoffman et al., with the Author's Guild as associational plaintiff, citing commercial use of works contained in libraries without license.[21] By reproducing for itself a copy of works which were not in the public domain without authorization, the plaintiffs claimed Google was engaging in a wilful, massive infringement of the 'electronic rights' of copyright holders of such

---

[18] See e.g. Band (2009), p. 230.

[19] Mathes (2005).

[20] The Google Library Project FAQ is available on http://www.google.com/googlebooks/common.html. Accessed 03 September 2023.

[21] The Author's Guild, Associational Plaintiff, Herbert Mitgang, Betty Miles and Daniel Hoffman, Individually and on Behalf of all Others Similarly Situated, Plaintiffs, v. Google Inc., Defendant; Class action complaint of 20th September 2005 to US District Court, Southern District of New York, ref. 05 CV 8136.

works for the purpose of attracting visitors to its website and generating advertising revenue. Demanding that Google be found in breach of Section 101 et seq. of the Copyright Act, the plaintiffs sought damages, injunctive and declaratory relief with respect to the infringement and planned unauthorised use of the works in question.

In its response to Author's Guild's complaint, Google admitted to scanning (and continued resolve to scan) literary works provided by participating libraries but denied all allegations of wilful infringement and stated that no permissions of copyright holders were required in the present case, citing applicability of fair use exceptions under Section 106 of the Copyright Act.

Less than a month after the first complaint, another lawsuit was filed by a number of publishing companies of the Association of American Publishers including McGraw-Hill and Penguin Group.[22] The companies, all members of the Google Partner Program at the time,[23] alleged violation of Section 101 et seq. of the Copyright Act by means of inflicting '*continuing, irreparable and imminent harm*' that they were suffering, would continue to suffer etc. due to wilful infringement by Google of exclusive rights of copyright of a variety of books, housed in, among others, the University Library of the University of Michigan in Ann Arbor, Michigan[24] again for the purpose of commercial benefit from increased website traffic. Interestingly, the complaint allowed that the fair use provisions of (a) Section 107 and (b) Section 108 would, '*in very different circumstances*' permit a library to make digital copies of works in its collection; still, they could not apply to '*Google's wholesale unauthorised copying*'.[25] The plaintiffs claimed that the actions of Google included unauthorised reproduction, public distribution and public display of books, with a '*substantially adverse impact on the potential market*' for such books.

Responding to the publishers' complaint, rather unsurprisingly, Google again claimed fair use and denied allegations of wilful infringement. It also made note of its opt-out mechanism by which the copyright holder could object to a particular book being included in the system. Moreover, Google reaffirmed that its policy was to enable users to search the index of words in the books as stored on its secure servers and the displayed snippets were truly minute for books covered by copyright and not submitted by the copyright holder: '*depending on the type of book, three or fewer very short excerpts of approximately one vertical inch each*'.[26] Thus began a court battle that, however decided, was expected to address the big questions of application of fair use doctrine for Web-based services.

---

[22] The McGraw-Hill Companies, Inc., Pearson Education, Inc., Penguin Group (USA) Inc., Simon & Schuster, Inc., and John Wiley & Sons, Inc., Plaintiffs, v. Google Inc., Defendant, filed 19th October 2005 with US District Court, Southern District of New York, ref. 05 CV 8881.

[23] Samuelson (2010).

[24] McGraw-Hill et al. v. Google, 05 CV 8881, p. 2.

[25] McGraw-Hill et al. v. Google, 05 CV 8881, p. 4, section 7.

[26] Answer, Jury Demand and Affirmative Defenses of Defendant Google Inc. of 8 November 2005, Civil Action No. 05 CV 8881 (JES), p. 2.

2.3.3.2 The (Attempted) Controversial Settlement of 2008

In spring 2006, a few months following the above responses, the parties sat down to negotiate the terms of a possible settlement, with the participation of representatives of libraries due to their planned involvement in the ultimately proposed scheme.[27] Google's willingness to explore room for settlement came as no surprise: with the amount of statutory damages set at USD 150,000 per book, assuming 24 million titles still under copyright, the court could technically hit Google with USD 3.6 trillion in statutory damages.[28] Allowing Google to continue scanning in peace, and letting the copyright holders have their slice of the cake, the settlement would have both cases (Author's Guild and AAP) joined and, if approved by the court (mandatory due to the suit being structured as class-action[29]), closed—unfortunately, leaving the potential for bringing new value to the fair use dispute largely unrealised.

With very little actual progress made in the actual cases despite the passage of time,[30] the parties filed their proposed settlement on 28th October, 2008 and obtained preliminary approval by Judge John E. Sprizzo on November 17, 2008.[31] The contents of the draft caused quite a stir: seemingly, the parties had devised a highly powerful tool that would grant Google what was often claimed to be a worldwide mandate to digitise distribute books, reaching far beyond the typical understanding of fair use allowing electronic distribution of potentially all works whose copyright holders would fail to opt-out.[32] The proposed draft gave rise to controversy on many fields, including anti-trust and competition policy,[33] class-action dispute resolution,[34] the future role of traditional libraries in the face of Google's 'world's largest library'[35] and social policy as a whole.[36]

---

[27] Samuelson (2010), p.6.

[28] Band (2009).

[29] Band (2009).

[30] Samuelson (2010), p. 5, referencing Objection of Scott E. Gant to Proposed Settlement and to Certification of the Proposed Settlement Class and Sub-Classes at 3, Authors Guild, Inc. v. Google, Inc., Case No. 05 CV 8136 (DC), available at http://www.publicindex.org/docs/objections/gant.pdf, as well as statement by Michael Boni, lawyer for the author subclass that that no depositions have been taken in the case. Transcript of Status Conference, Oct. 7, 2009 at 9, Authors Guild, Inc. v. Google, Inc., Case No. 05 CV 8136 (DC), archived copy available at https://web.archive.org/web/20130309055424/http://thepublicindex.org/docs/case_order/Status%20Conference%20Transcript.pdf.

[31] ECF No. 64.

[32] Sag (2010).

[33] Picker (2009).

[34] The Department of Justice advised the court to undertake a 'particularly searching analysis' to verify whether the requirements of Federal Rule of Civil Procedure 23 concerning procedural and substantial fairness, adequacy and reasonableness under applicable case law. See Statement of Interest of the United States Regarding Proposed Class Settlement at 27, Authors Guild, Inc. v. Google, Inc., Case No. 05-CV-8136-DC (S.D.N.Y. Sept. 18, 2009); see also Sag (2010).

[35] Darnton (2009).

[36] Sag (2010), p. 3.

Ultimately, the proposed settlement, despite its revision and preliminary approval of the amended version in November 2009,[37] was rejected by the District Court in March, 2011.[38] Voicing the final refusal, Judge Denny Chin cited failure of the settlement in the fields of fairness, adequacy and reasonableness. The ASA was also criticised as building upon a lawsuit where Google's scanning of books and display of 'snippets' for on-line searching were challenged on grounds of copyright protection to create a '*forward-looking business arrangement that would grant Google significant rights to exploit entire books without permission of copyright owners*'. Thus, Google would be granted an unfair competitive advantage and, at the same time, be rewarded for unauthorised wholesale copying of copyrighted material, all on basis of a settlement reaching far beyond the scope of the original lawsuit.[39] In the opinion of March 22nd, Judge Chin dismissed the request for final approval of the ASA, thus shutting the door on this scenario becoming reality.

2.3.3.3 Towards Proclaiming Google Books Fair Use: The Road to the 2013 SDNY Judgment

Among the numerous concerns raised against the ASA on grounds of class-action procedure, privacy, competition law, congressional supervision over the subject matter, even international law,[40] the great absentee in the settlement was the matter of fair use considerations, and their applicability to Google Books in its basic form (i.e., comprising unauthorised scanning for purposes of book search and snippet view, not taking into account the proposed expanded business model). Just as the ASA failed to address the core question of the case, i.e. applicability of the fair use exception claimed by Google, it was also not covered in the District Court Opinion of March, 2011.

Interestingly, despite the kerfuffle surrounding the ASA, the obvious criticism from the publishing industry[41] and the shadow of astronomical statutory damages looming over Google, it appeared that—despite the obvious criticism from the publishing industry[42]—the ultimate pro-fair use outcome of the Google Books litigation was quite expected in some scholarly circles.[43] Addressing the fair use consideration of 'affecting the market for the original work', some authors argued, in

---

[37] Amended Settlement Agreement, Authors Guild, Inc. v. Google, Inc., No. 05 CV 8136 (DC) (S.D.N.Y. Nov. 13, 2009); hereinafter referred to as the '**ASA**', preliminary approval by Judge Chin of 19th November 2009, ECF 772.

[38] United States District Court, Southern District of New York, The Author's Guild et al., Plaintiffs, v. Google Inc., Defendant, Opinion 05 Civ. 8136 (DC) of March 22, 2011.

[39] *Author's Guild v. Google*, Civ. 8136 (DC).

[40] Ibid., pp. 11–13.

[41] See e.g. Schroeder (2005).

[42] Id.

[43] Samuelson (2010) fn. 31; see also Arthur (2006).

regard to the nature of books as 'experience goods' (i.e. where the utility received is not known until consumed; in most cases, after purchase),[44] that although the digital reality may sometimes allow to substitute the sample for the original, thus reducing the incentive for creation of new works, the offering of preview solutions such as the snippet view was not likely to adversely affect the sale of printed books. Quite the contrary: it helped avoid erroneous purchases based on incomplete marketing information.[45] By allowing users to eventually sample all available books of the world (unless their copyright holders were to choose to opt out from the project), Google Books was praised for both the scale of the project and the 'targeted' flexible selection of previews, always based on the input search criteria—thus largely solving the inherent 'experience good' problem of the books of the world.[46] It was also observed that the Library Project litigation was unique in that the plaintiffs did not seek preliminary relief in the form of a temporary restraining order, and were clearly not interested in removing their works from the system as the same result they could achieve by merely opting out of the Google index, or using the Partner Program to control electronic distribution and share the profits. This led to claims that the Author's Guild was primarily litigating on principle[47] to react to 'copyright law being flipped on its head' where a commercial company, acting in its own commercial interest, '*could copy and distribute the property of another person without the property owner's permission simply because if (Google) believes that its commercial interests will benefit and in its view of the public interest, if it can obtain assistance from entities (e.g., libraries) who do not own the relevant copyrights*'.[48]

In presenting its fair use argument, Google claimed precedent by referring to two fair use cases,[49] both involving unauthorised yet transformative commercial use of thumbnail images: *Kelly v. Arriba Soft Corp.* and *Perfect 10 Inc. v Amazon.com Inc.* As will be discussed in detail further on, the use being **'transformative'** or **'creative'** in nature is deemed as highly significant by U.S. courts in applying the fair use guidelines and requires to establish whether the use serves a new purpose, distinct from that of the original work.[50]

In *Arriba Soft*, the dispute pertained to creation and use of image thumbnails by a company operating an image search engine. Arriba's software created local copies of graphics found on the web and displayed them when presenting search results; upon

[44] See McCannon (2012); on the paradox of experience goods' marketing in the context of Google Books, see also Travis (2007).

[45] Amazon book previews actually boost book sales. See Travis (2006).

[46] Travis (2007).

[47] Band (2009), p. 236.

[48] Nimmer (2005).

[49] Band (2009), p. 237.

[50] Campbell v. Acuff-Rose Music, Inc. 510 U.S. 569 (1994), 510 U.S. This test was failed e.g. in *A&M Records v. Napster* where format-shifting was not found to be transformative use and therefore not allowed. See A&M Records, Inc. v. Napster, Inc., 239 F.3d 1004 (9th Cir. 2001), affirming, 114 F.Supp.2d 896 (N.D. Cal. 2000).

clicking on a thumbnail, the user was shown the original image as hosted on its native site.[51] In examining the applicability of fair use, Ninth District Court held that, although the commercial nature of the business weighed slightly against fair use, the use of images was transformative due to a significant reduction in size. Moreover, the court observed that creating thumbnails to display search results constituted the creation of a new purpose for the images without superseding the purpose of the original work.[52] While they did not supplant the need for the originals, Arriba's thumbnails were found by the court to benefit the public by enhancing information-gathering techniques on the internet.[53] While the nature of the copyrighted work was undoubtedly creative[54] and the copyrighted work being used in whole,[55] the court decided that thumbnails did not harm the market for the original images and therefore Arriba's use of thumbnails was fair use.[56]

The other case used by Google to make its fair use point, *Perfect 10 v. Amazon.com,* consolidated two lawsuits filed by Perfect 10, an online adult website, against Google and Amazon for infringement of copyright by displaying thumbnail images as search results. The district court hearing the case ruled that, due to the fact that Google earned revenue via AdSense by displaying thumbnails of copyrighted pictures, and often leading users to infringing sites hosting said pictures, there was more of a 'commercial use' than in *Kelly v. Arriba Soft.*[57] However, this ruling was then reversed by the Ninth Circuit, rejecting the distinction made by the district court based on deriving revenue from infringing sites via AdWords, finding that '*while Google's use of thumbnails to direct users to AdSense partners containing infringing content* [added] *a commercial dimension that did not exist in Kelly, the district court did not determine that this commercial element was significant.*'[58] The court concluded that '*the significantly transformative nature of Google's search engine, particularly in light of its public benefit, outweighs Google's superseding and commercial uses of the thumbnails in this case.*' and ruled that Google's use of Perfect 10's thumbnails sufficiently met the criteria for being considered fair use.[59]

---

[51] Kelly v. Arriba Soft Corp., 336 F.3d 811, 815 (9th Cir. 2003).

[52] *Kelly v. Arriba Soft*, para. [8].

[53] *Kelly v. Arriba Soft*, para. [9].

[54] *Kelly v. Arriba Soft*, para. [10–13].

[55] *Kelly v. Arriba Soft*, para. [16].

[56] *Kelly v. Arriba Soft*, para. [20].

[57] Perfect 10, Plaintiff, v. Google Inc., et al., Defendants. Case no. CV 04-9484 AHM (SHx) United States District Court for the Central District Of California, 416 F. Supp. 2d 828; 2006 U.S. Dist. LEXIS 6664; 78 U.S.P.Q.2D (BNA) 1072; p. 18.

[58] Perfect 10, Inc. v. Amazon.com, Inc. United States Court of Appeals for the Ninth Circuit 487 F.3d 701 (9th Cir. 2007); https://www.law.berkeley.edu/files/perfect10.pdf. Accessed 03 September 2023.

[59] An analogous position was adopted by the 9th Circuit in a twin case of Perfect 10 v. Google, 508 F.3d 1146 (9th Cir. 2007) http://cyber.law.harvard.edu/people/tfisher/IP/2007%20Perfect%2010%20Abridged.pdf (accessed 03 September 2023). Aside from the fair use argument, the claims of unlicensed display and distribution, the judgments applied a 'server test' to demonstrate that, by

Aside from public benefit, *Kelly* and *Perfect 10* shared a crucial element for establishing unauthorized use of copyrighted material as fair: in both cases, the affected copyrighted material was **transformed** and used for a **new purpose** that was distinct from that of the original work which follows the views expressed on the subject by the Supreme Court in its *Campbell v. Acuff Rose* ruling of 1994.[60] Proving Google Books to be transformative was to be highly significant for Google's case: as demonstrated in *A&M Records v. Napster*, plain distribution of **format-shifted copyrighted work** was not likely to be seen by judges as transformative or creative enough to benefit from the fair use exception.[61]

2.3.3.4 Authors V. Universities: The HathiTrust Litigation

Months after the ASA was finally rejected by the District Court, another suit was filed in relation to Google's digitization effort; this time, Author's Guild was joined by organisations of authors and individual plaintiffs in going after educational institutions that collaborated with Google Books via HathiTrust.

HathiTrust is a project of research institutions and libraries established for the purpose of preservation and ensuring ongoing accessibility of the cultural record via operation of a digital library. The list of participants, now comprising over 100 entities, includes Michigan State University, Princeton University, Stanford University, University of California Berkeley, Harvard Library and Yale Library.[62] With the Digital Library sometimes being reported on simply as a spinoff of the Google Library Project,[63] HathiTrust is a platform comprising research tools for browsing its extensive archives, also for people with print disabilities. One of the fields of its activity comprises digitization of print materials of the participating libraries; in this regard, a partnership with Google was established; in exchange for lending Google books for scanning and allowing it to retain a copy for display in the form of snippets on the Google Books website, the HathiTrust Digital Library ('HDL') received digitised copies of the material (The Mass Digitization Project, 'MDP').[64] Four HathiTrust universities also joined an initiative for identification and making available to university students, faculty and library patrons of orphan works, where the copyright holder could not be located by HathiTrust procedures. Dubbed 'The Orphan Works Project', the system would, after having exhausted the prescribed

never coming obtaining possession of the full-size images, the defendant could not be deemed as engaging in their communication. This view has been later criticized for being overly broad and disregarding the definition of display embodied in the Copyright Act (see footnote 161). For extensive comment on the 'server test', or 'server rule', see also Ginsburg and Budiardjo (2018).

[60] Campbell v. Acuff-Rose Music, Inc. 510 U.S. 569 (1994).

[61] Crews (2001).

[62] For more information, see http://www.hathitrust.org/community.

[63] This framing is used e.g. in the Wikipedia article dedicated to the case; see http://en.wikipedia.org/wiki/Authors_Guild,_Inc._v._HathiTrust. Accessed 03 September 2023.

[64] Author's Guild et al. v. Hathitrust, et al., 11 CV 6351 (HB), Opinion & order, p. 2–3.

means to contact the copyright holder, make the works available to students, professors, and other authenticated users and visitors to university libraries.[65] Conversely, where the authors were known, HDL used the works in three ways: full-text searches, preservation and access for people with certified print disabilities.[66] It was noted that prior to its establishment, print-disabled students could only access works which were converted to braille or read aloud, which significantly restricted the usability of the text as human narration cannot be navigated like text.[67] Following introduction of the program, these students have gained access to the entire repository of digitised books. Using screen readers, they became able to navigate, search, access, read and re-read text just like a sighted person would.[68]

The plaintiffs claimed copyright infringement and their demands left little to the imagination: declaratory and injunctive relief to prevent the reproduction, distribution, or display of copyrighted works by HathiTrust, as well as provision of such works to Google for the purpose of digitization, declaratory relief against the Orphan Works Project[69] and impoundment of all unauthorised digital copies held by the HathiTrust. Not surprisingly, HathiTrust responded claiming fair use and massive public benefit of the project.[70]

In examining the fair use defence, Judge Harold Baer of the District Court first observed that a defendant in a fair use case, despite having the burden of proof, '*need not prevail with respect to each of the four enumerated fair-use factors*[71] *to succeed on a fair use defence*',[72] citing *NXIVM Corp. v. Ross Institute* of 2004.[73] Instead, it was the role of the court to weigh the factors together as the '*ultimate focus is the goal of copyright itself, whether promoting the Progress of Science and useful Arts would be better served by allowing the use than by preventing it.*'[74] In short, Judge Baer declared that he was not going to expect HathiTrust to fully meet all four fair

[65] Author's Guild et al. v. Hathitrust, et al., 11 CV 6351 (HB), Opinion & order, p. 4.

[66] Ibid., p. 3.

[67] Kerscher (2012), p. 5 et seq.

[68] Kerscher (2012).

[69] The OWP claims were declared not ripe for adjudication by the Court as the project was suspended before goinv online, following filing of the original complaint due to serious errors in the processes for identifying orphan works. See also Authors Guild, Inc. v. HathiTrust, No. 12-4547 (2d Cir. 2014), p. 9.

[70] Available online at http://www.hathitrust.org/documents/HathiTrust_Authors_Guild_Statement.pdf. Accessed 03 September 2023.

[71] 17 U.S. Code § 107. On a side note, at times the doctrine also speaks of a fifth rule. See Stim, R., Getting Permission: How to License and Clear Copyrighted Materials Online & Off, 5th Edition, October 2013, p. 289.

[72] Author's Guild et al. v. Hathitrust, et al., 11 CV 6351 (HB), Opinion & order, p. 15.

[73] NXIVM Corp. v. Ross Inst., 364 F.3d 471, 477 (2d Cir. 2004).

[74] Cases cited: Campbell v. Acuff-Rose Music, Inc., 510 U.S. 569, 569 (1994); Swatch Grp. Mgmt. Servs. Ltd. v. Bloomberg L.P., No. 11 Civ. 1006, 2012 WL 1759944, at *3 (S.D.N.Y. May 17, 2012) (quoting Castle Rock Entertainment, 150 F.3d at 141; U.S. Const. art, 1, § 8, cl. 8).

use criteria, choosing to go for the big picture instead, citing precedent as aforementioned.

Regarding the purpose and character of the use, the court noted the significant benefits of the MDP to scholars, its usefulness in preserving the library collections against damaging factors and, last but not least, providing print-disabled individuals with a broad access to literary works on an unprecedented scale. It was also noted that, for works which are not public domain, only print-disabled library patrons are provided full access to the text. Noting how the HDL was a non-profit operation[75] and seeing as the search capabilities of the HDL had already caused new methods of academic inquiry such as text mining to arise, it was observed that the use was both non-commercial and transformative, thus satisfying the first fair use guideline[76] and affecting the consideration of the second, i.e. the nature of the copyright works. Here it was noted that indeed 76 percent of the copied works identified by plaintiffs were fiction, and thus deserving greater protection than factual works. Still, in view of existing case law, the court ruled that where a use is transformative, the nature of the original work whether being prose or non-fiction is of lesser importance and not dispositive.[77] Existing case law was also used to address the remaining factors, i.e. portion of the work taken (‘*sometimes it is necessary to copy entire works*’ quoting *Bill Graham* 448 F.3d at 613 and *Arriba Soft*, 336 F.3d at 821) and usurping the market for the original work (NXCIM Corp., 364 F.3d at 482: ‘C*ourts consider only those [markets] that the creators of original works would in general develop or license others to develop.*’ *Campbell*, 510 U.S. at 591, 592 ‘*[W]hen* [. . .] *the second use is transformative, market substitution is at least less certain, and market harm may not be so readily inferred.*’) Having said this, the court also addressed the alleged substitution claimed by plaintiffs *(‘[e]ach digital copy of a book that Defendants [. . .] rather than [purchased] through lawful channels, represents a lost sale.*’) by noting that merely purchasing another copy would not allow either full-text searches or access for the disabled—two transformative uses granted by HathiTrust’s Mass Digitization Project. The court also made an important observation concerning the alleged loss of licensing opportunities: a court of law cannot automatically conclude impairment of potential licensing revenues where a new use for the work is found: ‘*a copyright holder cannot preempt a transformative market*’.[78] Therefore, in view of the prohibitively expensive cost of creating a licensing scheme for the works gathered at HDL of over USD 500 million in comparison to the

[75] Thus the court rejected the view of the plaintiffs who claimed that the primary purpose was commercial as the libraries saved the expense of purchasing authorised copies. See Author’s Guild et al. v. Hathitrust, et al., 11 CV 6351 (HB), Opinion & order, p. 17.

[76] Author’s Guild et al. v. Hathitrust, et al., 11 CV 6351 (HB), Opinion & order, p. 16–17. The significance of transformative use is also covered in detail in the next paragraph of this paper, against the backdrop of the SDNY opinion on Author’s Guild v. Google.

[77] Citing Bill Graham, 448 F.3d at 612 (‘[T]he second factor may be of limited usefulness where the creative work of art is being used for a transformative purpose’) as well as Campbell, 510 U.S. at 586; see also Harper & Row, 471 U.S. at 546.

[78] Citing Bill Graham, 448 F.3d at 614.

anticipated revenue, the court concluded that this would not be a 'commercially viable endeavour'. For this reason, it could not be claimed that a likely and foreseeable viable market could ever be established for the goods in question, thus defeating the argument that '*it is permissible to steal the goods if it is too expensive to buy them*': 'buying' cannot be discussed where there is no market in the first place.

Having weighed all the factors of fair use and the benefit to the public against the interests of the authors who would '*stand to gain very little if the public* [was] *deprived of this resource'*,[79] as well as the potential for actually enhancing the market for the original works by attracting researchers to the titles they sought, Judge Baer famously concluded '*although I recognise that the facts here may on some levels be without precedent, I am convinced that they fall safely within the protection of fair use such that there is no genuine issue of material fact. I cannot imagine a definition of fair use that would not encompass the transformative uses made by Defendants' MDP and would require that I terminate this invaluable contribution to the progress of science and cultivation of the arts [...].*'

This ruling received praise for 'rightly solidifying the growing body of jurisprudence protecting uses that have a transformative purpose and that pose no threat of artistic substitution while providing a public benefit'[80]; it should also be noted for showing great caution concerning impairment of 'potential future market' for any use of copyrighted work that did not exist earlier, and has only been made possible because of the innovative technological solution introduced by the defendant. Some criticism addressed Judge Baer's approach to full-text copies for the print-disabled students as going a step too far and one that could be narrowed on appeal. Still, the fact remained that the HathiTrust ruling was the first to openly declare that transformative use of copyrighted books, digitised and used in whole without consent from the copyright holders, could indeed be seen as fair use.[81]

2.3.3.5 Author's Guild v. Google SDNY Fair Use Ruling of 2013

Eight years after the initial complaint by the Author's Guild, the District Court for the Southern District of New York issued an opinion by Circuit Judge Denny Chin, ruling in favour of the defendant.[82] The court made strong points about the fair use doctrine in itself, reaffirming how it requires an 'open-ended and context-sensitive inquiry'[83] and a case-by-case analysis. The court also stressed how the four factors

[79] Hathitrust Opinion & Order, p. 21.

[80] Diaz (2013).

[81] For a discussion on the assessment of transformative uses in fair use cases, see Chap. 3.

[82] Author's Guild v. Google Inc., SDNY Opinion of 14th November 2013, 05 Civ. 8136.

[83] Citing Blanch v. Koons, 467 F.3d at 251.

provided in the statute[84] (the purpose and character of the use, the nature of the copyrighted work, the amount and substantiality of the portion taken, and the effect of the use upon the potential market) are merely general guidance and should be explored and weighed together, *i.e.* not as cumulative requirements.[85] Judge Chin took the opportunity to reaffirm that fair use permits fulfilment of the 'copyright's very purpose', that is, by providing '*sufficient protection to authors and inventors to stimulate creative activity, while at the same time permitting others to utilise protected works to advance the progress of the arts and sciences.*'[86] Following an extensive review of the benefits of Google Books (as cited earlier), the Judge stressed the importance of establishing the transformative nature of a use of copyrighted work in establishing whether the use is fair.[87] Quoting *Campbell v. Acuff-Rose Music* of 1994, the court stated that '*the goal of copyright, to promote science and the arts, is generally furthered by the creation of transformative works'*.[88] In this regard, the digitization of books by Google was found to be 'highly transformative' in a similar manner to display of thumbnails in *Kelly v. Arriba Corp.*[89] as it caused words in books to be '*used in a way they* [had] *not been used before*'.[90] It was also noted that Google Books would not supersede or supplant books because it was not a tool to read them; instead, the service created a new way of using the text contained in the books, thus '*adding value to the original*'.[91] It was also noted that fair use could still be claimed despite commercial benefit being attained in the process; since Google did not sell its scans, sell its snippets, run ads on the 'About the Book' page, the commercial profit for Google was found to be less than significant taking into account the important educational purposes of the project; hence the first factor was deemed to 'strongly favour' fair use.[92]

In regard to nature of copyrighted work, it was observed that the majority of digitised books are non-fiction, which translated into a lesser standard of copyright protection than in the case of fiction.[93] Not surprisingly, the third criterion (portion of the original work used) was found to weigh against fair use, although it was also observed that in some situations copying the entire work is necessary to make a fair

[84] 17 U.S. Code § 107. On a side note, the doctrine also speaks sometimes of a fifth rule. See Stim, R., Getting Permission: How to License and Clear Copyrighted Materials Online & Off, 5th Edition, October 2013, p. 289.

[85] Author's Guild v. Google, SDNY 05 Civ. 8136, p.19.

[86] Author's Guild v. Google, SDNY 05 Civ. 8136, p.19.

[87] Citing Campbell v. Acuff-Rose Music, Inc. 510 U.S. 569 (1994), 510 U.S.; Leval, Toward a Fair Use Standard, 103 Harv. L. Rev. at 1111); Bill Graham Archives v. Dorling Kindersley Ltd., 448 F.3d 605, 608 (2d Cir. 2006) Am. Geophysical Union, 60 F.3d at 923.

[88] Campbell, 510 U.S. at 579.

[89] Kelly v. Arriba Corp, 336 F.3d 811 (9th Cir. 2003).

[90] Kelly v. Arriba Corp, p. 20.

[91] Kelly v. Arriba Corp, p. 21.

[92] Kelly v. Arriba Corp, p. 21.

[93] As stated by the Court of Appeals in Stewart v. Abend, 495 U.S. 207, 237 (1990): 'In general, fair use is more likely to be found in factual works than in fictional works.'

use of the image[94] and full-work reproduction is critical in Google Books; at the same time, the displayed results were always a fraction of the copyrighted material.[95]

Finally, addressing the concerns made by plaintiffs in regard to the negative impact on the market for books by becoming a 'market replacement' for the digitised material (and the alleged possibility to recreate the entire book by entering a few searches) the court responded with quite strong language, striking down these claims as nonsensical.[96] It was stressed that libraries could indeed download digital copies of books that they provided for scanning in the first place; hence, they already have the books in question. Moreover, it would take one to 'input countless searches', and still have the printed original as reference, to put together a book out of scanned snippets. The court observed that 'a reasonable factfinder' could only find that the only effect on the market was that of *enhancing* sales of books for benefit of rightsholders, especially in the world of online shopping—since for a title to be successful, the individual must first learn of its existence.[97] Consequently, the fourth factor was declared to strongly favour fair use: not only was Google Books not found detrimental to sales of the original works, it actually brought added value to the market and helped stimulate demand. From this perspective, Judge Chin's choice of words when describing the plaintiffs' position can be seen as indeed substantiated.

2.3.3.6 HathiTrust as Fair Use

Seven months after the first instance ruling in its crusade against Google, the Author's Guild's case against HathiTrust was ruled on appeal by the United States Court of Appeals for the Second Circuit. The Court took the opportunity to cite the position of the Supreme Court that the chief purpose of copyright was to *'promote the Progress of Science and useful Arts'*[98] and reiterate how crucial it was for the use in question to be of 'transformative' nature.[99] However, it also observed that it is not the '*valuable contribution to the progress of science and cultivation of the arts'* that constitutes a transformative use as according to Judge Baer; the use must indeed serve a new and different function than the original work did, and at the same time not be a substitute for it.[100] Nevertheless, the Circuit Court still found the creation of a full-text searchable database to be a '*quintessentially transformative use*' observing that authors do not write for the purpose of enabling text search in their books

[94] Bill Graham Archives, 448 F.3d at 613.

[95] Author's Guild v. Google, SDNY 05 Civ. 8136, p. 23.

[96] Author's Guild v. Google, p. 24.

[97] Author's Guild v. Google, p. 25.

[98] Citing Campbell v. Acuff-Rose Music, Inc., 510 U.S. 569, 574 (1994) (quoting U.S. CONST. art. I, § 8, cl. 8); see also Twentieth Century Music 20 Corp. v. Aiken, 422 U.S. 151, 156 (1975).

[99] Quoting Campbell as did Judge Baer in the first instance, the more transformative the use, 'the less will be the significance of other factors [. . .] that may weigh against a finding of fair use.'

[100] Authors Guild, Inc. v. HathiTrust, No. 12–4547 (2d Cir. 2014), p. 17.

and the HDL did not substitute, repackage or republish the original work in a new mode of presentation; what it offered was a new functionality with a different purpose and of different character.[101] The Court approved of Judge Baer's analysis concerning the remaining fair use prerequisites and held his ruling in regard to the fair use aspect of the case, reiterating in particular that no cognizable market harm can be effected where there is no market substitution. The fair use nature of creating copies accessible for disabled persons was also confirmed by citing a House Committee Report of 1976 noting that '*blind-accessible formats are not usually made by publishers for commercial distribution*', and '*the making of a copy as a free service to blind persons would properly be considered fair use*'.[102] The Circuit Court held the ruling of Judge Baer in regard to its fair use considerations.[103] On January 8th, 2015, Author's Guild declared that they had dropped the litigation.[104]

The language used by the court was praised for having made references to the constitutional purpose of copyright '*to promote progress of science and the useful arts—not a blunt instrument for rightsholders to regulate all downstream uses*'.[105] It also appears that, despite minor differences on what exactly constitutes transformative use (valuable contribution to progress v. creating an entirely new use for the work), the courts seemed so far consistent in applying a flexible approach to balancing the rights of copyright holders and the benefits of new technologies of text digitization for the purpose of large-scale indexing. It has also been observed that Google's book project was clearly designed *in anticipation* of lawsuits and sought to balance the interests of rightsholders with the provision of the new services.[106] Notably, as mentioned above, even in the proposed settlement, fostered by both Google and the Author's Guild, the terms accepted by publishers *did not significantly differ* from those offered before the lawsuit.

2.3.4 *Google's Defeat in France*

From the outset, it was obvious that Google's book project would not remain geographically limited to the United States. As with other areas of activity stemming

[101] Authors Guild, Inc. v. HathiTrust, No. 12–4547 (2d Cir. 2014), p. 18.

[102] H.R. REP. NO. 94-1476, at 73 (1976), reprinted in 22 1976 U.S.C.C.A.N. 5659, 5686, quoted by Authors Guild, Inc. v. HathiTrust, No. 12-4547 (2d Cir. 2014), p. 28.

[103] However, the court remanded the issues on long-term preservation of books, expressing doubt whether the Authors Guild has standing in this regard. The matter was left for the District Court to examine whether Author's Guild can prove standing to challenge the preservation use of the HDL (Authors Guild, Inc. v. HathiTrust, No. 12-4547 (2d Cir. 2014), p. 32.

[104] Authors Guild (2015).

[105] Higgins (2014).

[106] See Diaz (2013), p. 713.

from its business model,[107] at some point the question would arise of running into disputes over Google Books that would be governed by a legal system that sees matters of copyright exceptions and infringement quite differently. A fitting example of how it fared in such circumstances is the case of *La Martinière v Google*, decided in late 2009.

2.3.4.1 La Martinière v. Google

French intellectual property law is built around author's moral and economic ties with the work ('*droit d'auteur*'), whereas the aim of copyright is often seen as to 'incentivise creation economically with the public's interest for culture and creativity in mind.[108] Similarly to a number of states in continental Europe including also Germany and the Netherlands, French law provides for an enumerative and exhaustive list of exemptions[109] and no 'overriding rule of fairness' in the case of economic intellectual property rights, thus strengthening their protection by setting forth precise norms and leaving little room for application of general normative principles.[110]

Under such circumstances, it should come as no surprise that, under fire by *La société Des Auteurs des Arts Visuels et de L'image Fixe Visual Auteurs* (SAIF) suing for copyright infringement by using thumbnail images for displaying search results,[111] Google invoked Article 5 (2) Berne Convention[112] claiming the infringing activity took place in the U.S. (where the servers were located) and thus applicability of U.S. copyright law, along with its fair use system. The move proved successful insofar that the Parisian court ruled in favour of the defendant, applying American law as *lex originis* and finding the thumbnails to indeed qualify as fair use.[113]

On 6th June 2006, Google Inc. and its French subsidiary Google France were sued by the publishing group La Martinière seated in Paris, for 'counterfeiting and

---

[107] For the Belgian lawsuit of newspaper publishers against Google over Google News, see Palmer (2011).

[108] Meyer (2011); See also Liemer (2011).

[109] Code de la propriété intellectuelle, loi no 92-597 du 1er juillet 1992 relative au code de la propriété intellectuelle, publié au Joural officiel du 3 juillet 1992, Article L122-5.

[110] Hugenholtz and Senftleben (2011), p. 6.

[111] Spelman (2011).

[112] Article 5 (2) of the Berne Convention for the Protection of Literary and Artistic Works of September 9, 1886; '[. . .]the extent of protection, as well as the means of redress afforded to the author to protect his rights, shall be governed exclusively by the laws of the country where protection is claimed.'

[113] This qualification was reversed in 2011 by the *Cour d'Appel* stating that French law should be applied. However, the court used the 'safe harbor' under the EU E-Commerce Directive for passive Internet Service Providers; see Cour d'Appel de Paris, 26 January 2011 (SAIF v. Google France), available at http://juriscom.net/wp-content/documents/caparis20110126.pdf. Accessed 03 September 2023.

breach of intellectual property rights'[114] claiming damages against its publishing houses: Editions du Seuil of France, Delachaux & Niestlé of Switzerland and Harry N. Abrams of the United States.[115] The suit was brought before *La tribunal de grande instance* (TGI) in Paris, with the French *Syndicat national de l'Edition* (SNE) joining the proceedings on 25th October 2006. The plaintiffs claimed that scanning books constituted unauthorised reproduction 'disregarding fundamental principles of law of intellectual property' and claimed damages of EUR 1,000,000 coupled with EUR 100,000 per day of each discovered infraction.[116]

In view of the lack of any flexible exceptions under French IP law that could be used to shelter itself from liability for unauthorised reproduction of the books it had scanned, Google attempted a defense used in an earlier case of SAIF v. Google (concerning use of thumbnail images) and again chose to seek refuge under American law. It claimed that under Article 5 (2) of the Berne Convention pointed to application of the law of the country where the infringing activity was conducted; in this case, it would again be the United States where the servers were located. Additionally, Google claimed that, under American law, said activity would be protected under the fair use provisions of Section 107 of the Copyright Act. However, this time the French court saw things differently: applying the principle of *lex locus damni*, it found that French law was applicable as being the most closely connected with the case. The court noted that it was French books copied and made available to French users located within the territory of France, the court and plaintiffs were French, as was the seat of Google France, the website was in French and it had a *.fr domain code.[117]

Unsurprisingly, the court deciding on application of French law marked the end of the case for Google. The court ruled that Google could not argue that '*creating a digital file from a book is not an act of reproduction*' and therefore it requires '*approval of the author or the copyright holders*'.[118] Google was found in breach of French intellectual property law and ordered to remove all offending books from its database and to pay damages; however, of significantly lesser amount than demanded by the plaintiffs. One could also see as significant that Google chose not to appeal the judgment; instead, it chose to pursue a settlement with the publishers and avoid further litigation.[119]

[114] Available online at http://news.bbc.co.uk/2/hi/entertainment/5052912.stm. Accessed 03 September 2023.

[115] Saltmarsh (2009).

[116] Lucke (2009), pp. 43–44.

[117] Lopez-Tarruella (2012), p. 347.

[118] See RFI (2009).

[119] Schechner (2012).

2.3.4.2 Comments

The decision of the TGI in the *La Martinière* case was noted for the construct applied for its choice of law: instead of applying *lex loci,* which effectively would allow 'forum shopping' by service providers to avoid any liability by establishing their servers in any friendly overseas jurisdiction that does not care much for their potentially infringing activities.[120] Notably, what seems to be missing from the discourse surrounding Google's proceedings in France is criticism of the merits of TGI's ruling on infringement. Indeed, it is difficult to find any fault in the court's reasoning in view of French law: where a digital copy is created, reproduction occurs. Where reproduction is unauthorised, an infringement has been committed.

As will be discussed in detail later in this work, ruling on the earlier case of *SAIF v. Google* on appeal in 2011, the *Cour d'Appel* apparently found a way to rule in favour of Google by applying the special regime of liability for passive internet providers with no knowledge or control of the information being processed, as provided by the E-Commerce Directive 2000/31/EC. However skilful a solution, it still makes the impression of Google getting off on a *lex specialis* provision of commercial law, instead of falling into an exonerating category of use that should be established (or allowed) by statutory copyright law.

2.3.5 *Epilogue: The Final U.S. Judgment and Conclusions*

In October 2015, Google's longest struggle arising from the Book Project on American soil seemingly came to an end. The judgment, passed by the Second Circuit Court was not surprising given the available material from discovery sessions. The appellants had built an argument against the transformative nature of Google's use of copyrighted material; points were also made about the commercial nature of the use in question, despite the lack of displayed advertising, creating a risk of hackers stealing the full digital copies stored on Google's servers, and, last but not least, about Google's operation infringing upon *derivative rights* of copyright holders who might have, at some point in the future, wished to capitalize upon offering a similar search service in regard to their works.

All the above claims were rejected by the court. The judgment again stated that the use of copyrighted property by the defendant was '*transformative within the meaning of Campbell v. Acuff-Rose Music Inc.*', did not offer the public a 'meaningful substitute' for the works used and satisfied the test for fair use, augmenting public knowledge '*by making available information about Plaintiffs' books without providing [...] a substantial substitute for matter protected by the Plaintiffs'*

[120] Lopez-Tarruella (2012), p. 346.

copyright interests in the original works or derivatives of them.'[121] Providing information about the work is not a licensable activity, the court added, and thus no infringement upon potential licensing markets can be claimed. The court added that, either at the time of judgment or earlier, no unreasonable risk of incursions of hackers can be claimed; lastly, the ultimate commercial goal of Google's activity is, in itself, immaterial to establishing fair use which, in view of the above considerations, was beyond doubt in this case.

The judgment, reaching again to the substantial case law mentioned on earlier stages of the proceedings, demonstrates how, with all the turmoil surrounding the cases, the strength of clashed interests and the years of court proceedings, with its open regulations and the flexibility of courts, the U.S. copyright regime has managed to create a space, on the fringes of traditional protection of intellectual property, where creativity and innovation—if indeed creating a novel and different quality, in other words ensuring that the use of other people's creations is *transformative*—are allowed to thrive and prosper.

One observation must be made from the perspective of this analysis. From the normative myriad that is statutory law, case law and views of the doctrine, emerged a fair use perspective on Google Books that was clearly foreseen by the creators of the product in regard to U.S. law. It could even be said that, despite being based on such a large number of factors and involving the necessary setting of certain precedents, it was indeed quite coherent and, to a degree, predictable. Based on assumptions built around the flexibilities of the U.S. copyright law system, this prediction was firm enough for the company to engage into a multi-million investment in the most ambitious digitisation project in history, risking horrendous statutory damages (put into perspective, the absolute-worst scenario of USD 3.6 trillion in damages is close to 20% of U.S. National Debt as at March, 2016[122]) that would have unquestionably ended the history of Google in a bang. So far, this approach has been successful in the United States; from a European perspective, it should be a reminder of how creativity and innovation can benefit from flexible exceptions in the very system of law that was devised to protect them.

At the same time, the chief reason of Google's success may be seen in how, despite its clear expectation of a finding for fair use, it had approached the matter of balancing conflicting interests and avoiding, in the final incarnation of its service, the risk of market substitution. This point has been reiterated in a more recent case which deserves a honourable mention when discussing the effectiveness of protection offered under a fair use system; one that, despite its similarities to *Authors Guild v. Google*, ended in a finding for infringement.

In late 2018, the U.S. Supreme Court denied certiorari in *Fox News v. TVEyes,*[123] a case where a service provider had been offering a text-searchable database of

[121] *Author's Guild v. Google, Inc.*, October 16, 2015, 2nd Circuit Court of Appeals, 13-4829-cv, p. 4, v. 5 and on.

[122] See http://usgovernmentdebt.us.

[123] See Barnes (2018), Brachmann (2018).

transcripts created on the basis of speech-to-text processing from over 1400 current TV and radio broadcasts that it had been recording. Customers of TVEyes were able to text-search the database of transcripts, retrieve time-stamped search results, play back related clips of up to 10 min, as well as archive, e-mail and download them to their own computers. The clips could be played one after another, with a tool preventing this being introduced only after the litigation had started. This attitude to copyrighted material, according to the 2nd Circuit, became the *differentia specifica* that set the case apart from *Authors Guild v. Google*. While Google Books' operation had been found to be 'testing the boundaries of fair use' but fair use nonetheless, due to being both transformative and protective of the interests of rightsholders, TVEyes had failed to demonstrate that its product protected these interests. By giving its subscribers access to 'virtually all of Fox's copyrighted audiovisual content',[124] despite the presence of a transformative purpose seen in allowing the user to filter out the desired content from the general body of broadcasted material, TVEyes' service was found to exceed the boundaries of fair use as laid out in the Google Books case.

It is important to note that, with the Supreme Court's refusal to review the TVEyes case, an important contribution was made to the body of case law on the fringes of copyright law and technology. While it may certainly be viewed as a course correction in the wake of a period marked by initial enthusiasm over the new capabilities offered by Google's online services, it can nonetheless also be seen as proof of a copyright system at work, where the existence of flexibilities and precedent in their application does not automatically result in depriving the copyright holder of protection.[125]

[124] *Fox News*, No. 15-3885 (2d Cir. 2018), p. 7.

[125] Seemingly, another example of this tendency could be seen in the 2018 SDNY judgment in *Goldman v. Breitbart* (1:17-cv-03144) which pertained to a pirated image that was embedded on a number of media websites. The Court refused to simply follow in the footsteps of 9th Circuit in *Perfect 10 v. Amazon* which had noted no distribution could occur as the image was not hosted on the defendant's server (as the only communication occurred in regard to 'HTML instructions that direct the users' browsers to Google's computers (for thumbnail images) or to a third party's computer (for full-size infringing images)'. The SDNY refused to apply this 'server test' noting that, in *Goldman*, the user was shown a full-size image immediately upon opening the website, as opposed to actively following a thumbnail link. The Court took the opportunity to question the extent of the test's actual compatibility with the Copyright Act (noting that its broad application could have a devastating effect on the licensing market) and ruled it inapplicable to display rights seeing as the Copyright Act did not mention the requirement of actual possession of the work for it to be publicly displayed (in fact, the Act defines such display as 'transmitting a display of the work, by means of any device or process').

References

Arthur C (2006) As Long as Google Sells Ads, Publishers Be Damned. The Guardian (London), available online at http://www.theguardian.com/technology/2006/feb/23/bookscomment.advertising. Accessed 3 Sept 2023

Authors Guild (2015) Court Filing Ends AG v. HathiTrust Copyright Litigation, January 08, 2015, https://www.authorsguild.org/industry-advocacy/court-filing-ends-ag-v-hathitrust-copyright-litigation/. Accessed 3 Sept 2023

Band J (2009) The long and winding road to the Google Books settlement. J Marshall Rev Intell Prop Law 9:227

Barnes A (2018) Petitions of the week: Fox News Network, LLC v. TVEyes, Inc., No. 15-3885 (2d Cir. 2018), petition for writ of certiorari denied by the Supreme Court on 3rd December 2018; via SCOTUS blog, http://www.scotusblog.com/case-files/cases/tveyes-inc-v-fox-news-network-llc/. Accessed 3 Sept 2023

Brachmann S (2018) Supreme Court Denies TVEyes v. Fox News, Leaves Intact 2d Circuit Ruling on Market Harm of Transformative Uses. IPWatchdog 31 Dec 2018. https://www.ipwatchdog.com/2018/12/31/scotus-declines-2d-cir-market-harm-transformative-uses/id=104181/. Accessed 3 Sept 2023

Crews KD (2001) Case summary, A&M Records, Inc. v. Napster, Inc.: Implications for the Digital Music Library, Indiana University Purdue University Indianapolis, http://variations2.indiana.edu/pdf/AnalysisOfNapsterDecision.pdf. Accessed 3 Sept 2023

Darnton R (2009) Google & the Future of Books, N.Y. Review of Books Feb. 12, 2009, at 9, available at http://www.nybooks.com/articles/22281. Accessed 3 Sept 2023

Davies P (2013) Aid, Abet, Counsel or Procure? In: Pitel SGA, Neyers JW, Chamberlain E (eds) Tort law: challenging orthodoxy. Hart Publishing, Portland, pp 413–440

Diaz AS (2013) Fair use & mass digitization: the future of copy-dependent technologies after Authors Guild v. Hathitrust. Berkeley Technol Law J 28. https://www.jstor.org/stable/24122033 Available at SSRN: http://ssrn.com/abstract=2231750

Ginsburg JC, Budiardjo L (2018) Liability for providing hyperlinks to copyright-infringing content: international and comparative law perspectives. Columbia J Law Arts 41:153

Goldstein P (2003) Copyright's highway: from Gutenberg to the Celestial Jukebox. Stanford Law and Politics, Stanford

Higgins P (2014) Another Fair Use Victory for Book Scanning in HathiTrust. Available via EFF.org, 10th June 2014, https://www.eff.org/deeplinks/2014/06/another-fair-use-victory-book-scanning-hathitrust. Accessed 3 Sept 2023

Hugenholtz PB, Senftleben M (2011) Fair use in Europe: In Search of Flexibilities. SSRN Electronic Journal. https://doi.org/10.2139/ssrn.1959554

Intellectual Property Office (2015) Quashing of private copying exception. Available via Gov.uk. https://www.gov.uk/government/news/quashing-of-private-copying-exception/. Accessed 3 Sept 2023

Kerscher G (2012) Declaration of George Kerscher In Support Of Motion For Summary Judgment, Author's Guild et al. v. Hathitrust, et al., Case No. 11-cv-6351(HB) https://cases.justia.com/federal/district-courts/new-york/nysdce/1:2011cv06351/384619/117/0.pdf?ts=1376355293. Accessed 3 Sept 2023

Liemer S (2011) On the origins of Le Droit moral: how non-economic rights came to be protected in French IP law. J Intell Prop Law 19(1):65

Litman J (2007) Lawful personal use. Texas Law Rev 85:1871–1920

Lopez-Tarruella A (2012) The international dimension of Google Activities. In: Lopez-Tarruella (ed) Google and the Law 2012

Lucke B (2009) Die Google Buchsuche nach deutschem Urheberrecht und US-amerikanischem Copyright Law, Lepizig 2009

Mathes A (2005) Preserving public domain books. Available via Google Blog http://googleblog.blogspot.it/2005/11/preserving-public-domain-books.html. Accessed 3 Sept 2023

McCannon BC (2012) Experience goods and risk preferences. SSRN Electronic Journal. https://doi.org/10.2139/ssrn.2194163. http://ssrn.com/abstract=2194163

Meyer T (2011) Political economies of copyright, Droit D'Auteur and the internet: convergence or clash? TPRC 39th edition, September 24, 2011. Available at SSRN: http://ssrn.com/abstract=1985692

Nimmer R (2005) Google lawsuit begins; fair use. Ipinfoblog.com. Archived version available at https://web.archive.org/web/20070216012037/http:/www.ipinfoblog.com/archives/50662-print.html. Accessed 3 Sept 2023

Palmer M (2011) Belgium proves a headache for Google, Financial Times 18th July 2011, https://www.ft.com/content/ea6c9f41-d4c7-3649-a9e5-3611842e47de. Accessed 3 Sept 2023

Picker RC (2009) The Google book search settlement: a new orphan-works monopoly? J Compet Law Econ 5:383–409. https://doi.org/10.1093/joclec/nhp013

RFI (2009) Google told to stop digitising French books. Available online at http://www1.rfi.fr/actuen/articles/120/article_6241.asp. Accessed 3 Sept 2023

Sag M (2010) The Google book settlement and the fair use counterfactual. New York Law School Law Rev 55, 2010; The DePaul University College of Law, Technology, Law & Culture Research Series Paper No. 10-001. Available at SSRN: http://ssrn.com/abstract=1437812

Saltmarsh M (2009) Google Loses in French Copyright Case, via NY Times ed. 18th December 2009, http://www.nytimes.com/2009/12/19/technology/companies/19google.html. Accessed 3 Sept 2023

Samuelson P (2010) Google Book search and the future of books in cyberspace. Minnesota Law Rev 503, Available at SSRN: http://ssrn.com/abstract=1535067, https://scholarship.law.umn.edu/mlr/503

Schechner S (2012) Google Settles Lawsuits Brought by French Authors and Publishers. WSJ June 11th, 2012, online at https://www.wsj.com/articles/SB10001424052702303901504577459971316136552. Accessed 3 Sept 2023

Schroeder P (2005) Google Cannot Rewrite U.S. Copyright Laws. Wall Street Journal 20 Oct. 2005, online at http://www.wsj.com/articles/SB112977420906974032. Accessed 3 Sept 2023

Spelman K (2011) La Société des Auteurs des arts visuels et de l'Image Fixe (SAIF) v. Google: a Parisian Story of the Berne Convention and online infringement claims. Calif Int Law J 19(1)

Travis H (2006) Building universal digital libraries: an agenda for copyright reform. Pepperdine Law Rev 33:819. Available at SSRN: http://ssrn.com/abstract=860784

Travis H (2007) Google book search and fair use: iTunes for Authors, or Napster for Books? Univ Miami Law Rev 61:605. Available at SSRN: http://ssrn.com/abstract=944048

Waelde C, Brown A, Kheria S, Cornwell J (2016) Contemporary intellectual property: law and policy. Oxford University Press, Oxford

Chapter 3
The Mechanics of Flexibility

3.1 Introduction

Returning to the famous quote by Judge Baer in the *Hathitrust* case, it is noteworthy that, when delivering his final points in a judgment to end a milestone battle of traditional intellectual property protection against an innovative investment that was shaking its very foundations, he chose to remark on the value of this novel contribution to the progress of science and creative arts being so immense that it could not have been deemed not to constitute a fair use of the protected works. This inspires the question: where exactly does the flexibility originate, as demonstrated by American judges (albeit not only, as will be shown), in fringe cases pertaining to IP protection in the context of digital innovation?

Until this point, it has been discussed how the flexible U.S. approach built around an intentionally vague and standards-based legislation has led actual court cases to an ending that favours digital innovation on the edge of copyright, contrasting them against their European counterparts. This chapter will continue and build upon this analysis, delving deeper into examining the rationale behind this flexibility in the United States, whose justice system is notably not famous for being flexible as a general characteristic.

The discussion is structured as follows: firstly, it will aim to analyse the wording of rulings to review the legal considerations, means and justifications mentioned directly by judges when taking (or advocating) a flexible stance in fringe cases and then to demonstrate how judicial flexibility extends beyond the vague wording of statutory law in cases where the judges feel the underlying rationale demands it. Then, a similar, yet more desperate search for flexibility in such cases will be demonstrated using a selection of European cases pertaining to digital innovation. A more detailed outline of this reasoning will be stated in the subsections below.

Judgments passed in Google Books cases, as well as in other relevant landmark fair use proceedings have something in common: they all appear to show a certain

K. Drazewski, *Copyright as a Constraint on Creating Technological Value*, Law, Governance and Technology Series 63,
https://doi.org/10.1007/978-3-031-51276-6_3

level of judicial flexibility that does not yet border on judicial activism (as could be claimed for some cases on EU soil) but is nevertheless going beyond what could be seen as simple application of the letter of the law. This subchapter will explore whether indeed it is a matter of the judge being intentionally flexible, notwithstanding what is naturally required due to working under open-ended statutory law. To this end, we will be delving into the justifications given by judges in high-profile U.S. copyright cases and exploring the nature of the transformative use doctrine since its introduction in 1990. As the argument would hardly benefit from discussing cases where the transformative use doctrine has served its purpose (like the examples given in Chap. 2), a closer look will be had on a handful of cases which have been offered by scholars as examples of the transformative use doctrine being too imprecise to fulfil its initial purpose, thus allegedly leaving too much latitude in the hands of the judges. While the criticism offered at the time may be taken with a grain of salt, it will be argued that this, in fact, signifies a utilitarian attitude towards the 'transformative use test' demonstrated by judges in order to preclude it from invading too far into the flexible system established by the deliberately vague four fair use factors.

Later on, a glimpse into analogous European cases will be made to illustrate how European judges are taking a similar stance, yet at a greater effort due to the far less permitting legislation, closing with a prime example of a CJEU case where the Court chose to apply an ostensibly flexible interpretation to relatively straightforward legislation in order to protect the freedoms of users of the Internet from the perils of overregulation. First, however, a look must be taken at the language of fair use cases before the transformative use doctrine came about, leaving an indelible mark on future fair use judgment substantiations.

3.2 Flexibility Considerations in 'Pre-Transformative Use' Justifications in the United States

Below are descriptions of example cases representative of the 'flexible' language used by American judges in reference to fair use considerations, before they were infected, or 'hijacked', by the transformative use considerations following the creation of the doctrine. Language is telling and it is important to look at the actual terms and phrasing used by judges to see how a flexible approach was advocated for, and applied by judges since the very beginnings of fair use cases.

3.2.1 'First' Fair Use Case: Advocating for Flexibility in Judicial Practice

The 1976 Copyright Act, upon introducing the fair use provisions, codified a doctrine originating from common law[1] and one that had long been thought necessary to fulfil 'copyright's very purpose to promote the progress of science and useful arts'.[2] The considerations that later became fair use provisions of the Act had been applied by judges for over a century and arguably arose as a framework ensuring the necessary level of judicial latitude surrounding the delicate matters of potentially fair uses. Indeed, in the landmark 1841 pirating case of *Folsom v. Marsh,*[3] Justice Story of the Circuit Court for Massachusetts made firm points on how, in certain cases, the question of piracy often depended '*upon a nice balance of the comparative use made in one of the materials of the other; the nature, extent, and value of the materials thus used; the objects of each work; and the degree to which each writer may be fairly presumed to have resorted to the same common sources of information, or to have exercised the same common diligence in the selection and arrangement of the materials*'. As an example, the court offered that '*a reviewer may fairly cite largely from the original work, if his design be really and truly to use the passages for the purposes of fair and reasonable criticism*'. More importantly, the court noted that a wide interval exists between uses which are clearly infringing and clearly fair, demanding exercise of great caution and warning against great difficulty in making such assessments. Every case of alleged fair quotation would need to be examined closely: '*a review will not, in general, serve as a substitute for the book reviewed; and even there, if so much is extracted, that it communicates the same knowledge with the original work, it is an actionable violation of literary property*'.[4] The court noted that such cases demanded great caution as much rested upon the nature of the secondary work, the value and extent of the copies, and the degree of injury inflicted upon the original authors.[5] Also included in the opinion, a consideration of using copyrighted material to create an '*original and new work*' may, from today's perspective, have a familiar ring in view of the 1990 work of Judge Leval dedicated to defining the transformative use doctrine as will be discussed further on.

Folsom v. Marsh is often cited as the first fair use case; still, the language used by Justice Story seems to suggest that some established practice had already been in place. It does, nonetheless, seem to take on a similar endeavour as Leval did over a century later; and that is to draw a framework around judicial practices developed in response to the challenges of a complicated and ever-changing matter where

[1] See e.g. Castle Rock Entertainment, Inc. v. Carol Publishing Group, 150 F.3d 132 (2nd Cir. 1998).

[2] Campbell v. Acuff-Rose Music, Inc., 510 U.S. 569, 575 (1994) (quoting U.S. Const., art. I, §8, cl. 8.

[3] Folsom v. Marsh, 9 F.Cas. 342, 348 (No. 4901) (CCD Mass. 1841).

[4] Folsom v. Marsh, quoting Lord Ellenborough, Roworth v. Wilkes, 1 Camp. 94.

[5] Lord Chancellor Cottenham, in Saunders v. Smith, 3 Mylne & C. 711.

statutory law may only aspire to codify flexible standards coined by judges,[6] taking great caution not to restrict them – even if, as it often was noted in regard to the codification of the fair use factors, such regulations sound too broad to be meaningful if they were to be applied without knowledge of the body of case law behind them.

3.2.2 *Harper & Row v. Nation Enterprises*

A memorable case of when the Supreme Court advocated for flexibility in applying fair use provisions, *Harper & Row* has its roots in 1977 when, shortly after the conclusion of his term of office, President Gerald Ford made a contract with publishers Harper & Row and Reader's Digest for the publication of his memoirs, still unwritten at the time. These were highly anticipated due to the expected background information about the Watergate scandal and Ford's pardoning of Nixon; consequently, excerpt pre-publication rights were bought by *Time Magazine*. The manuscript was then leaked to *The Nation*, who produced a short article entitled 'The Ford Memoirs - Behind the Nixon Pardon' using material from the manuscript. As a result, *Time* cancelled its agreement and the licensees sued for infringement. The court of the first instance ruled for the plaintiffs; then, on appeal, the ruling was reversed on grounds of public usability. The Second Circuit Court of Appeals stated that it was not 'the purpose of the Copyright Act to impede that harvest of knowledge so necessary to a democratic state' or 'chill the activities of the press by forbidding a circumscribed use of copyrighted words.'[7] Notably, this wording was later upheld by the Supreme Court, who nevertheless reversed the opinion on grounds of 'insufficient deference' to the scheme of protection established by the Copyright Act.[8] This notwithstanding, quoting the Constitution Copyright Clause[9] in

[6] 'Congress meant § 107 "to restate the present judicial doctrine of fair use, not to change, narrow, or enlarge it in any way" and intended that courts continue the common law tradition of fair use adjudication. H. R. Rep. No. 94-1476, p. 66 (1976); S. Rep. No. 94-473, p. 62 (1975)' – quoted by U.S. Supreme Court in Campbell v. Acuff-Rose Music (92-1292), 510 U.S. 569 (1994).

[7] 723 F.2d 195, 205 (1983) at 197, 209.

[8] Harper & Row v. Nation Enterprises, 471 U.S. 539 (1985).

[9] The Copyright Clause in Article I, Section 8, Clause 8 of the United States Constitution empowers the Congress to '[p]romote the Progress of Science and useful Arts, by securing for limited Times to Authors and Inventors the exclusive Right to their respective Writings and Discoveries'. Its history dates back to the Constitutional Convention in 1787 where proposals were submitted to the Committee of Detail for the wording of the new provision. Some proposals of simply referenced 'securing to literary authors their copyrights for a limited time' were along similar lines as the concurrent British optic of the law affirming a natural right, rather than granting it, still, the one that affected the final wording in terms of defining the goal of copyright was James Madison's clause on aiming 'to encourage, by proper premiums & Provisions, the advancement of useful knowledge and discoveries'.

connection with *Sony Corp. of America v. Universal City Studios,*[10] it observed that the purpose of copyright was to serve as '*a means by which an important public purpose may be achieved. It is intended to motivate the creative activity of authors and inventors by the provision of a special reward, and to allow the public access to the products of their genius after the limited period of exclusive control has expired.*'

It is worth observing that the Copyright Clause of the Constitution is quoted by courts both in judgments finding in favour of fair use and those that do not,[11] suggesting that the 'progress of Science and of useful Arts' formulation may indeed be interpreted quite flexibly.[12] What is also notable in *Harper & Row v. Nation Enterprises* from the perspective of this analysis, is that the case was later quoted for the Supreme Court's flexible approach to the very construct of fair use itself, by stressing the importance of *tailoring fair use analysis to the particular case.*[13]

3.2.3 *Sony Corporation of America v. Universal City Studios*

Deserving analysis as a landmark Supreme Court case involving a flexible approach in dealing with a novel technological solution, *Sony v Universal* is commonly referred to as the *Betamax* case. It is also one where, amidst the political turmoil that surrounded it, the Supreme Court stated, in a straightforward manner, that the Constitution had set forth an overriding goal: that of promoting the Progress of Science and useful Arts in opposition to securing a private benefit.

Sony Corp. was sued as the supplier of Betamax video tape recorders which were used by their owners to record shows off commercially sponsored broadcasts on television, thereby infringing copyright; another claim was that Sony was actively marketing such capabilities of the devices and was thus liable for the infringements committed by their users.[14] Plaintiffs demanded pecuniary damages and an equitable accounting of profits, as well as an injunction against the manufacture and marketing of the Betamax device. The case was lost in District Court[15] and then won on appeal,[16] with the 9th Circuit Court of Appeals ordering the District Court to provide

---

[10] Sony Corp. of America v. Universal City Studios, Inc., 464 U.S. 417, 429 (1984).

[11] See e.g. 13-4829-cv Authors Guild v. Google, Inc., decided October 16, 2015.

[12] As will be shown later, the situation did not change significantly after the introduction of the transformative use doctrine.

[13] See e.g. Salinger v. Random House, Inc., 811 F.2d 90 (2d Cir. 1987).

[14] It was the logic offered decades earlier by Justice Holmes in the *Ben Hur* case, Kalem Co. v. Harper Brothers 222 U.S. 55 (1911); parallels can also be drawn to the 'willful supplier of the murder weapon' reasoning as offered in the Amstrad and Brennan JB7 cases as discussed in Chap. 2.

[15] 480 F.Supp. 429 (1979).

[16] 659 F.2d 963 (1981).

adequate relief. In the atmosphere of a political uproar after the appellate ruling, the Supreme Court granted certiorari and reviewed the case.[17]

Verification of the findings of fact made on earlier stage of the proceedings included studies showing that most Betamax users would use it to a) record television shows to watch them at a later date (time-shifting), and b) record in the process and for the purpose of building their own video libraries. Observing how viewing of television programs has not decreased since the market introduction of the Betamax devices, the Supreme Court commented on the Copyright Clause of the Constitution and the primary public benefit goal that it established. The Court noted that that the monopoly privileges that the Congress may authorize [by means of passing statutory copyright law—KD] have, as its primary object, the '*general benefits derived by the public from the labors of authors*', while rewarding the creator '*serves to induce release to the public of the products of his creative genius*'.[18]

Interestingly, thanks to a public disclosure of court documents by the Library of Congress years later, it became known that the Supreme Court was initially in favour of finding for infringement. Overshadowed by the approaching end of the Court's term, the hot debate among the justices continued around the matters of a statutory exemption of private copies. Over its course, Justice John P. Stevens listed three factors in favour of such an exemption: (1) privacy aspects of the law seeking to control activities conducted at home, (2) the risk of branding millions of users as lawbreakers without a fair warning, (3) the economic interest in '*not imposing a substantial retroactive penalty on an entrepreneur who has successfully developed and marketed a new and useful product*', particularly since no evident harm has been demonstrated.[19] This opinion was countered by Justice Blackmun who noted that the existing limitations on private use already included in the wording of the Act[20] would be '*wholly superfluous if an entire copy of any work could be made by any person for private use*'. As noted later by Goldstein, Blackmun's point was that seeking such intentions in an act of Congress was pointless in view of the existence of the fair use provisions.[21] Eventually, the majority opinion left out any mention of a statutory exemption for private copying and focused on 'substantial non-infringing use' of the device. Justice Blackmun dissented, noting that in ruling thus the Court shied away from duly addressing technological change in view of the 1976 Copyright Act: '*Perhaps a better and more accurate description is that the Court has tended to evade the hard issues when they arise in the area of copyright law. I see no reason for the Court to be particularly pleased with this tradition or to continue it. Indeed, it is fairly clear from the legislative history of the 1976 Act that*

[17] Sony Corp. v. Universal City Studios 464 U.S. 417 (1984).

[18] Stevens J, Opinion of the Court, in Sony Corp. v. Universal…, quoting United States v. Paramount Pictures, Inc., 334 U.S. 131, 158 (1948).

[19] Goldstein (2003).

[20] U.S. Copyright Act, §§ 108(d)(1) and (e)(1).

[21] Goldstein (2003).

Congress meant to [. . .] *enact a statute that would cover new technologies as well as old'*.[22] The dissenting opinion of Justice Blackmun favoured a finding against fair use in this case on grounds of non-productivity of the new use, with a 'potential' for market harm which, in this context, needed not be proved.[23] The 'productivity' as a factor for finding for or against infringement was, however, soon to be replaced, by the 'transformative use' interpretational framework as proposed by Judge Pierre N. Leval.

3.3 Transformative Use: A (Vague) Remedy to Vagueness?

3.3.1 Toward a Standard: Attempting to Bring Order Into Chaos

On the basis of the example cases described in the preceding chapter, it should be observed that a major point made in both the substantiations given by judges (and reused in the submissions of defendants) is the aspect of frequently cited transformative use. To an analyst arising from the civil law tradition, it may be striking how the frequently cited concept is, in fact, not a creation of the lawmaker. Dating back to the judicial concept of 'productive use' describing the act of (unlicensed) taking, or 'borrowing' of copyrighted content in order to create a new value with measurable social utility (as described in the case of *Sony v. Universal*,[24]) the term it is not mentioned among the fair use factors set forth in the 1976 Copyright Act, and only found its way into courtrooms after the landmark publication of *Towards a fair use standard* article by Judge Pierre N. Leval in 1990.

Leval sought to address the perceived lack of guidance in weighing the statutory pre-requisites for an unauthorized use to be declared fair. He observed that decisions in fair use cases were not governed by consistent principles; they were resulting from 'intuitive reactions to individual fact patterns', rendering the system unpredictable.[25] This, he feared, caused the very nature and character of fair use to become lost; instead of a '*disorderly basket of exceptions*' or abandonment of the principles of

[22] *Sony v. Universal*, dissenting opinion by Justice Blackmun, with whom Justice Marshall, Justice Powell, and Justice Rehnquist join.

[23] *Sony v. Universal*, dissenting opinion by Justice Blackmun, with whom Justice Marshall, Justice Powell, and Justice Rehnquist join.

[24] In the proceedings concerning the Sony Betamax recorder, it has been noted by the 9th Circuit Court of Appeals that taping television programs off the air could not be considered fair use due to the 'unproductive nature' of an activity based on pure reproduction. [Universal City Studios v. Sony, 480 F. Supp. 429, 432]. The definition of the term was then amended by the Supreme Court, stating that productive nature of uses of copyrighted material needed to be evaluated by applying a test of utility of the copying, i.e. for educational or entertainment purposes. See Zimmerman (1999), p. 1.

[25] See Leval (1990), p. 1107.

protection, he argued, it should be seen as a '*rational, integral part of copyright, whose observance is necessary to achieve the objectives of that law*'. In this quest for a solid base of fair use evaluations, the most crucial consideration, he argued, was the first of the factors enumerated by Section 17 of the Copyright Code, this being the purpose and character of the use—and examination of whether the use is, in fact, *transformative*. The term he defined as one encompassing the earlier considerations of a *productive* use, but also *employing the quoted matter in a different manner or for a different purpose from the original.* In other words, the test would be passed by a use that is both productive and serves goals different than those of the original work; the examples given included using the borrowed property as raw material for creating '*new information, new aesthetics, new insights and understandings*'.[26]

Leval scrutinized the connections between the first and last statutory fair use factors, that is between the purpose and character of the unauthorized use and the manner and degree to which the market for the protected work was affected. He objected against the most attention being received at the time by the latter factor (dubbed 'undoubtedly the single most important element of fair use' by the Supreme Court in 1985[27]). This, he cautioned, would always lead to leaning the scales in favour of the original creator who always loses some potential revenue as the secondary user does not pay royalties. The fourth factor should only be weighed against the finding of fair use when the secondary work—again—acts as a substitute for, or *supersedes* the original creation.[28] Thus, in one broad stroke, Leval drew a firm parallel between the first and the fourth statutory fair use factors, making the latter dependent on how the first one is fulfilled according to the optic he proposed.[29] In other words, in the offered mode of reasoning, the degree to which the potential market is affected is of secondary significance if the first factor is satisfied by establishing that the unlicensed use of copyrighted work may be deemed as transformative. Interestingly, echoes of this reasoning may be found in the last judgment in the Google Books case (with Judge Leval sitting in the bench). To the claim that by scanning books, Google had been usurping the rights of copyright holders to offer or license a similar service within existing licensing markets for 'substantially the same function that Google provides', the judgment responds that the services offered by Google go beyond the range offered by existing licensing markets. Still, likely in order to avoid the impression that finding a use to be *transformative* could override the fourth consideration (hinted at in *Campbell v. Acuff-Rose*, quoting strongly from *'Toward a fair use standard…'*), the court still noted that '*even if the purpose of the copying is for a valuably transformative purpose, such copying might nonetheless harm the value of the copyrighted original if done in a manner that results in widespread revelation of sufficiently significant portions of the original as to make*

[26] Leval (1990), p. 1111.

[27] Harper & Row v. Nation Enterprises 471 U.S. 539 (1985) at 566.

[28] Leval (1990), p. 1125.

[29] This parallel was later also used by courts; notably in Campbell v. Acuff-Rose Music (92-1292), 510 U.S. 569 (1994).

available a significantly competing substitute'.[30] Given the involvement of Judge Leval in providing the basis on which *Campbell* was decided, this distinction may be viewed as marking the frontiers of his previous argument in protection of the validity of the fourth of the statutory factors.[31]

In the years that followed, the 'transformative use' factor became widely popular in the arguments surrounding fair use cases, referred to by the Supreme Court as being 'central' for finding of fair use and gladly reused by other courts.[32] As originally intended, it indeed allowed to do away with the previously dominating consideration of *productive use*[33] and establish a seemingly predictable line of case law.

3.3.2 Non-paradigm Cases: A Flexible Approach to the Doctrine

Despite Leval's effort to keep the founding analysis straightforward (which may be particularly observed in his strong rebuttal of the 'false' considerations for fair use applied by courts *extra legem*, such as the good or bad faith of the infringing party, protection of artistic integrity (sometimes invoked in court as a reference to the European (*droit moral*) and invasion of privacy,[34] the term 'transformative use' was faced with criticism for being too indeterminate to serve a valid purpose in court in the years that followed. As observed by Diane Leenheer Zimmerman, this indeterminacy has led to cases of strong disagreements between appellate panels of the same court: one bench would support that finding a 'transformative purpose' renders it irrelevant whether the borrowed material is included in a 'new mode of presentation' or not'; another would claim the exact opposite.[35] This lack of uniform agreement on whether the term 'transformative' was even to be applied to the use itself, or, conversely, not to the use at all but to its very purpose, Zimmerman named it a 'Humpty-Dumpty sort of word', meaning whatever is at the time convenient for the party using it and leading to appellate rulings citing the absence of a finding of transformative use, despite the creativity and originality involved.

---

[30] Authors Guild, Inc. v. Google Inc., No. 13-4829-cv (2d Cir. Oct. 16, 2015), p. 34, lines 14–17.

[31] Campbell v. Acuff-Rose Music (92-1292), 510 U.S. 569.

[32] See Campbell, 510 U.S. at 579 and American Geophysical Union v. Texaco Inc., No. 1479, Docket 92-9341; see also e.g. 126 F.3d 70 (2d Cir. 1997) and 150 F.3d 104 (2d Cir. 1998).

[33] One of the last high-profile cases where *productive use* considerations played a strong part in deliberations on the ruling (and remained voiced in the dissenting opinion by Justice Blackmun) was *Universal* v. *Sony* (see footnote 155).

[34] The example given was the *Prince Albert v. Strange* case concerning privately created etchings of Queen Victoria and Prince Albert which were not meant for public display and were illegitimately obtained by a publisher. See also Warren and Brandeis (1890).

[35] Zimmerman (1999), p. 1.

The following rulings will be cited as an illustration of the ambiguity or, to borrow from Durkheim's *Le Suicide*, the anomy that surrounded the first years of the 'transformative' doctrine while settling in, and, to a degree, continue to this day. From the perspective of this analysis, they offer a valuable insight into what really happens when the transformative use doctrine becomes inconvenient in view of the statutory considerations that the judges apply when hearing copyright cases.

3.3.2.1 Dr. Seuss v. Penguin Books

In 1995, Alan Katz and Chris Wrinn created an illustrated book meant as a rhyming-verse satire on O.J. Simpson's murder trial that made a reference to the 1957 novel 'Cat in the Hat' by Theodor S. Geisel, published under the pseudonym of Dr. Seuss. The title, the name 'Dr. Seuss' and the distinctive depiction of the title character in a stove-pipe hat are registered trademarks; still, this is of no significance to the fair use judgment. The book by Katz and Wrinn, entitled 'The Cat NOT in the Hat – a Parody', was published with Penguin Books under the pseudonym of Dr. Juice. It included a drawing of a character wearing a similar stove-pipe hat and made general references, both style- and graphics-wise, to the characteristic style of the original. Dr. Seuss Enterprises, the holder of copyright and trademarks, sued Penguin for both copyright and trademark infringement, seeking injunctive relief. In responding to the claims, the defendants stated that infringement could not be based on the title of the parody (since, as a matter of statutory construction, titles could not claim statutory copyright); similarly, no claim of ownership could be made on the design of lettering, stylized neologisms and onomatopoeia; in the event this reasoning were to fail, Penguin claimed a fair use defence as the work in question was a parody. Still, injunctive relief was granted and the case was appealed.

In examining the non-copyrightability defence, the 9th Circuit Court of Appeals dismissed the claims on the basis that the injunctive relief had been granted on the basis of the back cover illustration and the Cat's Hat, not the typeface, poetic meter, whimsical style or visual style. Having said this, the Court moved on to examine the parody-based fair use defence by weighing the four statutory factors.

Analysing the nature and character of the use, the Court observed that a distinction must be made between a parody (as claimed in the appeal) and satire. In doing this, it reached for the *Pretty Woman* spoof case of *Acuff-Rose* and the reasoning offered by Justice Souter of the Supreme Court.[36] In that case, the Supreme Court

[36]The judge's argument was as follows: 'For the purposes of copyright law, the nub of the definitions, and the heart of any parodist's claim to quote from existing material, is the use of some elements of a prior author's composition to create a new one that, at least in part, comments on that authors works. . . . If, on the contrary, the commentary has no critical bearing on the substance or style of the original composition, which the alleged infringe merely uses to get attention or to avoid the drudgery in working up something fresh, the claim to fairness in borrowing from another's work diminishes accordingly (if it does not vanish), and other factors, like the extent of its commerciality, loom larger.' (Justice Souter, Acuff-Rose).

had observed that a parody must target the original work being parodied[37] and satire, conversely, merely borrows the means of expression to poke fun at a different target: '[parody] *needs to mimic an original to make its point, and so has some claim to use the creation of its victim's (or collective victims) imagination, whereas satire can stand on its own two feet and so requires justification for the very act of borrowing.*' This distinction was crucial as the Penguin book did not make an attempt to ridicule the original 'Cat in the Hat'; *au contraire*, it merely copied its distinctive style without actually conjuring neither its substance nor its content in the context of the O.J. Simpson trial. As such, the work could not be seen as a parody of the original work as '*no effort was made to create a transformative work with 'new expression, meaning, or message"*'.

This 'non-transformative' verdict in *Dr. Seuss Enterprises v. Penguin Books* has been cited as surprising not as much in view of its finding against fair use; it was criticised for stating a non-transformative use when the public was clearly provided 'with a new or reworked product'.[38] This makes the language used in the verdict seem counterintuitive. The work in question was made in a way that would seem highly 'transformative' by the popular understanding of the word; there also was clearly no market substitution. Notably, referring back to the original considerations made by Judge Leval in 1990, it could indeed be claimed that Penguin had indeed the right to claim a fair use defence. Still, the fact remained that, being a satire and not a parody, the work did not stand the test of the first factor, one whose importance Leval had stressed. That test was thus failed and there was no fair use; still, the court clearly felt compelled to also address the 'transformative' aspect and find against it. This shows an interesting dynamic between the statutory considerations and the transformative use doctrine which had become such a useful tool in the judiciary practice that the court would fret to undermine it by admitting that there was indeed a clash between the two in the case—or at least that there was a need of a very serious redefinition of what is being understood as a transformative use. If this were the case, this would constitute a reverse application of the observation made by Geiger in *Flexibilising Copyright*, by reaching for an internal rule to protect the coherency of the subject against the contradictions caused by external principles.[39]

---

[37] Justice Kennedy in Acuff-Rose.

[38] Zimmerman (1999), p. 4.

[39] In 2008, Christophe Geiger made observations on how, at times, the fundamental idea for a rule is controversial; in such cases, the court would reach for external principles, e.g. from other branches of the law, to ensure coherency of the subject. In our case, this would be a reversal of this mechanism. See Geiger (2008).

3.3.2.2 Castle Rock Entertainment, Inc. v. Carol Publishing Group

Another case that has been offered as exemplary of the ambiguity of the doctrine was Castle Rock Entertainment, Inc. v. Carol Publishing Group,[40] decided on appeal by the United States Court of Appeals for the Second Circuit in 1998. Castle Rock Entertainment was the holder of rights to the *Seinfeld* television series, revolving around the New York lives of four single adult friends. The defendants were Beth Golub (author) and Carol Publishing Group (publisher) of *The Seinfeld Aptitude Test, or The SAT*, a book comprising tests of fan knowledge revolving solely around trivia from the series' episodes, divided according to their level of 'expert' knowledge about the series that was required to answer. The questions pertained exclusively to the plot and characters featured in the series. Castle Rock sued Golub and Carol Publishing for copyright infringement and won in the first instance. The Second Circuit's reasoning in regard to establishing derivative nature and 'substantial similarity' in view of similar case law, including the *Twin Peaks* case,[41] is less than relevant from the perspective of this analysis; however, the fair use and transformative use considerations of the court should be reflected upon as they have, similarly to *Dr. Seuss*, become the subject of criticism.

In evaluating the purpose and character of use, the court first noted that the commercial nature of the allegedly infringing action was of lesser importance, since—in the words of James Boswell—'*no man but a blockhead ever wrote, except for money*'. To inquire into the first factor, it was deemed fit to evaluate whether it was a case of the secondary work 'superseding' the original, or adding value to the original by '*adding something new, with a further purpose or different character, altering the first with new [. . .] meaning or message*' in a manner described in Pierre Leval's landmark paper, i.e. by using the original work as a raw material, '*transformed in the creation of new information, new aesthetics, new insights and understandings*' which, as the court noted, could be summarised with the quote from Campbell that '*the goal of copyright, to promote science and the arts, is generally furthered by the creation of transformative works.*'[42]

Having noted that the criteria for finding an exonerating purpose and character of the use would be those defined by Leval as transformative use, the court proceeded to evaluate the defendants' claims that the SAT was to qualify as 'criticism, comment, scholarship' given that would be the nature of a text testing the knowledge of *Ulysses* or *Hamlet*. The argument was that the mundane nature of the subject matter should not alter the result of the fair use analysis since a comment, as such, was just as allowed irrespective of artistic value of the work commented upon.

[40] Castle Rock Entertainment, Inc. v. Carol Publishing Group, 150 F.3d 132 (2nd Cir. 1998).

[41] The case pertained to an unauthorized compendium entitled *Welcome to Twin Peaks: A Complete Guide to Who's Who and What's What*, containing exhaustive information about the plot and characters. Due to significant market substitution, it was declared not to be fair use. See *Twin Peaks v. Publications Int'l, Ltd.*, 996 F.2d 1366 (2d Cir. 1993).

[42] Campbell, 510 U.S. at 579.

Secondly, the defendants claimed that the SAT was also a critical text, '*decod[ing] the obsession with . . . and mystique that surround[s] 'Seinfeld," by 'critically restructur[ing] [Seinfeld's mystique] into a system complete with varying levels of 'mastery' that relate the reader's control of the show's trivia to knowledge of and identification with their hero, Jerry Seinfeld.*'[43] This earned a witty response from the plaintiffs, observing that '*had defendants been half as creative in creating The SAT as were their lawyers in crafting these arguments about transformation, defendants might have a colorable fair use claim.*'

Both the critical nature and the general transformative nature of the work were rebuked by the court, noting that the purpose was clearly neither to educate viewers nor to comment on, or criticize the series, but to 'repackage' *Seinfeld* for its fans. What seemed to be the straw that broke the camel's back in this case was the cover, which—instead of promising comments or critique of the series, or a research tool—promised to 'capture *Seinfeld*'s flavor in a quiz book fashion'. There was no effort of parody (which, as the court noted, would have built a stronger case) and no effort to 'educate, criticize, parody, comment, report upon or research the original work, or otherwise serve a transformative purpose'. As a result, the judgment of the district court was affirmed.

Castle Rock v. Carol Publishing has been criticized for not finding transformative use where the original work had been clearly transformed to serve a new purpose, as the book 'relied on the fans' knowledge of the episodes but did not directly reproduce them or even something close to them.'[44] Some attributed this move to the earlier precedent in the case of *Twin Peaks*[45] where an unlicensed book of trivia went further as to tell the story of the original creation. Just as Carol Publishing would have had a stronger defence had there been a parody element to meet one of the sample criteria, Castle Rock would have had a more straightforward case of infringement had the SAT book followed the earlier example and included the original story, instead of just a set of trivia quizzes.[46] Still, despite the criticism based on the typical understanding of the term *transformative*, one could possibly agree with the position of the court—perhaps even more easily than in *Dr. Seuss*—given that, as observed earlier, the ambition of the publisher had not been to create anything new, but to serve the consumers of the original work a 'repackaged version' of *Seinfeld*. In this regard, however narrow a meaning was attributed by the court to *transformative use*, it not being affirmed by the court is not overly surprising given the rationale provided. On the other hand, Zimmerman (1999) commented on the case as an 'obvious' example of a confusing understanding of '*transformative use*'.

---

[43] Castle Rock v. Carol Publishing, para. 26.

[44] Zimmerman (1999).

[45] Twin Peaks Prods., Inc. v. Publications Intern., Inc., 996 F.2d 1366 (2d Cir. 1993).

[46] From a current perspective, one could even ask the question about transformative use the way it was defined in the *Seinfeld* or even *Twin Peaks* cases, in comparison to the *Google Books* defense which, among other factors, relied upon providing information about the content of the original work. Still, one could say the value of the search functions offered, combined with information about the searched book would suggest that it is entirely a different matter.

While perhaps remaining agnostic on the 'obvious' part, this view may generally be seen as justified.

3.3.2.3 AP v. Meltwater[47]

A more recent case to demonstrate the vagueness of the 'transformative use' term and its loose application, the 2013 *Associated Press v. Meltwater* was a copyright dispute over *Global Media Monitoring*, a news-monitoring service offered by Meltwater, a Norwegian-founded SaaS (Software-as-a-Service) company, to its subscribers since 2005. Meltwater's crawlers indexed and scraped news stories off the Web, and then sent daily snippets to its subscribers, matched to their 'standing agents', i.e. pre-defined search queries. It also allowed ad-hoc searches conducted in real time, with results being also offered as snippets. Every matched article was labelled with information identifying its source, such as the publisher and the country of origin, and contained two snippets: a 300 characters-long opening of the article, and then a 140-character line of text with the highlighted search phrase that triggered the march. The user could then click the provided link to be transferred to the original material.[48] Where the original material had been already removed, the redirected reader would see 'whatever content the operator of the webpage had chosen to display in place of the original article'.[49] Associated Press felt it infringed copyright in the materials in question and filed suit on February 14, 2012. In its response, Meltwater argued that their use was transformative, using content for a new purpose, this being as an 'information-location' tool.

The SDNY court observed that AP's business mode included licensing of access to the news stories it created; this included licensing to entities offering a similar snippet functionality as that of Meltwater. It noted that Meltwater had been marketing its service as one to trace and monitor media coverage and to stay informed on current events; it also observed that the Meltwater service had been described by an employee as allowing 'not to read the whole article' and thus saving time. The snippet function came with a multitude of other functions, such as charts and graphs showing geographic distribution of hits to search queries; tools available to users also included automated classification of coverage depending on its tone (negative, positive or neutral), analyses of current trends etc. The snippets being of generally standardized length covered a varying percentage of the original article; at times as low as 4.5%, in regard to very short pieces the percentage grew significantly, reaching 61% in one demonstrated case.

In the fair use analysis, the court made the customary reference to Campbell 'fair use defense permitting courts to avoid the 'rigid application of the copyright statute'

[47] The Associated Press v. Meltwater U.S. Holdings, Inc. et al., No. 1:2012cv01087 - Document 156 (S.D.N.Y. 2013).

[48] Masnick (2013).

[49] AP v. Meltwater, p. 14.

when 'it would stifle the very creativity which the law is designed the foster.'[50] Having presented the statutory fair use criteria, the court cited Infinity Broadcast to say that 'use of copyrighted material that merely repackages or republishes the original is unlikely to be deemed a fair use' and a 'change of format, though useful' is not transformative'.[51] Then, quoting from Leval and Castle Rock, made a point about the original content being used as 'raw material, transformed in the creation of new information, new aesthetics, new insights and understandings'.[52] On this basis, the court found the use in question to be non-transformative, by virtue of using computer programs to '*automatically capture and republish designated segments of text from news articles, without adding any commentary or insight in its News Reports.*' The court had refused to consider Meltwater a search engine facilitating access to information; on the contrary, due to its business model and its marketing which to some extent had made references to substituting the original material, it was considered to have built a business model around 'consistent copying of creative expression' that was not transformative. Meltwater was found to make money directly from 'undiluted use' of protected material, conveying an intent of serving as a substitute for AP's news service. The court ended on a strong note that 'permitting Meltwater to take the fruit of AP's labour for its own profit, without compensating AP, [would injure] AP's ability to perform this essential function of democracy' and added comments on public interest in enforcement of copyright laws and ensuring a level playing field on grounds of competition: *'the public interest in the existence of such commercial enterprise does not outweigh the strong public interest in the enforcement of the copyright laws or justify allowing Meltwater to free ride on the costly news gathering and coverage work performed by other organizations. Moreover, permitting Meltwater to avoid paying licensing fees gives it an unwarranted advantage over its competitors who do pay licensing fees'.*

The AP position and the SDNY ruling were met with multi-faceted criticism that many hoped would be addressed on appeal.[53] In its amicus curiae brief of 2013, the Electronic Frontier Foundation had criticized AP's approach citing a multitude of cases where transformative use has been defined in favour of electronic search services[54]; some authors noted the court became unnecessarily focused on matters of competition, since AP had been licensing access to companies offering news monitoring and snippet view[55]; others addressed the brusque manner the court displayed towards transformative use, despite strong similarities to other content indexing/snippet view cases (citing the use as 'highly transformative') as discussed earlier in this work. Similarly as in the *Dr. Seuss* case, the fact that the use of source

[50] Campbell, 510 U.S. at 577.

[51] Infinity Broadcast Corp., 150 F.3d at 108 & n.2.

[52] Leval (1990); see also Castle Rock v. Carol Publishing.

[53] An appeal was never filed. Months after the judgement, AP and Meltwater signed an agreement to regulate their future collaboration.

[54] See https://www.eff.org/document/amicus-brief-14. Accessed 03 September 2023.

[55] Masnick (2013).

material had clearly served a new purpose and offered a range of possibilities with hardly any market substitution had not swayed the court and its use of the transformative use doctrine, putting into question the very sense of its application.

3.3.2.4 Righthaven v. Jama[56]

The Centre for Intercultural Organizing ('CIO') was a non-profit entity that republished on its website an entire article on the police targeting minorities, originally by the Las Vegas Review Journal ('LVRJ'). Righthaven LLC was a litigation company with a business model which involved having copyright claims assigned to it (in a limited and revocable manner) by the aggrieved parties, and then, acting as the copyright owner, pushing alleged infringers to settle or taking them to courts. The LVRJ assigned its rights to the article in question to Righthaven, and Righthaven sued CIO over copyright infringement.

Examining the four fair use factors, the court determined that the use had been transformative, non-commercial, informative rather than creative, impractical to cut down, and not harmful to the market as the use was non-commercial and the plaintiff had failed to establish that there was a market in the first place.

The ruling was criticized on some levels. For example, the 'informative' and non-creative aspect was put in doubt given that the article in question was not a simple news story; on the contrary, it '*totaled 33 paragraphs and involved planning, research, multiple interviews and probably a good amount of work in the writing and editing process*',[57] or that the 'educational' character made it impractical to use less than an entirety of the article.[58]

What seems to have merited more attention, however, is the loose approach taken by the court to the matter of transformative use. Leaving aside the obvious observation that the CIO '*did not alter a single word of the article*',[59] in a clear move to punish Righthaven for its business model based on trading claims and copyright trolling, the court disregarded the fact that the use in question was exactly the same as that of the original publisher, as it did Righthaven's weak assignment of rights, limited effectively to the right to sue and revocable in the event of no suit being filed.[60] From this perspective, the argument of the use being 'transformative' due to it being different than that of the copyright trolls is one more proof that Leval's attempt to render the copyright system more strict had not been entirely successful, and that Zimmerman was right in her critique of the term 'transformative' having

[56]Righthaven v. Jama D. Nev. April 22, 2011, 2:10-cv-01322-JCM -LRL.

[57]Green (2011).

[58]Neuburger (2011).

[59]Generalpatent.com, Picking Your Battles, 18 May 2011.

[60]For more on the nature of Righthaven's business model and the resulting lack of standing see Righthaven LLC, Plaintiff–Appellant, v. Wayne Hoehn, Defendant–Appellee, 9th Cir., Nos. 11–16751, 11–16776, decided 9 May 2013.

essentially become a loosely applicable term of art to bring additional justification to a judgment based on other considerations.

3.3.3 Conclusions

From the above non-paradigm judgments emerges a much clearer glance at the nature of the transformative use doctrine. In all these cases, the 'transformativeness' aspect was not really of any use (and, particularly in *Dr Seuss* and *Castle Rock*, it seemingly became a burden on the courts in cases otherwise easily resolved under the statutory considerations). In seeking to explain the 'twisting and turning' done by judges in their context, Zimmerman offers that perhaps the courts felt compelled, faced with a growing body of case law, to address the 'transformative' aspect in the context of the analysis.[61] This could be seen as indeed likely. However, one more observation comes to mind, of a more systemic nature: the application of the 'transformative use' term in the cases shows that, using the perhaps mundane analogy to Arthur C. Clarke's Monolith, in judicial practice, transformative use doctrine may have become a Swiss-Army knife: a highly useful, universal and flexible tool for reaching and substantiating conclusions which the judges have reached based on an analysis often, but not necessarily involving simple application of the original characteristics offered by Judge Leval. This demonstrates how, despite the unquestionable value of Leval's proposed standard, intended to bring a solid base into fair use cases (setting aside the possible pressure to at least address it in applicable cases), judges are willing to accept it only as far as is does not restrict the flexibility allowed to them under the original statutory factors in furtherance of ultimate goals of copyright law.

3.4 Looking for Flexibility: Examples of European Copyright Cases

3.4.1 Bildersuche (Vorschaubilder I)[62]

On the other side of the Atlantic, a strong example of a case where a circumscribed legal framework forced the court to look for flexibilities in a manner extending well into the area of judicial activism was the 2010 *Vorschaubilder I* (also referred to as *Bildersuche I*) case argued before the German Federal Supreme Court (*Bundesgerichtshof*). It pertained to the allegedly infringing use of thumbnail pictures by an operator of an Internet search engine, in this case Google. The

[61] Zimmerman (1999), p. 260.

[62] BGH, Urteil vom 29. 4. 2010 – I ZR 69/08 – Vorschaubilder I.

functionality being challenged was not far different from that discussed in the American cases of *Kelly v. Arriba Soft Corp.* and *Perfect 10 Inc. v Amazon.com Inc.* and pertained to using an automated service for making and storing smaller-sized copies of protected images located on websites (thumbnails of approx. 100x150 pixels and a file size of 4–5 kilobytes, yet still 'retaining the essential creative features'), without asking permission of the respective copyright holders, and then using them in the course of commercial activity, particularly by displaying image thumbnails in search results in response to textual search phrases. By doing so, Google violated § 15, subsec. 2, item 2 of the Author's Law *Urheberrechtsgesetz* (UrhG) in connection with § 19a which secures the exclusive right to make one's works available to members of the public, via wired or wireless access, at a time and place individually chosen.[63]

The plaintiff was a visual artist, who had been running a website containing pictures of her works since 2003. In February 2005, she entered a search phrase into Google that included her name; in return, she was presented with search results involving thumbnail pictures created using her own art presented on her website. Seeing this as a copyright infringement, the plaintiff sought injunctive relief in court, seeking for the defendant to be prohibited from conducting reproduction, making available on the Internet and modification/alteration of her copyrighted work, as was the case with Google.

Google rejected the claims of the plaintiff. In its defence, it stated that the use of the images did not infringe the rights of the plaintiff and that it fell under copyright exemptions for transient or incidental reproduction of no economic significance (*flüchtige oder begleitende Vervielfältigungshandlung ohne eigenständige wirtschaftliche Bedeutung*, §44a of the UrhG)—and even if it was not found to be the case, the plaintiff had herself made the images available on the Web by publishing them on her website and thus making them freely accessible (*frei zugänglich*) on the Internet which signified an 'implicit acquiescence' (*eine konkludente Einwilligung*) of the plaintiff for the images to be accessed and processed by services such as Google's Image Search function. According to the defendant, this was signified by the fact that the plaintiff had the technical possibilities of programming her website scripts to the effect that the pictures could not be accessed by automated services like the ones used by search engines, and yet did not include any such scripts on the website. Moreover, the website had undergone a search engine optimization to 'lure' search engines to it by inclusion of characteristic 'meta' elements also influencing the behaviour of the image search function. The case was dismissed in the first instance and again on appeal,[64] then submitted to the Federal Supreme Court for review.

[63] 'Das Recht, das Werk drahtgebunden oder drahtlos der Öffentlichkeit in einer Weise zugänglich zu machen, dass es Mitgliedern der Öffentlichkeit von Orten und zu Zeiten ihrer Wahl zugänglich ist.' - UrhG §§ 19a.

[64] OLG Jena 27.02.2008 - 2 U 319/07 GRUR-RR 2008, 223.

The Jena court of appeals (*Oberlandesgericht*) observed that the pictures were indeed protected works of art whose digitalization did not deprive them of protection, and that including them in search results may have infringed the right to make available to the public as mentioned in § 19a in connection with § 15, subsec. 2, item 2 of the UrhG. Nevertheless, the creation and use of thumbnails constituted a transformation of the original work which, in order to be used or published, required consent by the author of the primary work under §23 UrhG, and this consent had not been granted.[65] Including thumbnails in displayed search results was the kind of use considered in § 15 Abs. 2. The court noted that shrunken versions of the images did not qualify as quotation; similarly, Google's 'transient or incidental reproduction of no economic significance' defense of § 44a was rejected, on the grounds that the use of thumbnails is of a lasting nature and would continue to bring about numerous earning opportunities, particularly through advertising.[66] Lastly, implied consent (*stillschweigende Einwilligung*) could not be claimed on the basis of posting images on a website without involving technological protective measures.[67] However, issuing an injunction against the search engine operator would be considered an 'abuse of rights' (*rechtsmissbräuchlich*) citing § 242 BGB.[68] This abuse was seen in the contradictory behaviour of the plaintiff: the artist had optimized the source code on her website to attract automated content-analyzing services, and then opposed a 'customary process' (*übliche Verfahren*) of the services in question in reference to transforming her content into thumbnails. On these grounds, revision of the judgment and issuance of an injunction was refused.

The *Bundesgerichtshof* affirmed that the defendant had interfered with the exclusive right of the applicant to exploit their works in tangible form[69] (§ 15 Abs. 1 UrhG). The digital image files stored by the plaintiff on her website constitute 'physical fixations' (*körperliche Festlegungen*) of her paintings and thus constitute copies within the meaning of the UrhG. The thumbnail pictures merely reduced the works of the plaintiff, but without any 'essential changes' (*wesentliche*

[65] 'Bearbeitungen oder andere Umgestaltungen des Werkes dürfen nur mit Einwilligung des Urhebers des bearbeiteten oder umgestalteten Werkes veröffentlicht oder verwertet werden', §23 UrhG, 1st sentence.

[66] 'Die Anzeige der Vorschaubilder sei keine lediglich flüchtige oder begleitende Vervielfältigungshandlung ohne eigenständige wirtschaftliche Bedeutung. Die Anzeige erfolge vielmehr dauerhaft und biete dem Verwerter eine Vielzahl von Einnahmemöglichkeiten, insbesondere durch Werbung' - BGH, I ZR 69/08, para. 13 quoting OLG Jena 2 U 319/07 GRUR-RR 2008, 223.

[67] 'Aus dem Umstand, dass die Klägerin ihre Bilder ins Internet eingestellt habe, ohne technisch mögliche Schutzmaßnahmen zu ergreifen, ergebe sich auch keine stillschweigende Einwilligung' - BGH, I ZR 69/08, para. 14.quoting OLG Jena 2 U 319/07 GRUR-RR 2008, loc. cit.

[68] Under § 242 BGB, the debtor is obliged to carry out their performance in good faith and observance of rules of social conduct ('*Der Schuldner ist verpflichtet, die Leistung so zu bewirken, wie Treu und Glauben mit Rücksicht auf die Verkehrssitte es erfordern.*').

[69] 'Das ausschließliche Recht der Klägerin eingegriffen hat, [die] Werke in körperlicher Form zu verwerten'. The cited regulation of § 15 Abs. 1 UrhG secures the author's exclusive right to exploit their works in tangible form, including in particular reproduction, distribution and exhibition.

Veränderungen) which made them – size aside – identical to the original works. In this regard, the court observed, even further reaching transformations that would still be devoid of their 'own creative expression' (*eigene schöpferische Ausdruckskraft*), would still be considered a remodeling (*Umgestaltung*) of the original work and thus still falling under the same category due to lack of originality and the 'matching overall impression' (*übereinstimmender Gesamteindruck*). The court then noted that, by storing thumbnails independently of their original source, and controlling their availability through its services, the defendant meets the criteria of § 19a (i.e. on making them publicly available). The fact that an Internet user first needs to enter a search phrase for the earlier created thumbnails to be retrieved and displayed does not change the legal qualification of the use, whose nature is as defined in § 19a UrhG and lies in the act of making available (*zugänglichmachen*) which is effected and controlled by the defendant. The court also ruled out the application of copyright exceptions as claimed by the defendant. The defendant could not claim that the thumbnail pictures constituted a standalone work created through free use of another person's work (*ein selbständiges Werk, das in freier Benutzung des Werkes eines anderen geschaffen worden ist*) which would have been allowed under § 24 UrhG. Merely by virtue of shrinking an image, yet retaining the essential creative properties of the original, it cannot be claimed that a transformation (*Umgestaltung*) has been created. Qualifying thumbnails as citation was also ruled out both on the grounds of the UrhG in its wording at the time of the infringement and the amended wording after implementation of the InfoSoc Directive.

Nevertheless, the court observed, the injunction as demanded by the plaintiff was rightly denied. Despite the violation of § 15 Abs. 2 Satz 2, § 19 a UrhG (making publicly available) as the search engine returned thumbnail pictures of the plaintiff's works upon entry of a search term containing her name, the defendant's action was not illegal on grounds of consent having been implicitly granted by the plaintiff, despite the lack of making an express declaration of intent (*Willenserklärung*) to this effect, the existence of which cannot be derived plainly from the inclusion of keywords in the source code of the webpage. However, the court of appeals had erred in assuming that such a consent would need to meet criteria as are generally considered under the applicable doctrine in transferring rights to use a copyrighted work. On the basis of the facts of the case as determined by the court of appeals, it should be deemed that, by positive action of the plaintiff, and despite the fact that no express consent had been granted, the defendant could assume that implied consent had been issued to the processing of the works by a search engine as no adequate safeguards (*hinreichende Sicherungen*) were implemented in order to prevent this processing. Also, the fact that the plaintiff objected against the images being displayed in the search results of one search engine has no impact on the interpretation of the discussed consent as the 'declaration of consent' is made to an indefinite circle of people.[70]

[70] 'Der lediglich gegenüber dem Betreiber einer einzelnen Bildersuchmaschine [...] geäußerte Widerspruch, mit dem Auffinden der Bilder durch dessen Bildersuchmaschine nicht einverstanden

The 2010 *Vorschaubilder* case is notable for the clearly technology- or, depending on perspective, innovation-friendly attitude adopted by the courts—and a commendable dedication to finding a legal solution amidst regulations of statutory law which clearly lacked either an applicable provision to govern such use of copyrighted intellectual property, or the flexibility to leave room for situations precisely like the one in question. The BGH had chosen to rest its decision on an 'implied consent' construct that made the tacit assumption of there being an 'opt-out' model with Google's search functions which had not been taken into consideration by the copyright holder in this case. More notably, the full BGH ruling is an extensive list of legal provisions that, absent the construct that was ambitious, yet legally of questionable strength (as evidenced in its ruling out by the appellate court in the same proceedings), demonstrate how a legalist approach would have led to the case being resolved against Google and its image search service. This 'activist' attitude has been praised as a sign of dedication to protecting the social benefits brought about by Google's business model.[71] Also the 'judicial resourcefulness' in coming up with the solution has been noted, yet with a grain of salt: the ruling reads almost like an indictment against the circumscribedness of copyright law. As commented by Paul Hugenholtz and Martin Senftleben, the case was one of many examples demonstrating that EU courts are aware of the lack of capacity in copyright law to recognize that certain free uses of copyright works may be desirable for social, cultural, economic or other reasons: '[w]*hile the courts' judicial resourcefulness deserves applause, these cases are* [...] *symptomatic of a legal system that lacks an appropriate escape valve. Flexibility should ideally be found inside the system of copyright proper*'.[72]

3.4.2 *Vorschaubilder II*[73]

A year after the first *Vorschaubilder* case, another one of a related, yet slightly different nature ended up ruled upon before the *Bundesgerichtshof.* The decision, significantly shorter than its predecessor, shows the court taking further its earlier line of reasoning (and further expanding its definition of consent).

The plaintiff was a photographer who had, at one point, done a photoshoot of the TV anchor Collien Fernandes. These photos were then licensed a number of online services. In December 2006 and March 2007, the photographer discovered, using the Google Image Search function, that that those pictures were featured on two

zu sein, ist für die Auslegung der Einwilligungserklärung, [...] schon deshalb ohne Bedeutung, weil diese Einwilligungserklärung als solche an einen unbestimmten Personenkreis gerichtet ist.' – BGH, I ZR 69/08, para. 42.

[71] Clark (2010).

[72] Hugenholtz and Senftleben (2011), p. 12.

[73] *Vorschaubilder II*, BGH 19.10.2011 - I ZR 140/10.

websites without his permission. Thumbnails of his pictures were displayed in Google search results displayed as links leading to those infringing websites. This use of his copyrighted work by Google he considered an infringement, and filed for injunctive relief prohibiting Google from displaying his works as thumbnails to the German public in its search results. The plaintiff also demanded that Google be obliged to provide information on the extent of the unauthorized use of his photographs and that it reimbursed both his legal fees and his estimated loss due to the said unauthorized use.

The case was ruled in favour of the plaintiff before the district court, but the ruling was reversed on appeal. The photographer then appealed to the *Bundesgerichtshof* which examined the case as against the background of the *Vorschaubilder I* ruling of last year. The court noted again that illegality is ruled out when copyrighted property is being put on display on the Internet without protective measures (*Schutzvorkehrungen*). The plaintiff stressed that the images in question were published without his consent; this, however, in the view of the court, was not the entire picture. As the court observed, the plaintiff had, in the past, licensed the online display of the images in question to third-party website operators. In doing so, the court reasoned, the plaintiff had granted 'effective consent' (*wirksame Einwilligung*) to his images being used as thumbnail pictures, not limited to the display of images which have been put online with the author's consent.[74] It is well known, the court observed, that search engines operate on the basis of automated processes which do not distinguish between images published by a duly authorized party and those posted by one lacking such authorization.[75] On the basis of the images being published, the court reasoned, the search engine operator 'can and may' (*kann und darf*) assume a consent that encompasses display of thumbnails also in regard to copies which have been put online without consent of the author.[76] The author is, nonetheless, entitled to bring claims against parties who conduct unauthorized publication of his images on the Internet.

Expanding on the construct it had earlier built in *Vorschaubilder I,* the BGH ruling does not surprise in holding to the presumption of implied consent which, seemingly, can only be contested on a case-by-case basis in regard to unauthorized parties engaging in publication of the content in question. It is however noteworthy

[74] 'Die von einem Dritten mit Zustimmung des Urhebers durch Einstellen von Abbildungen des Werkes ins Internet wirksam erklärte Einwilligung in die Anzeige in Vorschaubildern ist – so der Bundesgerichtshof – nicht auf die Anzeige von Abbildungen des Werkes beschränkt, die mit Zustimmung des Urhebers ins Internet eingestellt worden sind.' – BGH Mitteilung 19. 10. 2011 – 165/11.

[75] 'Es ist allgemein bekannt, dass Suchmaschinen, die das Internet in einem automatisierten Verfahren nach Bildern durchsuchen, nicht danach unterscheiden können, ob ein aufgefundenes Bild von einem Berechtigten oder einem Nichtberechtigten ins Internet eingestellt worden ist.' – BGH Mitteilung 19. 10. 2011 – 165/11.

[76] 'Deshalb kann und darf der Betreiber einer Suchmaschine eine solche Einwilligung dahin verstehen, dass sie sich auch auf die Anzeige von solchen Abbildungen in Vorschaubildern erstreckt, die ohne Zustimmung des Urhebers ins Internet eingestellt worden sind' – BGH Mitteilung 19. 10. 2011 – 165/11.

for how it addresses a different and more complex case by further expanding the opt-out concept of publishing on the Internet. Exonerating a search engine provider on the basis that any legitimate earlier publication online without due protection on a presumption of consent for the content, also when illegally copied, to be processed on a meta level by Internet crawlers, referred to by some as 'impenetrable logic',[77] could be deemed a highly realist perspective in regard to how the Internet works, effectively creating a safe space for search engine operators. Still, the rules of this presupposed opt-out scheme paint a rather grim picture for rightsholders: they are only safe as long as their licensees include due means of protection on their websites against automatic indexing services. Without getting into debate on what standards of protection would be considered sufficient, without much effort one could imagine a scenario where uncontrolled dissemination of pictures (along with the associated thumbnails) begins once a licensee website drops its protection e.g. as a result of a webmaster error a long time after the publication; the same doubts apply to a situation where a licensee website were to fail to meet its obligations to apply such means of protection from the upstart. Would this tip over the search engines' safe space in this regard? Alongside a common root of the issue, these questions appear to be another link to the first *Vorschaubilder* case: the 'implied consent v1.1' as proposed by the BGH in *Vorschaubilder II* remained an elaborate yet prosthetic solution by its very nature; and by testing the devised legal construct against a variety of theoretical, yet highly possible situations it would soon begin to show its deficiencies rendering it unsustainable over a long term.

3.4.3 SAIF v. Google Inc. and Google France[78]

Also decided in 2011, already touched upon in the preceding chapter in antecedence of Google Books' legal adventures in Europe, the case of *La société Des Auteurs des Arts Visuels et de L'image Fixe Visual Auteurs* (SAIF) against Google France is a strong example of courts actively looking for a way not to shut the door on a new technological solution that is clearly beneficial to the public. As will be demonstrated, this was done in the face of an overwhelmingly precise IP legislation which, to a judge taking the legalist approach, would leave little doubt as to ruling in favour of existing rightsholders who felt the new solution had threatened their legitimate interests.

On 17th April 2005, SAIF filed suit before the Paris *Tribunal de grande instance* (TGI) against Google Inc. and its local subsidiary Google France for committing acts of infringement by reproducing and offering Internet users the viewing of 'thousands

[77] Clark (2012).

[78] Cour d'Appel de Paris, Pôle 5 - Chambre 1, Arrêt du 26 janvier 2011, http://juriscom.net/wp-content/documents/caparis20110126.pdf. Accessed 03 September 2023.

of works' belonging to its repertoire and without its permission.[79] This violated the provisions of Articles L 122-4, prohibiting any full or partial reproduction,[80] and L 335-2 of the French Code of intellectual property (*Code de la propriété intellectuelle*), setting forth a rigid definition of counterfeit works.[81] The plaintiffs also demanded EUR 50,000 in damages, 60,000 in legal fees and EUR 80,000,000 as 'restorative compensation' (*l'indemnité réparatrice*). Google was to be banned from further reproduction of images as thumbnails unless an agreement were to be executed to this end with SAIF.

Google countered that French law should not apply due to the location of its servers, and that the Paris court should review the case under U.S. federal copyright law, in particular its fair use provisions. Google invoked Article 5.2 of the Berne Convention,[82] stating that the extent of protection, as well as the means of redress afforded to the author to protect his rights, shall be governed exclusively by the laws of the country where protection is claimed. This country, according to Google's interpretation, was the United States. Alternatively, it claimed that the said search services did not affect 'normal exploitation of the works of authors' (*l'exploitation normale des oeuvres des auteurs*) and that the image search did not differ, in essence, from the text search services that were offered.

The TGI observed that all of Google search services were hosted within its premises in Mountain View, California. Search engines, it observed, do not store images, videos or news but only the addresses of the websites that fit the user's query and direct them to the site containing the answer to the query (*les moteurs de recherche ne stockent pas les images, les vidéos ou les actualités mais seulement les adresses des sites internet qui permettent de répondre à la question que se pose l'internaute et de le diriger vers le site qui contient la réponse à sa question*).

---

[79] See https://www.legalis.net/jurisprudences/tribunal-de-grande-instance-de-paris-3eme-chambre-1ere-section-jugement-du-20-mai-2008/. Accessed 03 September 2023.

[80] Under Article L 122-4, any full or partial representation or reproduction (*toute représentation ou reproduction intégrale ou partielle*) made without the consent of the author or his successors or assigns is deemed unlawful. The same applies to translation, adaptation or transformation, arrangement or reproduction by any technique or process (*la traduction, l'adaptation ou la transformation, l'arrangement ou la reproduction par un art ou un procédé quelconque*).

[81] Under Article L 335-2, forbidden as counterfeiting, under pain of 500,000 EUR penalty and five years' imprisonment, is any edition of writings, musical composition, drawing, painting or any other production, printed or engraved in whole or in part without consent of authors (*Toute édition d'écrits, de composition musicale, de dessin, de peinture ou de toute autre production, imprimée ou gravée en entier ou en partie, au mépris des lois et règlements relatifs à la propriété des auteurs*). The same applies to stocking and dealing in such materials.

[82] Article 5.2. states: 'The enjoyment and the exercise of these rights shall not be subject to any formality; such enjoyment and such exercise shall be independent of the existence of protection in the country of origin of the work. Consequently, apart from the provisions of this Convention, the extent of protection, as well as the means of redress afforded to the author to protect his rights, shall be governed exclusively by the laws of the country where protection is claimed.' – Berne Convention for the Protection of Literary and Artistic Works (Paris Text 1971), https://www.law.cornell.edu/treaties/berne/5.html. Accessed 03 September 2023.

Google France was found to be unrelated to the operation of the search engine; the court noted that it did not receive any power on the search engine administration on French territory, or to represent France in American society (*n'a reçu aucun pouvoir quant à l'administration du moteur de recherche sur le territoire français, ni pour représenter en France la société américaine*) and it is, in fact, Google Inc. that 'controls, manages and makes all decisions regarding search engine activity that represents the heart of its business, including the google images written in French and accessible via the address www.google.fr'.[83] As such, the claims pertained in reality to the business operations of Google Inc. as the true operator of the search engine; the action against Google France was considered misdirected and thus became dismissed.

The court then agreed with Google's position on the Berne Convention Article 5.2 and its interpretation that the country where protection is sought is 'not necessarily that of the court hearing but that of the country where the event occurred, and where the damage is suffered'. Citing an interpretation offered in recent cases of SISRO of 5 March 2002 and Lamore of 30 January 2007 the court chose to apply the law of the U.S. on the grounds of the location of both the servers and the registered office of Google Inc. in California; on this basis, the court decided that the case needed be tried under the fair use provisions of the 1976 Copyright Act and found that the actions of Google Inc. constituted fair use.

Read from the perspective of the *Vorschaubilder* rulings, the initial analysis conducted by the TGI may first raise some eyebrows (particularly the statement that search engines do not store images) due to its disregard of the copying of images for the purpose of creation of thumbnails and their storage. This could be seen as negligence or perhaps deliberate downplaying the infringement, at a price of displaying a degree of technological naivety. What is more important, however, is the position taken by the court in connection to Article 5.2 of the Berne convention. The applied interpretation of the Berne article 5.2. has been widely criticized in the doctrine as referring back to applying the domicile law of the infringer while disregarding the law of the jurisdiction where the infringement was committed, the harm was done and protection was being sought; hence, in Article 8(1) of the Rome II Regulation the phrase is included as 'the country for which protection is claimed'. Otherwise, this construal would lead to a disjunction between the law of the jurisdiction where the infringement was committed and that applied to the claim; it would also go against the intention of the Berne Convention that was to ensure that authors be protected in the most uniform manner possible.[84] As mentioned earlier in Chap. 2, if upheld, the construct would constitute a gateway to forum-shopping by

[83]'la société Google Inc. est l'entité qui contrôle, dirige et prend toutes les décisions concernant l'activité du moteur de recherche qui représente le coeur de son l'activité, y compris celui de google images rédigé en français et accessible à l'adresse www.google.fr' SAIF v. Google France, TGI Paris, 20 May 2008.

[84]Thus e.g. Ginsburg and Treppoz (2015), p. 653; Stamatoudi and Torremans (2014), p. 1052.

allowing infringers to escape liability by establishing their businesses and server room is remote locations without adequate protection of intellectual property.[85]

When hearing the case on appeal in 2011, the *Cour d'Appel* (CA) overturned the considerations on applicable law made in the TGI hearing. This was not unexpected considering that the TGI itself had long decided against continuing down this alley[86]; as observed by the CA, the sole fact that the alleged actions were originated outside of France was not enough to rightly consider attachment to the French territory insufficient in the case. The services in question had been made available to the French public; moreover they were primarily intended for this public given how they were rendered via a *.fr domain which indicated that the French territory was 'deliberately targeted' by the service provider. The receiving country was thus considered to be far more related to the case; hence, French law would apply.

The court then delved deeper into the nature of creation of thumbnails and noted that search results are displayed via a cache or buffer memory (*au moyen d'une mémoire cache ou mémoire intermédiaire*) and that this function allows access to images for a few days or weeks after the original has ceased to exist. The storage of thumbnails is thus conducted over a certain period, but still is temporary. This function, the court reasoned, indicates therefore a 'transitory' nature (*un caractère transitoire*), involving a temporary reproduction for speeding up the flow of information and constitutes an 'integral and essential' part of an image search engine. The fact of offering a thumbnail that can be clicked to view the full-size image cannot be regarded as exerting control over legal content; the search function provider is thus a neutral link between the user and the website operator and does not venture beyond its role of a passive intermediary. It cannot be held liable for the misuse of data found by users of its search engine and advises that 'some images may be subject to copyright'; to advise less experienced users that some images are not royalty-free. The search provider, noted the court, does not confer any right of reproduction and advises users to verify the legal status of the images it links to. On this basis, the court noted that the role of Google qualifies as 'purely technical, automatic and passive' (*purement technique, automatique et passif*) and this its service, which boils down to content indexing posted on the Internet by third parties and automatic, intermediate and transient storage of the information transmitted which is regulated in Article L. 32-3-4 of the *Loi du 21 juin 2004 pour la confiance dans l'économie numérique* (LCEN), implementing the E-Commerce Directive 2000/31/EC.[87] On these grounds, all claims of SAIF were dismissed.

Conducting a more thorough analysis of the technical aspects of thumbnail creation and storage than on earlier stages of the proceedings, the court had found

[85] The TGI did not continue this line of interpretation and in the next case involving a conflict of laws, André R. and H & K v. Google France (2009) ruled on the application of the law of the territory where the damage occurred. See Matulionyte (2011), pp. 38–39.

[86] See the preceding footnote.

[87] Directive 2000/31/EC of the European Parliament and of the Council of 8 June 2000 on certain legal aspects of information society services, in particular electronic commerce, in the Internal Market ('Directive on electronic commerce') Official Journal L 178, 17/07/2000 P. 0001 – 0016.

a way to exonerate Google on the basis of a regime liability for passive service providers with no knowledge or control over the processed content. Reaching out to the e-Commerce Directive to reduce Google's role to a 'passive-only' automatic Internet provider with no control over content, while certainly praiseworthy, is also weak. The assumption of a 'transient' nature of reproduction has been rejected in the German cases; also the 'lack of control' over displayed content by Google could be up for debate. Even without looking for holes in the proposed argument on the grounds of e-commerce law, the fact remains that the case of SAIF v Google, which is a copyright case by its nature, has been decided with no regard to copyright law. The lack of a copyright argument may be easily explained given the fate of the short-lived concept offered by the TGI earlier; the simple fact is that French copyright law does not allow for such acts of reproduction as conducted by Google Image Search, and no sustainable reasoning could be built by the court to give Google a free pass.

3.4.4 *Megakini v. Google*[88]

As another example of the court venturing beyond the copyright statute, April 2012 saw the end of a case argued before the Spanish Supreme Court, concerning caching of websites and displaying snippets of text in search results. The plaintiff, Megakini.com, had claimed copyright infringement and sued Google Spain demanding that it be prohibited from further operation of a search engine.

The court of first instance applied a construct of non-abuse of rights and presumed consent not unlike that used by the German courts, stating that the reproduction of minor parts of the page was temporary and provisional,[89] and necessary for the operation of search engines. Moreover, the caching of the entire site was seen as falling under 'proxy caching' by ISP's[90] under the implementation of the e-Commerce Directive as was later applied by the CA in Paris.[91]

On appeal, the Provincial Court in Barcelona also ruled against the plaintiff, albeit on different grounds.[92] While agreeing that the search results displaying fragments of text were of minimal and incidental nature, it did strike down the construct offered under the e-Commerce regime for passive service providers as Google was not, after all, an access provider. It also noted that Google could not benefit from a safe harbour releasing search engines of liability for linking to infringing content[93]

---

[88] Sentencia n.172/2012, of 3 April 2012, Supreme Court, Civil Chamber.

[89] Article 31.1 Texto Refundido de la Ley de Propiedad Intelectual (TRLPI), implementing Article 5.1. of the e-Commerce Directive.

[90] Article 15 Ley de Servicios de la Sociedad de la Información (LSSICE) implementing Article Art. 13 e-Commerce Directive.

[91] See Juzgado Mercantil n.5 de Barcelona, ruling of 30 March 2007.

[92] Sentencia de la Audiencia Provincial de Barcelona (Section 15), of 17 September 17, 2008.

[93] Article 17 LSSICE.

since it was its own act of infringement that was being discussed. The court of appeal did, however, offer an extensive argument why Google's actions did not constitute an infringement. Noting that the TRLPI featured a closed list of exceptions, the court applied a construal of Article 40a TRLPI, (introducing the Berne restrictions on unreasonably prejudicing legitimate rights of the author and normal exploitation of the work) stating that it could also be interpreted in a positive manner, by application to limiting the author's rights, relating it to the concept of harmless use of movable property of third parties (*usus innocui*). The court also noted that the Anglo-Saxon fair use doctrine should be taken into account as guidance that the author's rights are not of absolute nature.

The Supreme Court generally agreed with these findings, noting that in situations not covered explicitly by statutory law, a judge must defer to applying general principles of the law, such as that of good faith and prohibition of abuse of rights,[94] in the context of the constitutional principle of property not being an absolute right. The Court also made a reference to the nature of the plaintiff's claim, aimed more at harming Google rather than protecting a legitimate right, which should not prevail on general principles despite the situation not falling within the exceptions allowed by Spanish copyright law. Lastly, the court made an express reservation that the ruling only applies to the given case.

From the perspective of this analysis, the dismissal of the e-Commerce safe harbour cannot be found surprising and it further undermines the findings of the CA in the French case. Similarly, the narrowness of the safe harbour under Art. 17 LSSICE precludes its applicability in a case where linking may be considered copyright infringement. This has been commented upon with some concern, pointing that the German presumed consent may, after all, be a more reliable solution.[95] While the general good faith and non-abuse of rights approach has earned praise as opening the door to a measure of flexibility under the European copyright regime,[96] others have noted that the construct it upheld had, in fact, created a new flexible exception despite other rulings in Europe noting that it is not the court's role to do that.[97]

3.4.5 *GS Media*[98]

Offering a considerable measure of flexibility in regard to the legal qualification of publishing links to content shared on file hosting websites, the CJEU judgment in *GS*

[94] Articles 7.1 and 7.2 of the Spanish Civil Code.

[95] Xalabarder (2012), para. 1.

[96] Xalabarder (2012), para. 5; see also Martinez de Aguirre (2012).

[97] See e.g. Ott (2008), making a reference to an earlier thumbnail case (LG Hamburg, Urteil vom 5. September 2004, AZ: 308 O 449/03).

[98] Sanoma et al. v. GS Media, C-160/15.

Media deserves an honourable mention to close this list of highlights of judicial creativity in the face of new uses enabled by technology. Importantly, in this case the national courts attempted to solve the case by applying a strict interpretation of the law and it was not until the CJEU stepped in that a creative interpretation of the law was offered.

In autumn 2011, Sanoma Media Netherlands BV, a publisher/media house in the Netherlands involved with the Dutch edition of the Playboy magazine,[99] commissioned C. Hermès, a photographer, to do a photoshoot with a Britt Geertruida Dekker, a Dutch TV anchor and media personality, set to appear in the December 2011 edition of the magazine. Mr. Hermès had granted Sanoma an exclusive license to publish the photos in question, as well as to exercise the rights and powers arising from his copyright.

GS Media, a subsidiary of Telegraaf Media Nederland BV runs the populist blog GeenStijl (The name and tagline translate into 'No Style: tendentious, unfounded and needlessly offensive'), bringing together celebrity gossip and political jokes on current affairs, which are at times received through a dedicated online form for submitting tips. On 27 October 2011, acting under an anonymous tip, the blog published a cut-out of one of the pictures of Ms. Dekker, advertising its own article that contained a hyperlink to a file hosting website based in Australia, FileFactory.com, where the photos had been shared. The subsequent request of Sanoma to remove the hyperlink was refused by GS Media, however the hosting site deleted the files in question. GS Media published another link on 7 November, this time to the images stored on Imageshack.us; once Imageshack removed the infringing content, GS Media published yet another article with a link to yet a third hosting website.

Sanoma, together with Playboy Enterprises and Ms. Dekker herself, filed suit with the *Rechtbank Amsterdam* (District Court for Amsterdam) on grounds of on breach of right to use of likeness and privacy as well as copyright infringement. The *Rechtbank* found in favour of the plaintiffs and awarded damages. In December 2012, GS Media filed an appeal on the grounds of not having published the infringing photos online.

Upon hearing the appeal, the *Gerechtshof Amsterdam* (Court of Appeals for Amsterdam) observed that it had not been established who posted the files on the hosting websites, thus justifying the assumption that it was done by an undisclosed third party. The court observed that, given the nature of the Internet as a '*free, open and accessible communication network for everyone*', the person placing a work on the Internet *'in such a way that it is accessible to the public (and thereby communicates to the public within the meaning of the Copyright Directive), is the person*

[99] By the time the 2016 judgment was passed, this was no longer the case as the Dutch Playboy had been sold to Pijper Media in 2014. See press release at https://www.sanoma.fi/en/news/2014/wp/sanoma-has-reached-an-agreement-to-sell-three-dutch-magazine-titles/. Accessed 03 September 2023.

who makes this work available to the public and thus discloses it'.[100] In other words, the act of disclosure was attributed solely to the unknown person who had been the original uploader of the infringing content. In the view of the Court, posting a hyperlink to already published content is no different than putting a footnote referencing an already published book or journal article.[101] The argument of Sanoma went towards FileFactory being a 'digital vault' ('*een digitale kluis*') which does not by default make files available to the public; it required a unique link to be generated. Also, until September 2013 the site was not indexed by search engines so that outside access was only available through the specific link pointing to the particular content. GS Media contested that, saying that the links can be found everywhere and also that indexing could be prevented in individual cases but, in general, without any guarantee that the files would not be found.

The Court sided with GS Media on the matter of privacy of files uploaded into file hosting services; in view of a lack of evidence to the contrary, it noted that the files on FileFactory being indeed 'untraceable and unreachable to the public' ('*onvindbaar en onbereikbaar is voor het publiek*') remains uproven. In consequence, the Court found that '*a third party has disclosed the photographs by placing them on Filefactory and that GS Media* [. . .] *has not provided the public with a new access channel for this purpose and therefore did not intervene within the meaning of the jurisprudence of the CJEU*'.[102] Still, the Court observed that a copyright infringement did take place in regard to publishing crops of the photos on the GeenStijl website.

The cassation appeal filed by Sanoma with the *Hoge Raad der Nederlanden* (Dutch Supreme Court) brought up the matter of communication to the public, stating that it also occurs where a hyperlink is provided pointing to a website that content that has been placed without due authorisation; moreover, the content in question has not yet at all been published under a licence at the time of the infringement. Reference was made to C-446 Svensson, rec. 31: '*where a clickable link makes it possible for users of the site on which that link appears to circumvent restrictions put in place by the site on which the protected work appears in order to restrict public access to that work to the latter site's subscribers only, and the link accordingly constitutes an intervention without which those users would not be able*

[100] '[. . .] het internet in zijn huidige vorm een vrij, open en voor een ieder toegankelijk communicatienetwerk is. Degene die een werk op internet plaatst zodanig dat dit toegankelijk is voor het publiek (en daardoor mededeling doet aan het publiek in de zin van de Auteursrechtrichtlijn), is degene die dit werk ter beschikking stelt van het publiek en dus openbaart.') Gerechtshof Amsterdam, 19 November 2013, 200.121.190/01 ECLI:NL: GHAMS:2013:4019, 2.4.4.

[101] 'Verwijzing met een hyperlink naar een aldus op een andere locatie openbaar gemaakt werk is niet veel anders dan met een voetnoot in een boek of tijdschriftartikel verwijzen naar een reeds gepubliceerd ander werk.' Gerechtshof Amsterdam, id., 2.4.4.

[102] '[. . .] een derde de foto's heeft geopenbaard door deze op Filefactory te plaatsen en dat GS Media [. . .] niet aan het publiek daartoe een nieuw toegangskanaal heeft verschaft en derhalve geen interventie heeft gepleegd in de zin van de jurisprudentie van het HvJEU', Gerechtshof Amsterdam, id, 2.4.7.

to access the works transmitted, all those users must be deemed to be a new public, which was not taken into account by the copyright holders when they authorised the initial communication, and accordingly the holders' authorisation is required for such a communication to the public.'[103] The Supreme Court noted that, thanks to the intervention of GS Media, the photos were made available to a larger audience than that for which the photos were placed into hosting in the 'digital vault'. In its own appeal, GS Media noted that, in the Bestwater case (C-348/13), where a video placed on YouTube without authorisation was then embedded by a website linking to it, the CJEU found that there was no communication to the public as there was, in fact, no new public. To this the Supreme Court responded that, in *Bestwater*, the video had already been '*freely accessible to all Internet users on another website with the permission of the copyright holders*' ('*auf einer anderen Website mit Erlaubnis der Urheberrechtsinhaber für alle Internetnutzer frei zugänglich*') and therefore there could be no question of a new public. Still, given the lack of sufficient certainty whether this would also be the case where the work was not yet made available with the consent of the rightsholder. In view of this, the Supreme Court submitted a preliminary question to the CJEU.

AG Wathelet noted that, before addressing the questions asked by the Dutch Supreme court, the CJEU should consider whether or not to depart from the concept of an 'act of communication' arising from the judgment in *Svensson*, being a prerequisite for 'communication to the public' to occur.[104] This communication to the public is, in light of Article 3(1) of Directive 2001/29, the exclusive right of the author. In regard to the matter of establishing an act of communication, the AG observed that the intervention of the linking entity ('the hyperlinker') must be 'vital or indispensable' in order to benefit from or enjoy the work in question. This criterion, in his view, can only be approached 'only in examining the existence of an act of communication'.[105] Consequently, GS Media's intervention not being indispensable for the making available of the photos to users, the AG offered that an act of communication could not have taken place.[106]

Despite the opinion of AG Wathelet offering a seemingly straightforward way of resolving the matter, the CJEU went in a different direction. The Court noted that the Directive's objective is to establish a high level of protection of authors, '*allowing them to obtain an appropriate reward for the use of their works, including on the occasion of communication to the public*', and that 'communication to the public' '*must be interpreted broadly, as recital 23 of the directive indeed expressly states*'. Still, another objective is for the harmonisation effected by it to maintain a fair balance between the interests of copyright holders and, on the other hand, the protection of interests and fundamental rights of users, in particular their freedom of expression and of information, safeguarded by Article 11 of the Charter, and of

[103] Svensson v. Retriever Sverige AB, C-466.

[104] Opinion of AG Wathelet, 7 April 2016, GS Media BV, para. 44.

[105] Opinion of AG Wathelet, 7 April 2016, GS Media BV, paras 57–59.

[106] Opinion of AG Wathelet, 7 April 2016, GS Media BV, para. 60.

the general interest.[107] As the Court observed, the rulings in *Svensson* and *BestWater* were only intended to refer to a situation where there had been a freely available copy published, duly licensed: '*the Court intended to refer only to the posting of hyperlinks to works which have been made freely available on another website with the consent of the rightholder, the Court having concluded that there was no communication to the public on the ground that the act of communication in question was not made to a new public.*'[108] The court also stated, perhaps most importantly, that the concept of 'communication to the public' required an '*individual assessment*'.[109] This assessment, the Court noted, must require an examination whether the person posting the links does so not in the pursuit of profit and '*does not know and cannot reasonably know*' that the linked content has been put online without consent of the rightsholder.[110] Such a person, according to the Court, does not—as a general rule—'*intervene in full knowledge of the consequences of his conduct in order to give customers access to a work illegally posted on the internet*'.[111] However, where such a person does have knowledge that the linked content has been posted without due consent, in particular due to having been so advised by the copyright holders, the provision of that link will constitute a communication to the public within the meaning of Article 3(1) of the Directive. The latter is the prevailing (yet rebuttable) assumption where the posting of links is effected for profit *as it can be expected that the person who posted such a link carries out the necessary checks to ensure that the work concerned is not illegally published on the website to which those hyperlinks lead, so that it must be presumed that that posting has occurred with the full knowledge of the protected nature of that work and the possible lack of consent to publication on the internet by the copyright holder.*[112]

The ruling in *GS Media* met with understandable criticism. On the surface of it, communication to the public, a straightforward concept in statutory law seems to be nothing if not a simple description of an act of publication adjusted to the realities of the early twenty-first century; choosing to interpret it into a vague and conditionally applied legal assessment was bound to raise many eyebrows. Why did the Court choose to go down this road, particularly in view of the sound approach of AG Wathelet?

It should be noted that the underlying motive for the CJEU to create the distinction that made *GS Media* famous had been clearly to not impose restrictions on the flow of information, or simply to create a margin of safety, for non-commercial users of the Internet who should not be reasonably expected to skilfully assess the copyright status of every work they link to. This was stated by the Court in para.

[107] See C-160/15, Judgment of the Court, para. 30–31.

[108] C-160/15, para. 41.

[109] C-160/15, para. 33.

[110] C-160/15, para. 47.

[111] C-160/15, para. 48.

[112] C-160/15, para. 51.

45: '(T)*he internet is in fact of particular importance to freedom of expression and of information,* [. . .], *and that hyperlinks contribute to its sound operation as well as to the exchange of opinions and information in that network characterised by the availability of immense amounts of information* [. . .] *it may be difficult, in particular for individuals who wish to post such links, to ascertain whether website to which those links are expected to lead, provides access to works which are protected and, if necessary, whether the copyright holders of those works have consented to their posting on the internet. Such ascertaining is all the more difficult where those rights have been the subject of sub-licenses. Moreover, the content of a website to which a hyperlink enables access may be changed after the creation of that link, including the protected works, without the person who created that link necessarily being aware of it'*. As offered in an observation submitted by the Portuguese Republic, the application of the *Svensson* judgment was likely to affect the dissemination of information and knowledge on the Internet; in that, the reference function of a hyperlink was likened again to that of a footnote. As similarly protective stance was taken by the Commission; in its observation it submitted that, where a hyperlink on a website directs to a protected work hosted on another website and where the users of the first website thus have access to that work, there can be no question of an 'act of communication' since there has been neither transmission nor retransmission in accordance with Directive 2001/29'.[113]

Notably, the CJEU decided this goal would be best served by forcing a flexible interpretation onto a straightforward concept, rendering its application conditional upon an 'individual assessment'. From the perspective of analysing the dynamics between legal flexibility and innovation this is particularly valuable, while it has little to do with fair use itself. Most likely, the technical availability of a fair use defence would hardly be of any help: linking to infringing content would be difficult to defend under the fair use factors and the CJEU would still be left looking for a solution that would allow to hold commercial entities accountable while not criminalizing private users. In this context, *GS Media* could be read as a case of the Court protecting fundamental freedoms of Internet users from a situation of overregulation that could ensue lest the strict interpretation of the law was replaced with a flexible one.

3.4.6 Epilogue: Vorschaubilder III

The decision of the Federal Supreme Court (*Bundesgerichtshof*) of 21 September 2017 (Case No. I ZR 11/16) marked the end of yet another battle waged in Germany over thumbnail images displayed as search results; this time, however, the legal situation in Europe had seen a new development as the CJEU judgment in *GS Media*

[113] Written submission by the European Commission in C-160/15 GS Media, para. 23; referenced by AG Wathelet in the Opinion of AG Wathelet, 7 April 2016, *GS Media BV*, para. 25.

had already been published, adding a level of flexibility to the interpretation of the terms of the Copyright Directive.

On 9 and 11 June 2009, the plaintiff, a California paywalled adult website, saw that by entering pseudonyms of two of its models into the Google search box on the Web portal (AOL.de) operated by the defendant, a number of thumbnail pictures from the plaintiff's database were displayed. The plaintiff served a warning letter upon the defendant, who consequently blocked these particular pseudonyms as search terms; still, the thumbnail search results kept showing the infringing pictures, some over a period of above 2 years, as they had been downloaded and put up on third-party sites by users of the plaintiff's website. Eventually, the plaintiff filed that the defendant be ordered to cease and desist, under penalty of fine, to make these thumbnails available to users within the Republic of Germany.

At the level of first and second instance, the case was dismissed. The *Bundesgerichtshof* followed suit, but not before it examined the dispute from the perspective of the recently published CJEU judgment in *GS Media*, and, in particular, its notion of the rebuttable presumption that commercial operators of websites can be assumed to know whether the content they are linking to has been published without consent of the rightsholder. In this case, the Court observed, the defendant could not demonstrate that the infringing images had been made available on the plaintiff's website for free; as such, it could not rely on the defence that no new public was reached as a result of its actions. Following further in the footsteps of *GS Media*, the Court observed that the defendant had been acting in a commercial context; moreover, posting of links on a website with protected works that are freely accessible on another website without the permission of the copyright owner could only constitute 'communication to the public' within the meaning of Art. 3 (1) of Directive 2001/29 / EC if the entity posting the links knew or ought to have been reasonably aware of the illegality of the publication of the works in question.[114] This, the Court noted, was based on the notion that the Internet is of particular importance for the freedom of expression and information guaranteed by Article 11 of the EU Charter of Fundamental Rights and that hyperlinks contribute to the good functioning of the Internet and to the exchange of views and information in that network.[115] Referencing the opinion of AG Wathelet in GS Media, the Court also noted that the functionality of the Internet would be unduly affected (*unangemessen beeinträchtigt*) if the users were made to be more reluctant to linking to content found on other sites. Search engines, the Court added, '*as an aid to finding content on the Internet make a significant contribution to the flow of information. In the interests of the information society, they ensure the functioning of the Internet.*'[116] As such, they cannot be burdened with the presumption formulated in *GS Media* by

[114] I ZR 11/16, para. 54–55.

[115] I ZR 11/16, para. 55.

[116] 'Suchmaschinen leisten als Hilfsmittel zum Auffinden von Inhalten im Internet einen wesentlichen Beitrag zur Informationsvermittlung. Sie gewährleisten im Interesse der Informationsgesellschaft die Funktionsfähigkeit des Internets.' Id, para. 56.

the CJEU. Taking into account the 'special significance' (*die besondere Bedeutung*) of search engines, their operators cannot be reasonably be expected to verify whether the images found by crawlers have been lawfully posted on the Internet before rendering those images as thumbnails. The Court concluded that, for an operator like the defendant, who provides the visitors of his website the search function by means of a link to the servers of the search engine operator, nothing else applies.[117]

Given the recent history of thumbnail cases resolved by the German *Bundesgerichtshof*, perhaps this judgment should come as no surprise; the Court has already demonstrated in the past how high a value it placed on the preservation of the functioning of the Internet even where written law seemingly left no leeway for such a maneuver. In *Vorschaubilder III,* from a functional perspective, the *Bundesgerichtshof* simply offered an application of *GS Media* to national law; one that examined closely the relevant reasoning and then rejected the presumption of knowledge or due diligence on the part of search providers in view of their special role and significance to the operation of the Internet. From a legalist point of view, however, the ruling could be claimed as being detached, to a considerable degree, from the letter of the law; particularly the provisions of Article 3(1) of the Copyright Directive. Following in the footsteps of the CJEU to adopt a flexible interpretation of the definition of 'communication to the public' judgment in *GS Media* that narrowed it down to cases of a reasonable presumption of illegality of the linked content, then went one step further and excluded the application of this presumption to search engines despite the nature of their operation as being quintessentially commercial and for-profit.

3.5 Summary

Building upon the discussion in the preceding chapter which focused on how the flexibilities of the American fair use system have proven to be more friendly to digital innovation occurring on the fringes of copyright, a deeper exploration into the tools and language used by judges when dealing with such cases leads to interesting conclusions.

Against the background of how judicial flexibility has been applied (and advocated for) since the very dawn of fair use exceptions appearing in case law, over a century before their introduction into statutory law with the passing of the 1976 Copyright Act, it is noteworthy how, in fair use cases, 'transformative use' has become a tool to further and secure judicial flexibility since the introduction of the

---

[117] 'Vom Anbieter einer Suchmaschine kann vernünftigerweise nicht erwartet werden, dass er sich vergewissert, ob die von den Suchprogrammen aufgefundenen Abbildungen von Werken oder Lichtbildern rechtmäßig ins Internet eingestellt worden sind, bevor er diese Abbildungen als Vorschaubilder wiedergibt. Für einen Internetanbieter wie die Beklagte, der den Besuchern seiner Webseite die Suchfunktion im Wege eines Links auf die Server des Suchmaschinenbetreibers zur Verfügung stellt, gilt nichts anderes.' Id, para. 60.

term and doctrine in 1990. Despite being devised to introduce a reliable standard and a measure of predictability into the 'flexible' regulatory sphere created by case law and then reinforced by the statutory provisions of the above Act, its own inherent vagueness and interpretative discrepancies have led to judges displaying a highly utilitarian, if slightly hypocritical, perspective on its application. On the one hand side, faced with a body of case law they clearly felt compelled to address the transformative use aspects of the case; from there, they would use it to reinforce and strengthen their position when finding in favour of fair use, but would have no second thoughts about casting it aside when the use in question failed to meet the four-factor test established in the doctrine. This has been demonstrated using a selection of 'non-paradigm' cases, dating from 1997 to 2013, all making references to the transformative use doctrine and then finding against fair use on general terms, irrespective of how transformative indeed the use in question appeared. This has been deemed as indicative of judges being protective of the flexible framework established under the original fair use case law and legislation, and accepting of the 'transformativeness' tool only in so far as it did not affect their original latitude within the traditional framework.

This very flexibility was shown to be desired and sought for by European judges in cases pertaining to digital innovation occurring at the expense of copyright protection. A detailed analysis of the reasoning offered in the cited cases of Germany and France shows how, lacking the statutory headroom to accommodate such innovation, judges have resorted to varying degrees of judicial activism—and how, while undoubtedly resourceful and heroic, still unsustainable the resulting legal constructs are; even despite having achieved their purpose 'here and now'. Ultimately, to reference again Hugenholtz and Senftleben, they remain symptomatic of a copyright system lacking an appropriate escape valve—seeing as copyright flexibility should always be found 'in the system of copyright proper'.[118] With the approach taken by the Spanish courts arguably being the boldest and potentially the most robust, the reasoning offered in the cited cases of Germany and France shows how, faced with a law too rigid to accommodate such innovation, judges were forced to display considerable creativity—and how, while undoubtedly resourceful, still questionable (and seemingly unsustainable) the resulting legal constructs were. It is now the time to ask yet another question: what it is about digital innovation that renders it so dependent on this flexibility in law and where lie the benefits of a flexible system from the perspective of creating new technological value in the digital age. This matter will be addressed in the next chapter.

[118] Hugenholtz and Senftleben (2011), p. 12.

References

Clark B (2010) Google Image Search does not infringe copyright, says Bundesgerichtshof. J Intellect Prop Law Pract 5(8):2010

Clark B (2012) Google image search still does not infringe copyright, reaffirms Bundesgerichtshof. J Intellect Prop Law Pract 7(11):2012

Geiger C (2008) Flexibilising copyright – remedies to the privatisation of information by copyright law. Int Rev Intellect Prop Compet Law 39:178–197

Ginsburg JC, Treppoz E (2015) International Copyright Law: U.S. and E.U. Perspectives: text and cases. Edward Elgar Publishing, ISBN: 978 1 78347 797 5

Goldstein P (2003) Copyright's highway: from Gutenberg to the Celestial Jukebox. Stanford Law and Politics, Stanford

Green S (2011) Judge grants summary judgment in favor of Righthaven defendant, via Vegasinc.com 22.04.2011 https://vegasinc.lasvegassun.com/business/legal/2011/apr/22/judge-grants-summary-judgement-favor-righthaven-de/. Accessed 3 Sept 2023

Hugenholtz PB, Senftleben M (2011) Fair use in Europe: In Search of Flexibilities. SSRN Electronic Journal. https://doi.org/10.2139/ssrn.1959554

Leval PN (1990) Toward a fair use standard. Harv Law Rev 103, 105, 1105

Martinez de Aguirre J (2012) El caso 'Megakini vs. Google' o la excesiva rigidez de nuestra Ley de Propiedad Intelectual, via PropiedadIntelectualHoy.com, 18 June 2012, https://propiedadintelectualhoy.com/2012/06/18/el-caso-megakini-vs-google-o-la-excesiva-rigidez-de-nuestra-ley-de-propiedad-intelectual/. Accessed 3 Sept 2023

Masnick M (2013) Sorry fair use, court says news clipping service infringes on AP copyrights, via TechDirt.com, 21 March 2013. https://www.techdirt.com/articles/20130321/13345322408/court-finds-meltwaters-news-clipping-service-infringes-ap-copyrights.shtml. Accessed 3 Sept 2023

Matulionyte R (2011) Law applicable to copyright: a comparison of the ALI and CLIP proposals. Edward Elgar Publishing, Cheltenham

Neuburger J (2011) Posting of Entire News Article is Fair Use, Says Judge in Righthaven Copyright Litigation. New Media and Technology Law Blog. https://newmedialaw.proskauer.com/2011/03/22/posting-of-entire-news-article-is-fair-use-says-judge-in-righthaven-copyright-litigation/. Accessed 3 Sept 2023

Ott S (2008) Spain: Google Cache is legal (the Megakini.com-case) via Linksandlaw.com http://www.linksandlaw.com/news-update60-megakini-case-spain.htm. Accessed 3 Sept 2023

Stamatoudi I, Torremans P (2014) EU copyright law: a commentary, 1st DRM edition. Elgar 2014

Warren & Brandeis (1890) The Right to Privacy. 4 Harv. L. Rev. 193. Online via MIT.edu https://groups.csail.mit.edu/mac/classes/6.805/articles/privacy/Privacy_brand_warr2.html. Accessed 3 Sept 2023

Xalabarder R (2012) Spanish Supreme Court Rules in favour of Google search engine... and a flexible reading of copyright statutes? JIPITEC 3:162. https://www.jipitec.eu/issues/jipitec-3-2-2012/3445/xalabarder.pdf. Accessed 3 Sept 2023

Zimmerman D (1999) The more things change, the less they seem 'Transformed': some reflections on fair use. J Copyright Soc USA, 46(2) 1999, Available at SSRN: https://ssrn.com/abstract=183474. Accessed 11 Dec 2021

Chapter 4
Jewels in the Sand: Supporting Creativity in a Mass Networked Environment

4.1 Introduction

Stories like the Brennan player, reuse of intellectual property by search engines or the various cases surrounding Google Books highlight a dimension of the interplay between copyright and innovation and an accompanying dynamic involving the role of the judiciary. The examples sourced from the European side showed remarkable efforts of judges seeking out possibilities to remedy the situation, leading to solutions which all showed a considerable degree of creativity, but were all flawed in being necessarily inconsistent and questionably sustainable over the long term,[1] particularly in going against the letter of the law which does not allow flexible exceptions that would apply to new technological developments. These dynamics will be analysed in more detail in the final chapter of this book. But before we delve deeper into the role of courts of law in safeguarding (or curtailing) technological innovation, an important question must be asked: is there a type of innovation that is uniquely bound to the history and nature of networked personal computing—and if yes, what makes it worth preserving?

Taking the spotlight away from the legal struggles of innovation driven by a corporate effort, this will require a focus on the potential for creating technological value that rests within large distributed networks of motivated individuals. The Internet reality bursts with a wealth of highly different examples, all sharing a common denominator of a creative effort resting upon a largely uninhibited exchange of information and the ability to build upon the results of others, leading eventually to achieving considerable goals. As we discuss these efforts, fair use

[1] The most remarkable attempt may be that by the Spanish courts in the *Megakini* case, building a line of reasoning involving both a flexible reading of the Berne three-step test and drawing parallels to the U.S. fair use system, but mainly building upon the transposition of the concept of harmless use (*usus inocui*) from property law. See Chap. 5.

K. Drazewski, *Copyright as a Constraint on Creating Technological Value*, Law, Governance and Technology Series 63,
https://doi.org/10.1007/978-3-031-51276-6_4

defined as involving creation of 'new aesthetics, new insights and understandings', in the words of Pierre Leval as he wrote about transformative use in 1990, will undoubtedly come to mind.

The examples that will be given here, including the cumulative investigative work of users on Internet forums, the collaborations underlying the cracking of DRM restrictions which were perceived by online communities as 'unfair', as well as such well-known efforts as the history of free and open software and the early days of personal computing, will aim to demonstrate how the large-scale creative projects that helped create the digital world as it is today have often relied on a certain culture of ongoing reuse and improvement of successful solutions, while being often confronted by those representing a more classic approach to intellectual property.

Open solutions built via processes of networked creativity can be used by business entities to develop new products; they can also be seized in an attempt to monetize one of the stages of their evolution. This creates a disruption which may lead to this strain of the digital genome to become abandoned if the entity manages to grab a hold on the technology with only the aim to collect rent and does not substitute the free flow of networked contributions with their own commercial effort. However slightly more complicated than the above simplification, the fight of Google and Oracle over Java APIs originally developed by Sun Microsystems will also be described, focusing on the commentary it sparked with scholars on its potential repercussions to the development of future solutions should Oracle's case (and the general philosophy it represented) prevail.

Importantly, this part of the discussion is not a sneaky attempt at furthering an extreme anti-protection agenda of the variety described by Boldrin and Levine in 2008.[2] Instead, it seeks to demonstrate, using real-life examples, that the birth of much of the digital world that we know employed, and was based on, social processes which still survive today. Just like in the case of Java APIs, their success is, to a large degree, conditional upon the possibility of creating further iterations of successful solutions without the transactions involved in seeking permission from incumbent holders of rights to earlier versions of the building blocks which comprise the new product, or ones that simply wish to monetize the product at one of the stages in its development.

4.2 Innovating in the Digital Age

4.2.1 The Efficiency of Distributed Effort

The following story, unfolding upon hundreds of forum pages documenting every stage of the investigation, deserves to be mentioned as a prime example of the

[2]Boldrin and Levine (2008).

efficiency of networked individuals at solving a seemingly impossible puzzle, with no incentive beyond that of entertainment and social recognition in their own circles.

In 2015, the online fan community of *Archer*, an animated spy-comedy series by FX (currently FXX), had gone berserk upon discovering that a secret website of a Dr Krieger, the series' mad scientist existed in real life as an Easter egg devised by the creators of the show, and that some pointers were leading to further hidden content. Soon, forum users worldwide became engaged in a wild hunt for clues within the series to see how deep down the rabbit hole went.

The first discovery took place when a user of a Reddit board translated the serial number of one of the series' secret agents into hexadecimal code and came up with a YouTube address pointing to a video of an abstract animation of coloured rectangles. The video featured a strange beeping sound in its audio track and a seemingly meaningless chain of characters for title. This chain of characters was then found to be the word 'tentacle' encoded in base64. The spectrogram of the audio, in the form of a chain of a few dozen capital letters and numbers, was then found out to be the decoding Vigenére cipher passphrase for yet another chain of characters, hidden in another of the episodes, leading to the decoding of a New York Craigslist advertisement which was posted in the name of the very Dr Krieger in question. In response to an inquiry e-mail, the ad poster responded to read each sentence from the beginning to the end; using this clue, the first and last letters of sentences within the listed ad were arranged to decode a tiny.cc URL which pointed to a comment on Krieger's Reddit account, thus leading to the discovery of the latter. The account's number was then found to be the Internet Movie Database code for *The Boys from Brazil*, a 1978 movie about Nazis in South America, which, incidentally, corresponded to Krieger's own family heritage in the series. At the same time, another user figured out that splitting the said comment into groups of two led to decoding the phrase 'tinyccyyz' which turned out to be the web address to Krieger's Flickr account, and the website stated in account data was algersoft.net—the website of Dr Krieger.

The Easter egg hunt went on and led to, *inter alia*, the discovery of the character's hidden Facebook account. Although many threads, including the significance of 'tentacle' (beside being a reference to the character's taste for a sub-genre in Japanese animation) remained unsolved, the operation itself, and the hundreds and hundreds of trial-and-error posts on Reddit forums, are remarkable for demonstrating both the scale of the collective effort and the success in finding and decoding seemingly random (and quite impossible to find) bits of information. It is, however, not an isolated case of a large number of Web users from around the world working together to solve a problem.

When describing the processes bringing together ad-hoc investigative and development communities, Yochai Benkler named entertainment value as a strong motivator, capable of bringing together considerable numbers of participants.[3] This was again confirmed in 2017, when a wave of panicked articles rolled over the media

[3] Benkler (2011).

after news of open-source face-swapping software having been released on Reddit, allowing a large network of users to 'train' the underlying AI in order to replace the faces of people in videos. The tech, dubbed 'Deepfakes' after the first user who launched it, owed its name to deep learning models used in its architecture. While still imperfect at close inspection, the illusion got better with community training, reaching results which were at times stunningly close to reality. To some extent, that ended up being the project's apparent downfall: as community members moved from training the AI on clips of politicians to inserting faces of celebrities into adult videos, the result was convincing enough to earn the 90,000-strong community[4] enough interest to get it banned from Reddit and other major sites.[5] Leaving aside the potential uses of the technology, which can indeed be murky in a world where wars between countries are seemingly powered by social media, one interesting detail may be fished out by a researcher interested in evaluating networked potential: in December 2017, the original analysis published by VICE magazine predicted a year before the technology would become automated. According to BBC.com, after its release on Reddit and the establishment of the training community, the automatic version was available within a month. Despite the ban from the original forum, the technology is still being perfected by a community of contributors on Github.[6]

A similar process, but much more structured and considerably better known was related to the origins and history of the Linux operating system as a collaborative effort of users worldwide. The processes behind Linux will be discussed in greater detail later in this chapter; for now, it is only mentioned to give an idea of scale that a successful collaborative non-commercial project may reach. In February 2017, Linus Torvalds, considered the creator and 'benevolent dictator' of the open-source Linux kernel, spoke at the Open Source Leadership Summit in California on how skewed a view on innovation gets perpetuated by the technological industry. His critique, complete with some strong language criticising the popular perception of tech innovation ('*The innovation the industry talks about so much is bullsh*t [. . .]. Anybody can innovate. Don't do this big 'think different'. . . screw that. It's meaningless. Ninety-nine per cent of it is get the work done*'), which mistakenly revolved around glorifying technology and neglecting the real effort put into getting any project off the ground. Following Torvalds' view successful projects are '99 percent perspiration, one percent innovation' and the Linux project has seen thousands upon thousands of contributors[7] doing the legwork over its history of 30 years. With procedures in place to allow the participants to work independently, the project has been relying on a strong social network of willing coders to add, remove and review tens of thousands of lines of code per day.[8]

[4]Farrokmanesh (2018).

[5]See online coverage in The Next Web (2018a, b) and Lee (2018).

[6]See e.g. https://github.com/deepfakes/faceswap. Accessed 03 September 2023.

[7]Vaughan-Nichols (2013).

[8]Claburn (2017).

Processes of this very nature were described by Benkler as driving innovation in the digital world.[9] Benkler argued that, with the advent of high-speed digital networking, a general shift was taking place, away from centralized ownership of means of production and management of information, towards a new distributed layout dubbed a networked information economy.[10]

Most prominent in areas that could be characterized as 'soft' such as entertainment, education or arts and sciences, it seems to entail a common denominator: its appeal to persons susceptible to nonmarket motivations in their creativity. This leads to production and processing of information that is, essentially, nonmarket in its nature and going against the 'economics 101'. Indeed, just as impossible it is to attribute economic motivations to the brave individuals that pooled their resources to bring us Wikipedia or the teams behind the early Linux, similarly the claims of rightsholders brought up in the Google Books cases of Google undertaking the task simply to earn advertising revenue with their intellectual property sound borderline naïve. The digital revolution has created a space for individuals to let their imaginations run wild and collaborate, often just to see whether something can be done—not necessarily in expectation of tangible returns. Distribution of production capacities brings along distribution of production means; differently from the industrial era, ownership of the latter is not concentrated in the hands of a limited number of entities but spread across the spectrum of participants. In this sense, individuals open to such collaboration schemes have at their disposal a platform armed with tools which are unprecedented in human history: low-cost processing power, affordable storage and, most importantly, high-speed connections that in many respects render distances between collaborating individuals irrelevant. Benkler noted that, in the absence of analytical tools to duly examine such processes, chapters in recent history like the creation of Wikipedia or the millions of users pooling CPU cycles for SETI@home can be easily dismissed as passing fads. Instead, he argues, they should be seen as a new mode of production that continues to emerge in the most highly networked economies of the world. It is one that involves individuals working for far more diverse motivations that just material gain; the feeling of social connectedness and creating something in a joint effort is just as important. Indeed, this can be seen as a shift that does not root out the traditional outlook on economy, but merely indicates that there are areas of human creativity, growing in importance through the joint effort of distributed networks—even though, through the goggles of a traditional industrial-era economy, they would be likely to appear just as group entertainment and get dismissed just as quickly.

In response to this, Benkler might point out that such projects are far more organized than they may seem, often offering their own social hierarchy with a strong decision-making centre (that would be e.g. Linus Torvalds for Linux, or the Wikipedia board) and a distributed structure, to mirror the granular structure of the project itself. Yet, it should be noted that neither this precisely outlined structure nor

[9] Benkler (2011), pp. 213–214. See also Benkler (2017).

[10] See generally Benkler (2011).

the existence of a powerful centre appear to be necessarily crucial for success. This will be discussed below as it ties in with the battles fought by such grassroots initiatives when moving against the established actors of the industry.

4.2.2 Clashes with Industry Incumbents

Reading Benkler's observations from today's perspective, it becomes obvious how the decentralized distribution of interests that he seems to truly appreciate (promoting topics which are highly interesting to smaller audiences, rather than moderately interesting to large ones) has also brought about its own risks; suffice to look at the growing concern with fake news, their political significance and the debates about freedom of expression they have caused to arise.

Still, the predictions he made about the 'incumbent' actors of the industry refusing to sit by and watch the balance of power being shifted to the users, using as excuses various trade regulations and copyright protection, now ring true more than ever. Every time copyright concerns are brought up by car companies attempting to use intellectual property protection to prevent car owners from working on their own vehicles[11] (due to their questionable qualification as 'mobile computing devices' and as such being protected from tinkering under the DMCA, but also offering more elaborate considerations[12]), these pushback tendencies become more evident. Another example of de-centralized, user-driven networked efforts going against restrictions imposed by the industry is the story of the ill-famed Protected Media Path in Windows Vista, and its short life when released, sheep amidst the wolves, into the hands of users who were more than happy to explore how resilient it actually was.

The story dates back to the origins of Vista and the considerations of the big actors of the recording industry in regard to allowing their latest premium product, high-definition content on HD DVDs and DVD-Audio, to be played on consumer PCs. Not unexpectedly, the main worries pertained to the PC being used as a copy machine, thus annihilating much of the anticipated revenues from sales. Microsoft was reluctant to part with their vision of a Windows PC as a media center and went to great lengths to ensure that the long-anticipated successor of Windows XP would constitute a safe environment for such content to be played. The result was creating an operating system whose main goal was to protect data from its user, or, paraphrasing Ed Felton of Princeton, to try and make water not wet. The technological solutions implemented in Vista were numerous: forced reduction of playback quality

[11] See The Alliance of Automobile Manufacturers (2014).

[12] Siding with other automakers in opposing an exemption relating to modifying motor vehicles, John Deere famously offered their own vision of farmers being able to use modified on-board entertainment systems in their tractors to listen to pirated music or audiobooks. See Brewster (2015).

(downsampling to 800×600), elimination of unified drivers, end-to-end encryption of signal between pieces of hardware within the PC, disabling of non-protected ports like S/PDIF, denial of service through blacklisting drivers and devices that were found to carry the risk of the premium signal being intercepted and prohibition of playback where content-protection could not be enabled due to hardware limitations (e.g. DVD content refusing to play on a non-TV-out machine due to failure of Macrovision protection to start, to protect the TV-out port that never existed in the first place). With other implications such as suddenly disabling video where Vista would decide that hi-def content is being played by heart monitors in a hospital, it has been commented by Peter Gutmann of Auckland that the Vista Content Protection specification read like the longest suicide note in history.[13]

The alleged undefeatability of Vista content protection caused quite a stir in user forums around the world; it was a painful example of efforts aimed at forcing manufacturers of computing devices to deliberately limit the functionality of their devices and make them tools of copyright enforcement, at the expense of the versatility that seemingly had been the underlying characteristic of every PC since the dawn of personal computing.

The unceasing debate on how DRM-related limitations annihilate the very latitudes left within the copyright system to ensure that overprotection does not stop people from being creative is a story for another rainy day. For now, suffice to mention that the PR image of such efforts by corporate rightsholders is rather poor, due to seriously (and often needlessly) undermining innovation and creativity. It may never come to light how many people worked on seeking out the vulnerabilities of the Vista protection system, but the results were as foreseen over a decade earlier in the infamous Microsoft Darknet Paper:[14] with all this effort that went in the creation of possibly the most hated and least reliable Microsoft operating system since the pre-SP1 Windows 95, Vista's famed Protected Media Path (PMP) was announced as broken **within days of its premiere**. More recently, with streaming services pushing fixed HD data carriers out of the market, echoes of the same struggle could still be heard in discussions about Microsoft Edge long being the only browser cleared to play Netflix at 1080p, and with further content protection arrangements with makers of peripheral devices concerning 4K video playback.[15]

[13] For extensive comments on the specifications of Windows Vista Protected Environment, the Protected Media Path and their technical implications, see Gutmann (2007).

[14] Users will continue to copy files, or 'objects' as long as (1) any widely distributed object is available to a fraction of users in a form that permits copying; (2) such copying is possible and interesting, (3) users are connected by high-bandwidth channels. Biddle et al. (2003).

[15] See Smith et al. (2016).

4.2.3 Creation Rooted in Chaos: The Non-structured Branch of Networked Creativity

Benkler identified three base characteristics of a networked information economy:

1. the hardware needed to participate in information and cultural production is widely distributed;
2. the primary raw materials—existing information, knowledge, and culture—are publicly available;
3. the problems that need solving have a granular structure.[16]

Looking in particular at examples like *Archer* and Windows Vista, it would seem that the distinction offered above does not cover the entire picture. While the first two listed characteristics are fair observations, it could be argued that the third unnecessarily narrows the field down. Certainly, a granular structure of a problem allows for an efficient distribution of tasks amidst a large body of collaborators, with a high level of duplication of results, and a central body making the decisions on which results to include in the official build. Still, it would seem that by adopting this optic we would be leaving out a broad spectrum of networked efforts which may be just as capable of producing results, however in a far less coordinated manner, rendering them more difficult to measure and to rely on. In their case, reliability in producing results would come from the same characteristics as Benkler identified, assuming availability of basic resources, existence of informal ties among involved users and an interesting topic capable of attracting enough attention to generate the effect of scale. In other words, if the topic is interesting and has a big mass of users working on it, solutions will eventually arise whether the structural prerequisites are met or not.

Exploring further down the non-structured rabbit hole, it is worth noting that the *Archer* story could likely be classified as a particularly challenging and elaborate rendition of an Alternate Reality Game (ARG)—a phenomenon based on real-world intellectual exercises planted for fanbases around areas belonging to the traditional reality. More classic (and simpler, by a few orders of magnitude) examples would be those built around faux user-recorded horror documentaries, such as the *Blair Witch Project* franchise or the *Cloverfield* ARG. Typically, the game does not necessarily involve such complex 'nerd-access-only' puzzles as those featured in the *Archer* case, but still involve a real-world investigation of the background of a publicly known story. in the case of *Cloverfield*, the ARG involved discovering the corporate schemes creating the much-needed background to the movie, a Godzilla-type monster mayhem story told from the perspective of amateur footage discovered in the aftermath. The Easter eggs for the fandom included websites for the featured companies, manufactured news stories, viral news coverage, advertisements of related products, as well as MySpace pages of the movie characters (which, as a

[16] Benkler (2011).

consequence of the 'recovered home video footage' storytelling style, were only featured on-screen in only a sketchy manner). The game led to the uncovering of a corporate plot by a fictitious company *Tagruato* involved in deep sea drilling around the world and its covert operations leading to the discovery and examination of dormant prehistoric monsters on the seabed, along with the subsequent disappearance of witnesses and whistleblowers. A similar scheme was employed earlier for the sake of the earlier *Blair Witch Project* horror movies.

What these stories have in common is the general viral marketing orientation and the mass involvement of users in a collective investigative effort with no promise of tangible profits due to it all being considered merely as entertainment. Applying the stencil coined by Benkler's analysis, it is worth to reiterate that he recognizes the networked collaborative potential in collective investigative efforts and does so in the aspect of investigative journalism. Interestingly, however, it may be worth to observe that such investigative projects also lack the granularity parameter, which Benkler offers as an important condition of success in a networked effort.[17] To put simply, investigative work—be it as part of a massive ARG, or as a real-world investigation—is not necessarily granular, and the scope of each participant's work is defined by their own progress. Success may come as a sum of all the individual efforts, but may as well be the work of one intellect that cracks the mystery and publishes the results. This suggests that Benkler was also aware of the non-structured pillar (or variety) of networked collective efforts, but likely chose not to include it in his three-characteristic typography.

Both the *Archer* Easter egg hunt and the Vista PE hacking case seem to indicate the very phenomenon. In both cases, there was a large pool of users, acting in a similar direction and powered by similarly non-economic motivations, taking on a seemingly difficult or impossible task. Yet, it should be observed that each of the two efforts lacked the distinct framework that is shared by the coordinated crowd projects such as Linux or Wikipedia. Similarly, neither had the benefit of an organized hierarchy among its participants or a distinct centre of operations; also, neither would allow to distinguish any considerable level of granularity in the subject matter. No technical architecture, social norms or legal rules different from those same that apply when browsing forums e.g. for pictures of cats could be readily identified.

The nature of the processes described here is clearly related to that observed in free software and open-source software in general. While the driving dynamic and motivations may be of a similar nature, free- and open-source programming has shown remarkable success in structuring and management of a large workforce, dedicated to what may well be a fantastically complex project. In this sense, the words of Steve Weber about how Apache and Linux demonstrate that 'a large and complex system of software code can be built, maintained, developed, and extended in a non-proprietary setting in which many developers work in a highly parallel, relatively unstructured way' may raise some eyebrows, particularly in the light of his

[17] See Benkler (2006), p. 101, citing the example of the failure of Wikibooks.

own observations about the structure required to keep Linux alive and updated, under the benevolent and charismatic dictatorship of Torvalds.[18] From a more general perspective however, looking back on the genesis of free software, these words are very correct, as will be explained below.

In 1983, Richard Stallman, a software developer with a Harvard BA in physics and a few years of operating system development in the Artificial Intelligence Lab at MIT, announced that a Unix-like operating system would be built that would be *entirely free*—not free because it is distributed for free, but free in terms of free speech, as he put it. [19] The system was to be called GNU—shortcut for GNU is Not Unix—which would be able to run Unix programs, but not be Unix itself. It would retain some of Unix' characteristics while offering something new in the areas where Unix felt lacking. According to Stallman's manifesto published in 1985, proprietary modifications would not be allowed; the idea was to keep all versions of GNU free. As regards the motivations of himself and other programmers willing to work on the project, he named disenchantment with the progressing commercialization of system software and retreat of the friendly environment that programmers used to create before their contracts forced them to treat each other as competition. Complete system sources would be available to all users, meaning that any user who would need to make any changes would be free to do so. [20] This was the beginning of the Free Software Foundation, and of the four freedoms that would determine free software in its intended meaning. Using Stallman's original numbering, those meant the following freedoms:

(0) to run the program,
(1) to study and change the program in source code form,
(2) to redistribute exact copies, and
(3) to distribute modified versions.

Due to the linguistic confusion surrounding the term *free*, a few years later, the term *open source* was coined. Its development, however, also involved the evolution of the original philosophy; suppliers of software or devices would now also offer solutions which were still open-source, but involved restrictions upon the user as regards their further software choices. Stallman, who opposed the direction open-source programming was headed, dubbed this process *tivoization*—from the TiVo playback and recording devices that used GNU GPL programming but actively blocked users from running modified versions of the software. Such practices were deemed as going against the original idea of free software, and, due to the restrictions

[18] Benkler (2006), p. 89.

[19] See Stallman (1985). Stallman actually made a specific reference to quitting MIT so that it would not stop him from 'giving GNU away', thus contributing to the understanding of free software mainly because of being available at no charge. Later, however, he became very strict about that not being the original idea behind the original wording, particularly when combating against the confusion of free software with open source.

[20] In the manifesto, Stallman cites a policy that was once upheld at Harvard, according to which no software was allowed to be installed unless its sources were on public display.

imposed upon the user and further software development, such devices were dubbed *tyrant devices*.[21]

The story of GNU and the ideals of free software rings familiar tones when analysed from the perspective of crowd-sourced innovation. The Free Software Foundation represented an effort at maintaining a framework for allowing unrestricted evolution of non-proprietary software along the lines of a very basic set of rules, and led to the creation of highly regarded pieces of Unix-compatible software. Steven Weber describes the GNU Emacs text editor, the GCC compiler and GDB debugger using terms like *most elegant, legendary, celebrated*.[22] Because of their popularity and dedication to writing enhancements, ports and updates to these applications, the main objective—building a new operating system was never completed. This task was fulfilled by another project that arose using GNU utilities and survives to this day, and that is the one supervised by Linus Torvalds.[23]

4.2.4 *Reinventing the Wheel: Oracle v. Google*

4.2.4.1 The Core of the Dispute

In mid-2016, the former CEO of Sun Microsystems, Jonathan Schwartz went on the stand in *Oracle v. Google* to offer the jury an explanation of what application programming interfaces (APIs) were. The 37 Java APIs in question were first developed and distributed by Sun Microsystems as open software, and as such reused and improved upon by generations of programmers, including those working for Google on development of the Android mobile operating system. Then Sun was taken over by Oracle, who had decided that it could sue Google for infringement. By the time Schwartz went to testify, Oracle's campaign had already seen a loss on grounds of patents, a loss on copyrightability, then a staggering win on copyrightability on appeal and was now being waged on the aspect of fair use.

When Schwartz's testimony famously likened APIs to items on a restaurant breakfast menu, presiding Judge William Alsup (who, incidentally, had actually learned the Java programming language himself to understand the case better) was quoted for saying '*I don't know what the witness just said. The thing about the breakfast menu makes no sense.*'[24] Schwartz did not give up and offered a more precise analogy: two restaurants could use the word 'hamburger' on their menus, and, instead of fighting over who was the first to come up with the name, (and, by implication, force the other to come up with a different name first) they should compete in who makes the *better implementation*—this being the better burger.

---

[21] Stallman (2011).

[22] Weber (2004), p. 49.

[23] Weber (2004), p. 49.

[24] Jeong (2016).

Despite jokes by commentators about Schwartz's apparent belief that hamburgers belonged on breakfast menus, this was an important point to make in proceedings that had been going on since 2010, with Oracle trying to *post factum* grab hold of 37 APIs which were distributed at the time of Java being owned by Sun as free and open software, widely used as such to ensure interoperability with Java, and then, as mentioned above, partly replicated by Google in the course of their development work on Android. The taking itself had been of extremely minor nature and comprised mainly of function names where the implementing code had been rewritten from scratch, and a small number of lines of code as a result of employing former employees of Sun Microsystems by Google. On a grand scale, the partial replication of the Java APIs had amounted to a neglectable small part of Android, and, in itself, may have a declining commercial significance in a world of Oracle's APIs being gradually abandoned in mobile devices.[25]

However, amidst the difficulties involved unavoidably when having die-hard nerds explain to a layman jury what APIs were and why they should not be copyrighted,[26] it had been widely commented that the significance of the case extended far beyond the 37 partially replicated APIs, beyond the struggle of two IT titans with $9 billion in damages on the table and beyond the clash of a nerd culture still living partly in Richard Stallman's realms of free-software with a world ruled by cold hard cash. What is truly important about Oracle v. Google were the possible implications of a final ruling in favour of the plaintiff, the full consequences of which could be difficult to fathom.

APIs are, in the simplest of terms, interfaces used by programs to interact with each other. As explained by Julie Samuels, Executive Director of Tech:NYC, '*it is safe to say that all software developers use APIs to make their software work with other software. For example, the developers of an application like Firefox use APIs to make their application work with various OSes* [operating systems] *by asking the OS to do things like make network connections, open files, and display windows on the screen. Allowing a party to assert control over APIs means that a party can determine who can make compatible and interoperable software, an idea that is anathema to those who create the software we rely on every day. Put clearly, the developer of a platform should not be able to control add-on software development for that platform.*'[27]

In a ruling that proved to be a reality check for many and 2 years before the case was re-examined by the District Court on the aspect of potential fair use, the U.S. Court of Appeals for the Federal Circuit famously ruled in 2014 that APIs

[25] See e.g. FOSSPatents (2015).

[26] In fact, also the lawyers involved in the case demonstrated having a rather basic idea about not only the subject matter itself but also the Internet in general. Benjamin Bicks, the main attorney for Oracle was reported to allege, when questioning Schwartz on the stand, that Schwartz was 'keeping a Google blog on himself' and present as evidence an e-mail Google Alert on Schwartz' name, leading to an article about the worse CEOs in history. To that Schwartz would famously reply 'I think you are mistaken as to what this is'. See Jeong (2016).

[27] Samuels (2012).

were, after all, copyrightable. In doing so, the USFC basically repeated the arguments presented on various occasions by the attorneys for the plaintiff.[28] In the words of Anette Hurst of Orrick, Herrington & Sutcliffe, APIs were simply code, and there could be no 'special' types of code that would not be copyrightable—just like there are no 'special' types of music which cannot be protected by copyright, or as one cannot dismiss abstract expressionist art as being too basic to merit protection. What mattered, Hurst said, was that there were universal rules, and these rules required to evaluate the creative and expressive value of the work. Hurst argued that APIs at hand clearly fulfilled these requirements, as well as they were not the only available—and thus inevitable—means of tackling the issues they addressed. This meant that APIs were copyrightable—and that is the way everyone interested in writing software should want them.

The USFC copyrightability decision was met with harsh criticism on the grounds of the judges being both unclear on what an API was, and in going against established law. At the ProgrammableWeb APIconSF API conference in June 2014, Pamela Samuelson of UC Berkeley made a point on how functional requirements for achieving compatibility, which are understood to be APIs, are part of what is unprotectable by copyright law under the provisions of 17 U.S. Code § 102b.[29] As she noted, it had been settled law since 1992 that the functional requirements for achieving compatibility are beyond the scope of copyright protection that is available to programs. On an even stronger note, Samuelson said that the matter of APIs being copyrightable '*essentially* [brought] *us back to the mid-1980s when the copyrightability of APIs had seemed to be a plausible interpretation of the statute*' before rulings from courts of appeal for both 2nd Circuit and 9th Circuit had seemingly put an end to the discussion. Samuelson observed that, however copyrighting software clearly merited its own special regime due to the functional aspects of software,[30] one cannot disregard the law says you cannot get a copyright for a process, procedure, system, or method of operation: '*there is a reason Congress put these words in the statute so that specifically the scope of copyright protection for computer programs would not be too broad.*' The grounds for this constitute the main reason for bringing up Oracle v. Google in this chapter and were dissected in the final judgment of the Supreme Court, which will be discussed below.

---

[28] See Oracle v. Google, United States Court of Appeals for the Federal Circuit, 2013-1021, -1022, Decided: May 9, 2014, https://www.eff.org/files/2014/11/10/oracle_v_google_13-1021.opinion.5-7-2014.1.pdf, p. 21 and on. Accessed 03 September 2023.

[29] 17 U.S. Code § 102b: 'In no case does copyright protection for an original work of authorship extend to any idea, procedure, process, system, method of operation, concept, principle, or discovery, regardless of the form in which it is described, explained, illustrated, or embodied in such work.'

[30] See Samuelson et al. (1994).

4.2.4.2 The Supreme Court Judgment of April 5th, 2021

4.2.4.2.1 The Trouble with Functional Nature of Software

'*Applying copyright law to computer programs is like assembling a jigsaw puzzle whose pieces do not quite fit*', the Supreme Court noted when reviewing the case, quoting *Lotus* v. *Borland*, to point out that the functional nature of computer programs renders it difficult to determine the adequate level of copyright protection. Historically, the functional nature of computer programs, oft accompanied with a near absence of an expressive or artistic aspect, had given rise to debates over whether software can at all be copyrightable. In an attempt to tackle the issue, in 1974 Congress appointed the National Commission on New Technological Uses of Copyrighted Works whose end report, delivered in 1978, took a clear position: software should be copyrighted, but copyright should not 'grant anyone more economic power than is necessary to achieve the incentive to create'. The report also pointed out that the unique [functional—KD] nature of computer programs meant a case-by-case application of the existing doctrines—including fair use—was sufficient to prevent copyright holders from stifling innovation.

In its opening analysis, the Court made an observation how fair use is useful in assessing the lawful scope of copyright protection as it can distinguish between technologies. This includes differentiating between 'expressive and functional features' in cases where they are mixed, as well as safeguarding the incentive to produce new material alongside examining the risk of harms 'in other markets, or to the development of other products'. Shortly put, this 'context check', as SCOTUS called it, can help keep the copyright monopoly 'within its rightful bounds'.

Notably, the Court's observations on usefulness of fair use in the assessment of software copyright cases were caveated by the dissent of Justice Thomas, who seemingly put into question the very applicability of fair use to computer programs. Thomas expressed reservations on whether distinguishing among types of computer code can be conducted while examining 'the nature of the work' (the second fair use factor) and offered that reuse of code in a new program can never have a 'valid purpose and character' (the first factor). The Court noted the dissent but disagreed, observing that Congress chose to place software in the copyright regime with no caveats, trusting in the existing doctrines to provide all the individual distinctions each case may require. Consequently, it was pointed out that just as fair use distinguishes between books and films, it must draw lines between computer programs; similarly, as it takes account of the market for scripts and paintings, it must give software the same consideration.

Notably, in its discussion of the dissenting opinion, the Court did not venture into more detailed examples that might reflect the nature of the dissent to a greater degree. Justice Thomas' reference pointed to a differentiation between types of 'raw' computer code rather than entire programs as used in the example. However, this choice of the Court appears deliberate. To object to this reasoning would be to claim that copyrightability of software programs should be guided by different principles than copyrightability of bits of raw code, which would also contradict the position Oracle has been firmly taking since the inception of the case.

4.2.4.2.2 SCOTUS' Fair Use Analysis

Starting its fair use analysis by commenting on the nature of the copyrighted work, the Court noted how the Java API contained three types of code. First, there was implementing code; this contained the actual instructions for tasks to be performed by the computer. This code had been written by Google. Second, 'method calls' which could be explained as commands associated with the calling up of each task. Oracle did not claim infringement by programmers' use of these commands. Thirdly, there was code which associated the given method call with the corresponding implementing code. This type of code labels the individual tasks and organizes these tasks or 'methods' into packages and classes. This function the Court likened to that of file cabinets, drawers and files. Despite being part of a computer program, this code was found to be 'inextricably bound' to the ideas of division of tasks, of organizing tasks, to use of specific commands, all of which are not copyrightable. It is also 'inextricably bound' to implementing code, which is copyrightable, but was not copied.

Declaring code and implementing code had obviously different capabilities but also required different types of creativity. Programming a task means choosing the most fitting out of many ways of achieving its purpose, factoring memory size, CPU power, or (on mobile devices) battery level. On the other hand, the function names in the declaring code were devised to be the most intuitive and easy to remember, to attract programmers who would use it and help develop it further. Due to extensive evidence showing the divide between the 'user-centred' declaring code and the 'innovative' implementing code, the Court concluded that declaring code—if copyrightable at all—is 'further than most' from what it called the 'core of copyright'. On this basis, this criterion was found to point to fair use.

Looking at the purpose and character of the use, the Court looked for evidence of the copier adding 'something new, with a further purpose or different character' that would give the work a new 'expression, meaning or message', or whether it fulfilled copyright's objective to stimulate creativity. In other words, this part of the analysis centred on whether Google added something 'new and important' that would make its use transformative. In assessing this, the Court noted, that Google, through Android, offered a new range of tasks which were labelled and organized using the structure that was copied, albeit only insofar as needed to allow programmers to work them using a language they were familiar with. Notably, reimplementing interfaces is considered standard practice in the software industry, which is paramount to creating interoperable software and competing in the market; for this reason, Sun had also used pre-existing interfaces in creating Java. In view of these considerations, the character of the use—despite taking place in a commercial endeavour, and in questionably good faith—was found to support fair use as well.

In examining the amount and substantiality of the portion that was used, the Court noted that 11,500 lines of code may objectively be seen as a lot of code. Still, when considered in context of the implementing code of the Java API, it was only 0.4% of the total set counting 2.86 million lines. This needs to be discussed in context: the Court pointed out that even a small taking can amount to a large part of the creative expression of the original work. In this case, however, the only purpose of the copied code was to call up the tasks it was bound to. Their copying was not dictated by their 'creativity' or 'beauty'; it was only to allow programmers to use the language they knew and apply it using their own creativity. Hence, this factor too was found to weigh in favour of fair use.

Perhaps the most important, from the perspective of this analysis, are however the Court's remarks when assessing the market effect of the copying and looking beyond the lost revenue. Market effects, the Court observed, can also kill the demand for the original work; these harms must be weighed against what the public stands to gain due to the copying. Sun had, in fact, tried to enter the smartphone market and started branding and licensing negotiations with Google. These failed as Sun insisted on necessary interoperability of all programs written for their platform; Google preferred to leave it open to developers. In reality, though, the two systems did not compete as they had their own market segments; simple devices like 'feature phones' or the Amazon Kindle would run on Java SE, while more advanced products like smartphones or the Kindle Fire would use Android. Evidence showed that Sun had sought to work with Google to expand the network of Java-trained programmers, while the attractiveness of its APIs to Google lay not in their creativity but in their widespread adoption and the fact that programmers were simply 'used to it'.

This also meant one thing: to allow Oracle, or other firms holding rights to interfaces, to enforce their copyright would risk harm to the public. The analogy used was that of a lock limiting the future creativity of new programs, with the rightsholder holding the only key. This, the Court found, was contrary to the basic objectives of copyright and again favoured fair use, thus bringing the analysis to a close.

4.2.4.3 Protecting Reusable Best Practices: Why Denying Protection Is Sometimes Important

Before being ultimately decided in favour of fair use, *Oracle* v. *Google* had kept stakeholders on the edge of the seat for many years. When the 2016 unanimous jury verdict in favour of fair use was reversed by the USFC, with the Supreme Court already having denied certiorari after USFC's decision of 2014, it seemed like the case was reaching its end—and not one favourable for Google. The possible implications of a win by Oracle had been widely covered in amicus briefs to the court and in other publications by scientists interested in the case.

One of the key considerations brought up was that of the detrimental effect that making interface specifications proprietary would have on creating new software that could be interoperable with existing systems, and thus able to compete in the market. This argument was shared in a number of positions put forward by computer scientists in the case. In its amicus brief, the Computer and Communications Industry of America offered a straightforward line of reasoning as to why software needs to be protected differently than literary works of intellect: a novel stands on its own as a standalone product, they argued, while a software product may only be operable '*in conjunction with hardware and other software, including an operating system.*' The hardware and operating system must be compatible, i.e. conform to the same set of technical rules—known as interface specifications.[31] In the words of Paul Goldstein, '*later-arriving hardware or software producers must, to compete, make their products compatible with the products sold by entrenched industry leaders, an effort that will characteristically require them to copy the industry leaders' interface specifications—the key that opens the lock to their operating systems.*'[32] The CCIA warned that making these specifications proprietary creates a toolkit for companies with a strong market position to reaffirm their dominance by deciding who of their small competitors may actually produce software to run on their system, much to the detriment of competition and the position of customers.[33] This touched upon what seems to be the heart of the issue in Google v. Oracle: by allowing companies to control the creation of any software compatible with theirs, its automotive equivalent would be that in order to market their new aftermarket onboard vehicle entertainment system, they could only do so if they first built their own car to offer it for. The aspect of disrupting a long-running assumption of openness of APIs and the possibility to reimplement them to create new software was also mentioned in the brief of computer scientists of November 7, 2014.[34]

Further down the alley of avoidance of overprotection as an important condition to allow software innovation, the CCIA reiterated that reverse engineering for interoperability and compatibility had long been recognized by U.S. courts and the USFC among them, as often leading to '*significant advances in technology*',[35] while disallowing access to interface specifications as a tool of large incumbents to hinder competition in the market has been discussed at large since *Franklin*[36] and *Whelan.*[37] These issues again sparked a debate at the time of *Lotus v. Borland,*[38]

[31] Computer and Communications Industry of America (2014), p. 3.

[32] Goldstein (2005), § 8.5.1.

[33] Computer and Communications Industry of America (2014), p. 4.

[34] Barlow et al. (2014).

[35] Bonito Boats, Inc. v. Thunder Craft Boats, Inc., 489 U.S. 141, 160 (1989).

[36] Apple Computer v. Franklin Computer, 714 F.2d 1240 (3d Cir. 1983) was the first instance when a court decided on the copyrightability of an operating system.

[37] Whelan Assocs., Inc. v. Jaslow D Pental Lab., Inc., 797 F.2d 1222 (3d Cir. 1986) was a case that led to software protection being extended beyond literal copying and into the realm of structure, sequence and organization. The ruling was criticized for commencing a period of overprotection stifling innovation. See Adamson (2001).

[38] Computer and Communications Industry of America (2014), p. 13. See also rulings in Lotus Dev. Corp. v. Borland Int'l, 49 F.3d 807 (1st Cir. 1995) and Lotus Dev. Corp. v. Borland Int'l, 516 U.S. 233 (1996).

illustrating the balance that courts must strike between overprotection and access to protect the innovation of future products,[39] but also leading to strong criticism on the basis that the existing software rights were incompatible with the basic principles of an IP system, promoting hoarding knowledge instead of sharing it and offering rewards for anticompetitive behaviours, leading ultimately to a sub-optimal incentive structure for innovation.[40] Interestingly, *Lotus* was also cited as precedent—as that was when the Federal Circuit ruled that control functional capabilities were a method of operation and thus uncopyrightable under § 17 USC § 102(b).[41]

Examples given by other *amici* on achieving progress and fostering competition by reverse engineering functional code included those dating back to the very dawn of the personal computer, when to create a computer that was compatible and (thus truly competitive) with the IBM PC, it was necessary to replicate its BIOS firmware.[42] This gave rise to an entire industry based on mutual compatibility and development of a practice become industry standard. In *Oracle v. Google* case, it has been mentioned at multiple times that the software industry of today depends to a considerable extent on repeatability of best practices. An embodiment of these practices are APIs—getting better with every iteration, with the technology behind a successful API being both used in existing solutions and further improved to create an even better API. In the words of David Berlind, EiC of ProgrammableWeb, we are all part of a world that is racing towards best practices. The emergence of patterns as to how APIs should be designed, make them much easier to use for developers. The jump from one API to the next can be very predictable: '*companies are building huge technologies and essentially baking these patterns into the technology in a way that the technology will produce an API that will often be the repeat of the last API created. This may completely wipe out all of that work*'.[43] The logic is clear: if one emerged and established pattern can be copyrighted, and the copyright holder chooses to protect that pattern, it becomes impossible to repeat production of that pattern and the industry standard established to-date.

When reading the numerous comments and submissions about *Oracle v. Google*, it is important to remember the deeper significance of the dispute, one that is being discussed here. A lot of ink had been spilled already in discussing whether or not Java APIs are (or should be) copyrightable, why the court felt they were and whether they have any business being copyrightable in the first place. On a level of code, this may be the point where our understanding of copyrightability does indeed become challenged—in the words of Lawrence Rosen of Rosenlaw & Einschlag, the way today's specifications are written is for them to be both 'code and spec' at the same

[39] Whong (1996).

[40] Adamson (2001).

[41] Lotus Dev. Corp. v. Borland Int'l, Inc., 49, F.3d 807, 815 (1st Cir. 1995), affirmed by an equally divided Supreme Court, 516 U.S. 233 (1996). Other cases considered as precedent included Sega v. Accolade, and Computer Associates v. Altai.

[42] Barlow et al. (2014).

[43] Berlind (2014).

time, which may be protected in some sense, but is primarily meant not as expression but as function and purposely written that way to enable widespread implementation.[44] What needs to be realized, however, is that—irrespective of the final result of the battle over 7000 lines of largely redundant code in Android—the case brought to the front pages an entire philosophy of innovating in the digital world that had been taken for granted as a tacit assumption with programmers and developers for years; one that has been unnoticeably underlying a major part of the digital progress achieved since the dawn of the personal computer as we know it today.

4.3 Wrap-Up: The Importance of Cumulative Selection

To provide additional commentary to the *Oracle* case and its takeaway message about holding the keys to future creativity (but also preservation of best practices), one more story deserves a mention which could be seen as an allegory of how networked digital creativity should ideally operate.

In 1986, Richard Dawkins published *The Blind Watchmaker*, offering his take on evolutionary biology and addressing a number of misconceptions related to it. One of those was the infinite monkey theorem, an example commonly used by creationists in their line of argumentation against evolution. In short, the concept is that a monkey with a keyboard, given enough time, would produce the whole works of Shakespeare. The time required for that to happen seems, quite correctly, so absurdly long that suddenly the entire concept involving random mutations indeed begins to look a tad naïve.[45]

The key element, however, is the term 'random'. In the real world, evolution is never pure randomness; new variations that appear in the genome are always based on a solution that already exists and has been tried and tested over time in terms of both survival and replication. In his work of 1986, Dawkins described evolution as a process combining random variation with non-random cumulative selection, devising his own thought experiment based on the infinite monkey theorem. By limiting the test to one 28-character sentence and using an algorithm that both ensured constant mutations and rejected variations which were too dissimilar to the target version, a random generator was able to line up the letters into a Hamlet quote after just about 30 min in the first version written in BASIC and 11 s after he switched over to Pascal.

What is striking about this example is its similarity to the type of networked innovation discussed in this chapter. In a way the grand-scale, low-entry cost,

[44]Other examples included HTML5 and W3C; see Berlind (2014).

[45]In 2003, an experiment, seemingly bordering on performance art, was conducted by a group of students of University of Plymouth, England who used a GBP 2000 grant to see if monkeys actually could write Shakespeare. Six Celebes crested macaques in Paignton Zoo in Devon were equipped with a keyboard and their literary output was recorded over a month. Not surprisingly, the said output was quite far from anything that actually made sense. See BBC News (2003).

common-failure model described here is not all too different from the random variation + cumulative selection scheme proposed by Dawkins to describe the evolution of living organisms. The driving factor for evolution is for the new variations to continue to occur, modifying existing genomes so that new combinations can be tested; here, there is a widespread pool of individuals making attempts to come up with something new on the basis of the knowledge they have and the means they have access to. In both cases, it is crucial that a new variation that has been tried and tested as successful, can then be used to form new developments. If an obstruction occurs at an early stage, the entire chain can never take place. In other words, every time a new generation of ideas reusing previous creations cannot be made into reality due to the barriers created by transaction costs and/or inflexible legislation, the entire chain of creation becomes disrupted. It is, therefore, a matter for the lawmaker to decide whether the time is ripe to reconsider the way statutory copyright law is drafted so as to reduce the risk of that happening. Some proposed ways of achieving this will be discussed in the final chapter of this book.

References

Adamson B (2001) Promoting Innovation in the Software Industry: A First Principles Approach to Intellectual Property Reform. Available via Academia.edu at https://www.academia.edu/69162006/Promoting_Innovation_in_the_Software_Industry_A_First_Principles_Approach_to_Intellectual_Property_Reform. Accessed 3 Sept 2023

Barlow JP et al (2014) Amicus curiae brief of Computer Scientists in Support of Petitioner, November 7, 2014. https://www.eff.org/files/2014/11/07/google_v_oracle_computer-scientists-certpetition-amicus-brief_14-410_final.pdf. Accessed 3 Sept 2023

BBC News (2003) No words to describe monkeys' play. BBC.co.uk http://news.bbc.co.uk/2/hi/3013959.stm. Accessed 3 Sept 2023

Benkler Y (2006) The wealth of networks. How social production transforms markets and freedom. Yale University Press, New Haven

Benkler Y (2011) Growth-oriented law for the networked information economy: emphasizing freedom to operate over power to appropriate. In: Litan RE (ed) Rules for growth: promoting innovation and growth through legal reform. Ewing Marion Kauffman Foundation, Kansas City, pp 313–314

Benkler Y (2017) Law, innovation, and collaboration in networked economy and society. Ann Rev Law Soc Sci 13:231–250. https://doi.org/10.1146/annurev-lawsocsci-110316-113340

Berlind D (2014) Oracle v. Google: Is there API copyright protection? ProgrammableWeb APIconSF API conference of June 2014, available at https://www.youtube.com/watch?v=FJ3-yFWYtrk. Accessed 3 Sept 2023

Biddle P, England P, Peinado M, Willman B (2003) The Darknet and the Future of Content Distribution. https://doi.org/10.1007/978-3-540-44993-5_10. Available at https://crypto.stanford.edu/DRM2002/darknet5.doc. Accessed 3 Sept 2023

Boldrin M, Levine DK (2008) against intellectual monopoly. Cambridge University Press, New York

Brewster T (2015) DMCA Ruling Ensures You Can't Be Sued For Hacking Your Car, Your Games Or Your iPhone. Forbes.com, https://www.forbes.com/sites/thomasbrewster/2015/10/27/right-to-tinker-victory/?sh=74a8e60c5d4c. Accessed 3 Sept 2023

Claburn T (2017) Talk of tech innovation is bullsh*t. Shut up and get the work done – says Linus Torvalds. TheRegister.com, 15 Feb 2017. https://www.theregister.com/2017/02/15/think_different_shut_up_and_work_harder_says_linus_torvalds. Accessed 3 Sept 2023

Computer and Communications Industry of America (2014) Amicus curiae brief on a petition for a writ of certiorari to the USCAFC. 7 Nov 2014

Farrokmanesh M (2018) Deepfakes are disappearing from parts of the web, but they're not going away. A community of that size doesn't need mainstream platforms to exist, via TheVerge.com, 9th Feb 2018, https://www.theverge.com/2018/2/9/16986602/deepfakes-banned-reddit-ai-faceswap-porn. Accessed 3 Sept 2023

FOSSPatents (2015) Google switches to open-source license for Java APIs in Android: will this limit Oracle's case to past damages? http://www.fosspatents.com/2015/12/google-switches-to-open-source-license.html. Accessed 3 Sept 2023

Goldstein P (2005) Goldstein on Copyright, 2nd edn. Aspen Publishers

Gutmann P (2007) A Cost Analysis of Windows Vista Content Protection. University of Auckland, NZ. https://www.cs.auckland.ac.nz/~pgut001/pubs/vista_cost.html#functionality. Accessed 3 Sept 2023

Jeong S (2016) In Oracle v. Google, a Nerd Subculture Is on Trial. Vice.com. https://www.vice.com/en/article/mg77dy/in-google-v-oracle-the-nerds-are-getting-owned. Accessed 3 Sept 2023

Lee D (2018) Deepfakes porn has serious consequences. BBC.com, 3 Feb 2018. https://www.bbc.com/news/technology-42912529. Accessed 3 Sept 2023

Samuels J (2012) Oracle v. Google and the Dangerous Implications of Treating APIs as Copyrightable, EFF.org. https://www.eff.org/deeplinks/2012/05/oracle-v-google-and-dangerous-implications-treating-apis-copyrightable. Accessed 3 Sept 2023

Samuelson P, Davis R, Kapor MD (1994) A Manifesto concerning the legal protection of computer programs. Colum Law Rev 94:2308–2431. Available via DukeLaw https://scholarship.law.duke.edu/cgi/viewcontent.cgi?article=1783&context=faculty_scholarship. Accessed 3 Sept 2023

Smith J, Mann J, Simmons J (2016) Get better quality video with Microsoft Edge. https://blogs.windows.com/windowsexperience/2016/07/13/get-better-quality-video-with-microsoft-edge/#vsqQUutIyUV3DWca.97. Accessed 3 Sept 2023

Stallman R (1985) The GNU Manifesto. Available GNU Operating System, https://www.gnu.org/gnu/manifesto.html. Accessed 3 Sept 2023

Stallman R (2011) Is Android really free software? The Guardian, 19 Sep 2011. https://www.theguardian.com/technology/2011/sep/19/android-free-software-stallman. Accessed 3 Sept 2023

The Alliance of Automobile Manufacturers (2014) Short Comment Regarding a Proposed Exemption Under 17 U.S.C. 1201 (Proposed Class #17). https://copyright.gov/1201/2015/comments-032715/class%2017/Alliance_of_Automobile_Manufacturers_class17_1201_2014.pdf. Accessed 3 Sept 2023

The Next Web (2018a) Someone is finally purging the AI-made fake celebrity porn from Reddit. The Next Web, 31 Jan 2018. https://thenextweb.com/artificial-intelligence/2018/01/31/fake-celebrity-porn-ai-reddit/. Accessed 3 Sept 2023

The Next Web (2018b) Reddit bans Deepfakes community that made AI-generated celebrity porn. The Next Web, 8 Feb 2018. https://thenextweb.com/news/reddit-deepfakes-ai-celebrity-porn. Accessed 3 Sept 2023

Vaughan-Nichols SJ (2013) Who writes Linux? Almost 10,000 developers. ZDNet.com, 16 Sep 2013 http://www.zdnet.com/article/who-writes-linux-almost-10000-developers/. Accessed 3 Sept 2023

Weber S (2004) The success of open source. Harvard University Press, Cambridge

Whong JA (1996) Lotus v. Borland: Defining the Limits of Software Copyright Protection. Santa Clara High Technol Law J 12:207. https://digitalcommons.law.scu.edu/cgi/viewcontent.cgi?article=1200&context=chtlj. Accessed 3 Sept 2023

Chapter 5
EU (Non) Remedies to Inflexible Copyright: Contracts as a Policy Tool

[A] real data economy [. . .] would be a powerful engine for innovation and new jobs [. . .] the reality is that 80% of industrial data is still collected and never used.—*Ursula von der Leyen's 2020 State of the Union address*

5.1 Introduction: Prescriptive Regulation, Data Economy and Generative AI

To paraphrase the question asked by the U.S. Supreme Court in *Google v. Oracle*: who holds the keys to innovation in a data-driven economy? A lot has been written about the personal data collection and generation ecosystem that rose from the ashes of the World Trade Center, born from an ambition to create a network of information collection as means of improving national security. The massive global network that emerged, employing a myriad of companies aiding the Big Tech giants' data collection by creating millions of data points in apps, websites and connected devices, siphoning data and monetizing it, had for many years evaded the attention of the general public. The eyes of the world began turning towards the issue around the time when Shoshana Zuboff's book on omnipresent data collection and monetization, *The Age of Surveillance Capitalism*, rose through the charts in 2019, with Barack Obama naming it one of his top books of the year. Around the same time, discussions on the market implications of the new data economy were on the rise again,[1] giving rise to literature demonstrating how the age-old mechanisms of some actors grabbing the means of production—in the traditional take, these were labor, land and money[2]—have now emerged again, giving rise to a new generation of industrial tycoons without an industry, massive platforms propertising intangible

[1] See generally Cohen (2019).

[2] Polanyi (1944).

K. Drazewski, *Copyright as a Constraint on Creating Technological Value*, Law, Governance and Technology Series 63,
https://doi.org/10.1007/978-3-031-51276-6_5

resources and giving rise to a new brand of information capitalism, ruled by economic actors that control the flows of data.[3]

In a gatekeeper-driven digital economy, yesterday's optimism about online innovation is now dwindling. The world's biggest tech companies, amounting to the top 25% tier of the S&P 500 market capitalization, continue to grow—but their input is rarely that of producing new and groundbreaking technologies; instead, they provide a constant influx of rent-seeking business practices attempting to squeeze out ever more profits, with the side effects of tribalism, societal frictions and innovation feudalism.[4] Looking at the sharp rise of TikTok as the primary source of news for its users, happening also at the expense of platforms like Facebook or Twitter,[5] one may wonder how little the world has changed—the market still rewards the bold and the affluent (in this case, data-rich) with little regard for the rules of the game,[6] in this case likely with considerable detriment to our societies and democracies.

However, the global outreach and market penetration of the new ruling caste of 'tech barons' is also where the difficulty lies. In a world of omnipresent personalization, if you are big enough, you become the eyes and ears of millions or even billions of people who will always be steered towards information and content that your algorithms consider the most likely to keep them engaged. In 2021, BEUC—The European Consumer Organisation published a series of reports on structural asymmetries in digital consumer markets, discussing the policy implications of this unprecedented power of data-driven Big Tech, but also pointing to one more issue: the 'essentiality' of their services to modern-day societies. In other words, not only do we now live in a market which is profoundly asymmetrical, with the domination of the few strongest actors who control our data and have the power to set the rules of the game by determining people's access to products, services and information; we have also come to rely on these actors for the functioning of the society, rendering them into the 'universal service' providers of the modern world—just as access to electricity or landline telephones was considered essential in the 1960s when the doctrine was first introduced.[7]

What are the drivers for these processes? Over the past years, a balance shift had been gradually occurring in the means of safeguarding the market positions of

---

[3]A term capturing the market implications was that of 'uberization' of the economy by platforms controlling both the centralized demand in certain markets (such as Uber or Airbnb) and but also centralizing supply realized by a myriad of service providers who cannot afford not to be on the platform. See Vercellone et al. (2019), p. 43.

[4]Ezrachi and Maurice (2022).

[5]https://www.pewresearch.org/journalism/fact-sheet/social-media-and-news-fact-sheet/?itid=lk_inline_enhanced-template.

[6]Thankfully, enforcers are not laying down their arms either. See Netherlands Authority for Consumers and Markets (ACM) (2022) Joint European consumer authorities force TikTok to make changes, https://www.acm.nl/en/publications/joint-european-consumer-authorities-force-tiktok-make-changes. Accessed 03 September 2023.

[7]Lynskey and Rott (2021). See also Ezrachi and Maurice (2022), Chapter 2.

industry incumbents. Existing means of intellectual property protection, both in terms of patents and copyright, had been reinforced with *de facto* protection resulting from technological monopolization of access to data. '*De facto*' in this case means exactly that: a strong player, placing on the market numerous data-driven products or intermediating in the operation of broadly used services, finds itself in a position of actual control over the data that they generate. On a big enough scale, this translates into an additional, highly effective safeguard of one's market position and until recently, there had been little to no legislative tackling of such monopolies. In the European Union, a major policy step towards changing this was meant to be the advent of the Data Act, giving rise to a discussion on whether and how the rights of data holders to the data generated by the use of their products should be addressed by lawmakers to boost innovation.

On 23 February 2022, Executive Vice-President Margrethe Vestager and Commissioner Thierry Breton co-hosted the launch conference of the new Data Act proposal. Vestager's opening speech brought forward imagery of fostering economic growth, competitiveness, innovation and job creation by enabling productive use (sic!) of data generated by operation of connected devices. Such reuse could foster the pursuit of all these goals, providing 'a multitude of possibilities for new products, new services, or they can foster research.' To unlock this potential for data to become an 'essential resource' for growth and innovation, barriers to data sharing would now be addressed in the Data Act.[8]

While setting a high bar for the introduced regulation, these words nonetheless rang true. The necessity of access to device- and service- generated data to enable and foster innovation and to prevent vendor lock-in (or, more broadly, incumbent lock-in) is unquestionable. In this context, copyright has a history of being the weapon of choice for protecting economic interests of established manufacturers and leading to much contention: suffice to recall the discussions on qualifying cars as 'mobile computing devices' and the resulting issues with tinkering and copyrightability of their onboard data,[9] then, in the EU context, the 2018 battle in European Parliament over an amendment to a resolution on autonomous transportation that would speak against the application of copyright to car telemetry data, which was eventually shot down by EPP MEPs[10] (the underlying rationale was clear enough; a connected vehicle is essentially a moving platform for a multitude of sensors and accessing the data they harvest would make reverse-engineering all the more simple).

This chapter takes a closer look at the apparent dissonance between the goals and ambitions formulated by EU lawmakers and the actual substantive input into the policy discussion. Always with growth and innovation on its banners, reconfirmed in

---

[8] https://ec.europa.eu/commission/presscorner/detail/en/speech_22_1312.

[9] See the discussion in Chap. 4.

[10] For coverage on the discussion, see e.g. Stolton (2018). For the JURI draft opinion, see here: https://www.europarl.europa.eu/meetdocs/2014_2019/plmrep/COMMITTEES/JURI/PA/2018/10-10/1156954EN.pdf. Accessed 03 September 2023.

the 2020 Action Plan,[11] the Commission's proposal for the Data Act (as well as the final text) ultimately shied away from addressing the big questions of value creation in the modern digital market. From the Commission's reports shutting down the need to flexibilise copyright, to the questionable added value of the *sui generis* right to databases, leading to the most recent example that was the proposed framework for the Data Act, which emerged out of big ambitions to ensure greater diversity in the innovation market and overcoming the lock-in effects—yet fell short from making any meaningful adjustments to the existing copyright framework that could favour innovators (even quite the contrary, as the analysis will show). The solution offered by the Data Act was based on case-by-case negotiations with data holders (tacitly assumed to have a sui-generis right of their own to the data generated by the devices they sold). This approach echoed earlier policy suggestions from analyses commissioned externally by the Commission at the time of early discussions over the (then) new Copyright Directive—and was burdened by the same assumptions, going against the logic presented by the U.S. Supreme Court in Google v. Oracle in 2021, and likely to end up risking solidification of big tech oligopolies instead of fostering distributed innovation and diversity.

This deepening of power asymmetries is being raised again now at the time of the first court battles being waged over the exploits of generative AI companies and the unavoidable policy discussions on how such technology should be regulated. Although the prescriptive approach to regulating AI had already been shown to be vulnerable to technological change (when the rise of ChatGPT and other generative models had laid bare the shortcomings of the circumscribed framework of the nascent AI Act, leading to an exercise in frantic last-minute rewriting),[12] this approach is again visible in the discussions on the desired regulatory approach to the text and data mining by generative AI models, both regarding the AI Act's requirement to make and publish detailed summaries on use of training data protected by copyright[13] and in the application of text and data mining copyright exceptions, which will also be discussed in this chapter.

---

[11] European Commission (2020a).

[12] For an overview of the blind spots of the AI Act proposal demonstrated by ChatGPT, see Helberger and Diakopoulos (2023). A similar example can be seen in the inherent weakness of Article 38 of the Digital Markets Act which mandates that '*recommender systems shall provide at least one option for each of their recommender systems which is not based on profiling*', which leaves out the newer (and highly efficient) recommender systems like TikTok's Monolith that do not build user profiles, choosing instead to dynamically allocate users to relevant clusters. On the mechanics of Monolith see Worb (2023), Kim (2022), Mage_AI (2022) and Smith (2021).

[13] See the Parliament's adopted text, Article 28b: https://www.europarl.europa.eu/doceo/document/TA-9-2023-0236_EN.html.

5.2 Exceptions and Secondary Market Failures: The European Commission 2013 Report

To begin discussing the chain of events that occurred on EU soil and will be described in this chapter, it is important to note how the debates that preceded the revision of the Copyright Directive had also given rise to interesting perspectives which are relevant to the issue of copyright flexibilities in the context of safeguarding innovation.

One such perspective was offered in a report ordered by the European Commission on the subject of copyright exceptions and their implications in the digital economy. The conclusions were remarkably relevant in the context of the earlier findings on the nature of distributed digital innovation and the entry barriers for it to come to exist. The report, produced in 2013 by Charles River Associates,[14] represents a valuable summary of an approach to copyright which could be called classically mercantile—with all the related shortcomings.

The report makes a note of copyright existing to create a market in the first place, for goods which are costly to develop yet cheap to duplicate. Thus, copyright's purpose is that of intervening where the market fails. From this perspective, the very rationale for copyright exceptions is that they prove their worth solely in the conditions where the market established by copyright fails; where this does not occur, copyright may function without imposing upon it any further limitations.[15] In other words, while copyright in itself is a remedy for a 'primary' market failure where one could not reap the benefits from valuable intellectual property in the absence of copyright protection, the system may lead, in turn, to a 'secondary' failure where an established licencing market does not perform its purpose. This 'secondary' inefficiency can then be remedied by appropriate copyright exceptions.

The report mentions three potential reasons for this market inefficiency:

1. substantial transaction costs, eroding gains from trading to prohibitive levels
2. inability of market powers to effectively discriminate in prices between user groups
3. private value of copyrighted work does not reflect its social value.

On this basis, the key underlying issue is shown in the transaction costs which, despite being considerably reduced in the digital world of today, may still lead to undesirable social outcome and market inefficiency. At the same time, having transaction costs hypothetically brought down to zero, along with ensuring that entitlements are clearly defined, would cause these reasons for a market failure to disappear.[16]

---

[14] Langus et al. (2013).

[15] As a follow-up in 2014, the Commission received another report by Charles River Associates, striving to analyse specific policy options. See Boulanger et al. (2014).

[16] Langus et al. (2013), p. 5.

Before addressing these considerations, a few observations need to be made about the 2013 report for a clear picture. In general terms, the report sought to address issues posed by the technological change, which had led to the emergence of new channels of distribution and new uses of creative work, reducing the cost of copying. Its approach is a cautious one, stating that the discussion is deliberately kept 'at a high level' (of abstract, presumably) to ensure wide applicability.[17] Regretfully, it also openly shies away from addressing the benefits of employing open-ended norms as in the fair use system against codified specific exceptions, thus limiting itself to a strictly continental approach to restrictions imposed upon copyright. On the upside, however, it also cautions that the development of technology and the introduction of new and innovative uses may likely render it difficult to produce, in advance, a list of circumscribed exceptions to cater for all the uses which should be exempted; hence 'to the extent possible, exceptions should allow for a certain degree of flexibility'.[18]

5.3 'Bespoke Negotiations' and Why They Do Not Matter for Networked Innovation

Having made these observations, the CRA report offered that, in a fully functioning market, market players (in this case, distributors and content rightsholders) will always reach an agreement on how to reuse content protected by copyright. The more complicated or innovative the new use is, the more 'bespoke' the negotiations, as will likely be the solution worked out in the end. The report admits, however, that intellectual property markets operate in ways which are often far from ideal and 'bespoke' negotiations may also carry considerable transaction costs. An example is given of a platform used in the aggregation and distribution of a wide variety of content; in this case, the costs would likely be found to be prohibitive and market entry would never occur.[19]

Applying the 'bespoke negotiations' optic to the types of innovation discussed here, the first tangible example that comes to mind is the endeavour of Google Book Project. It had little to do with the networked, fragmented innovation that was described earlier in this work; still, it had a lot to do with a powerful market player creating a way of using a humongous volume of other people's intellectual property in a networked environment, in ways which did not adversely affect the market for the original work. Nonetheless, irrespective of the fact that the entity in question was certainly one of means,[20] the fact remains that it would likely be unable to enter and conduct such negotiations due to the scale of the project. In the earlier chapters, the estimate of statutory liability was given in the case of a copyright failure of the

[17] Langus et al. (2013), p. 1.

[18] Langus et al. (2013), fn 1.

[19] Langus et al. (2013), pp. 3–4.

[20] Solomon (2016).

project, resulting in a figure which was best compared to the gross national product of the United States. However, applying the transaction costs optic offered by the 2013 CRA report, going about Google Books in a traditional way, seeking agreements with each publisher out of the 100+ million book pool would be prohibitive; thus, the 'bespoke' negotiations would likely never even commence. In such a case, the market failure could be seen in that project would have never even left the drawing board.[21]

It could be claimed that in a way, this also touches upon the heart of the problem. Mass low-cost innovation, the Benkler-type innovation, is the most fragile as it often does not come with the means to negotiate with established market players. It will thus almost always suffer from a market failure where it hits upon inflexible legislation: a low-cost innovator/experimenter will not acquire licenses for the new uses they come up with. Further on, this chapter will offer a thought experiment to see how such licensing arrangements would need to be structured, and whether they would be compatible with a hive mind of networked actors.

5.4 The Sui Generis Right to Databases

5.4.1 The Elusive Problem of Market Impact

In 2015, the European Parliament ITRE and IMCO committees published a report calling for the abolishment of the 96/9/EC Database Directive as an impediment to the development of a European data-driven economy.[22] Coming with its own copyright standard for protection of the intellectual creativity embodied in databases[23] and an entirely new *sui generis* right to protect databases which do not feature that creative element, based instead on a criterion on 'substantive investment',[24] the Directive had long been causing controversies as regards its impact on the market.

The Directive met with harsh institutional criticism in 2005, when the Commission published the results of its first evaluation.[25] The critique was broad: between a wave of litigations in European courts and a lack of empirically measurable benefits in encouraging growth in the European database industry (in fact, there had been a

[21] It should be noted that Google Books, while technically illegal in France, secured its position in that market by means of Google's settlement with publishers, the details of which have not been disclosed. Still, it was taking place at a time when it was becoming obvious that the project has succeeded worldwide and that the economic rights of rightsholders were not being adversely affected in a measurable manner, particularly in the light of the counterbalance of benefits offered by the system to legal merchandise providers.

[22] European Parliament (2015).

[23] Article 3 DBD.

[24] Article 7 DBD.

[25] European Commission (2005).

noticeable decline, concurrent with a rise in the U.S.)[26] the 'sui generis' right was found:

- to be difficult to understand,
- to come close to protecting data as property,
- to have an unproven overall economic benefit.

The policy options presented in the report were to kill off the entire Database Directive, to repeal or amend the sui generis right, or keep things as they were. In the end, the latter option prevailed.

If the first report had been critical but ultimately left the policy options open, the same cannot be said about the follow-up evaluation. Three years after the IMCO report calling for the abolishment of the Database Directive, a new study was prepared on commission for DG CNECT[27] taking into account the Principles of Better Regulation,[28] which embedded a requirement to evaluate for whether legislative measures had achieved their stated objectives effectively and efficiently, whether they were relevant and coherent, and, perhaps most importantly, whether there was any European added value. The analysis did not bring about a breakthrough: it noted that most stakeholders had experienced low, if any, benefits from the Database Directive except in terms of improved legal certainty, while at the same time the associated costs were also not significant. On this basis, the Database Directive was assessed this time as providing a relatively good cost/benefit outcome for the consulted stakeholders. However, the most important question—being the cost/benefit impact of the Directive in the broader data economy context—was still left unanswered.

5.4.2 Reliance on Contract Empowering Incumbents

The Database Directive reinforces a legal framework which relies on presupposing exclusive rights with very narrow exceptions, primarily relying on contract as means to gain access to protected property and placing the burden of proof on the aspiring creator in the latter case. This is aligned with the philosophy seeking to avoid regulatory burdens while relying on the market to find solutions; however, it also creates externalities where a more nuanced approach would be needed.

Martin Senftleben notes that this results in a system that is geared 'almost intuitively' towards the grant of exclusive rights which right holders can invoke as veto rights against use without prior authorization.[29] Examples given include the

[26] European Commission (2005), p. 23.

[27] Joint Institute for Innovation Policy and Technopolis (2018).

[28] https://ec.europa.eu/info/law/law-making-process/planning-and-proposing-law/better-regulation-why-and-how_en.

[29] Senftleben (2022).

very practical implications for researchers seeking to make use of the exceptions that are granted. Senftleben's 2022 report for the European Commission points out that this is not merely about the *expressis verbis* exclusion of collaborative projects which may involve partial commercialization of the results[30] but also restricting use rights to cases which do not cover communication and making available to the public, in effect preventing the sharing of research data with members of a larger research consortium, the academic community and the general public.[31] To make things worse, the burden is placed on anyone willing to rely on the exceptions to refute allegations of their use being in conflict with normal exploitation of the databases and/or unreasonably prejudicing the legitimate interests of the right holders,[32] all the way assuming that the Member State in question has even transposed the *optional* research exemptions of the Information Society Directive and the Database Directive without introducing more nuanced requirements on its own.

The Database Directive's protection model is mentioned here to provide an overture to a much more current initiative which reproduces—at the functional level—the policy mindset based on presupposition of exclusive rights of industry incumbents, with very narrow exceptions based predominantly on negotiations and individual bargaining power. Be it by design or simply due to the substantive proximity, this phenomenon is best illustrated by the philosophy embedded in the proposed Data Act which will be discussed further in this chapter.

5.5 Text and Data Mining in the Age of ChatGPT

5.5.1 Why Text and Data Mining?

> Unfortunately, I expect a flood of litigation for almost all generative AI products—Heather Meeker, OSS Capital, for TechCrunch in January 2023.[33]

One of the less intended contributions of early 2020s' generative AI models to the field of policymaking had been the mainstreaming of discussions about infringement of copyrights in the massive amounts of data required—and used—to train these models. A wave of front-page lawsuits targeting StabilityAI,[34] GitHub Copilot, Microsoft and OpenAI,[35] Midjourney[36] and others started rising in late 2022 to

[30] Article 5(3)(a) ISD; Article 9(b) DBD.

[31] Article 9(b) DBD; Article 3 DSMD.

[32] Article 5(5) ISD; Article 7(2) DSMD.

[33] Wiggers (2023).

[34] https://newsroom.gettyimages.com/en/getty-images/getty-images-statement. For comments see https://www.theverge.com/2023/2/6/23587393/ai-art-copyright-lawsuit-getty-images-stable-diffusion.

[35] https://githubcopilotlitigation.com/pdf/06823/1-0-github_complaint.pdf.

[36] https://stablediffusionlitigation.com/pdf/00201/1-1-stable-diffusion-complaint.pdf.

seek protection from unlicensed use of copyrighted works to train generative AI models. In an attempt of subsumption of existing legal concepts to machine learning, the class action against StabilityAI, operating the image generator *Stable Diffusion*, spoke of the model 'remixing' copyrighted works to create competing images, even if they did bear 'outwardly resemblance' the scrubbed originals.[37] The AI 'outputs' discussion on whether or not AI-assisted (or entirely AI-produced) creative works compete in the market against their input material, and whether they are at all copyrightable[38] is still on the rise, with different approaches depending on jurisdiction.[39] However, from the perspective of this analysis, what is more relevant is the 'input' side of things; namely the right (or lack of one) to reuse existing works for training machine learning models.

While a good case can be (and has been) made for training AI models on protected works to be fair use under the U.S. system[40] (not least due to their focus on generalizing insights, leading more to 'capturing ideas' rather than specific expressions, as well as little similarity to input data, little risk of market substitution, as well as the models actually storing very little data from the input material—apparently less than one byte per ingested image in the case of *Stable Diffusion*),[41] the same cannot be said about the European side of things, where the operators of such models would need to rely on the prescriptive text-and-data mining (TDM) exceptions granted in the 2019 Copyright Directive.

5.5.2 *The 'Art of the Deal': TDM Exceptions and AI in Europe*

Applicable since 2021 and window-dressed in language on how text and data mining benefits the research community and supports innovation, allowing to 'gain new knowledge' and to 'discover new trends' (Rec. 8), two mandatory copyright

[37] https://stablediffusionlitigation.com/.

[38] See e.g. Guadamuz (2023); for an account on how copyright protection was granted, then denied to a partly AI-generated work, see https://ipwatchdog.com/2022/11/01/us-copyright-office-backtracks-registration-partially-ai-generated-work/id=152451/.

[39] The United Kingdom is an example of a jurisdiction where no human creative input is required for the work to be copyrightable. See https://www.gov.uk/government/consultations/artificial-intelligence-and-ip-copyright-and-patents/artificial-intelligence-and-intellectual-property-copyright-and-patents#:~:text=Works%20generated%20by%20a%20computer,be%20protected%2C%20as%20described%20above [retrieved 28 July 2023]; see also the discussion in Guadamuz (2017).

[40] For a general discussion on why databases *should* be fair game for machine learning, see (from the technical perspective) Lemley and Casey (2021) and (for a legal argument) Sag (2019).

[41] For a description on the training process and a brief fair use discussion of training AI image generators see Walsh (2023). For a more in-depth discussion on applying the fair use factors, see Gervais (2022). A more cautious analysis was published by the Copyright Alliance, suggesting that the ultimate qualification must be done on a case-by-case basis depending on the specific facts of the case; see Coffman (2023).

exceptions to allow automated processing of digital text and data falling under copyright protection were introduced by the Copyright Directive.[42] The first of the two was enshrined in Article 3 CDSM and adding to the existing exceptions in the Infosoc Directive,[43] was designed to benefit research institutions and cultural heritage organisations in the field of 'natural and human sciences',[44] allowing them to store copies of the scrubbed data for research purposes with appropriate protection measures.[45] It was also safeguarded by a number of restrictions (including the requirement of having 'lawful access' meaning either the data being free, open-access, or licensed[46]).

The second exception, featured in Article 4, was introduced later in the legislative process as means to tackle the 'commercial' uses[47] of the mined data, its aim being to allow licensing outside of the Article 3 'scientific use' exception, as well as the earlier exceptions and limitations of the Information Society Directive 2001/29/EC. It is similar in structure to the scientific research exception, but imposes no limits on the range of entities that can benefit from it, while at the same time allowing rightsholders to opt out of data collection by making a 'reservation' of rights e.g. by use of machine-readable means such as metadata, thus in practice making a contract with data holders the main tool for enabling the scraping of information.

These two exceptions, arguably critical for innovation in general and for the development of artificial intelligence systems in particular, have faced strong critique for being 'conceptually wrong, theoretically flawed and normatively unambitious'.[48] From the broad definition of TDM[49] (capturing all forms of modern data-driven digital analytics that rely on 'training' on data, including such use cases as natural language processing (NLP) systems, image recognition, as well as content filtering[50]) to the inherent issue of enabling AI development in the EU only by meeting the criteria for an exception or by securing a contract with rightsholders, to the long-term risks caused by such an approach, including the petrification of market

[42]Directive 2019/790 of the European Parliament and of the Council of 17 April 2019 on copyright and related rights in the Digital Single Market (Copyright Directive, CDSM).

[43]Ducato and Strowel (2021) note that in some cases TDM work might not require reproduction and thus could benefit from the Infosoc Directive's exceptions for temporary reproductions in Article 5(1) and illustration for teaching or scientific research under Article 5(3)a).

[44]Recital 12 CDSM.

[45]Article 3 CDSM.

[46]Recital 14 CDSM. For a discussion on how to remedy the shortcomings of this provision, see Ducato and Strowel (2021).

[47]Article 4 CDSM.

[48]The quote is by Margoni and Kretschmer (2022). See also generally Griffiths et al. (2022), Ducato and Strowel (2021) and Geiger (2021). For a critique of the TDM exceptions and particularly the 'opt-out' feature in Article 4, see particularly Quintais (2023) and Rosati (2020).

[49]Defined by Article 2(2) CDSM as 'any automated analytical technique aimed at analysing text and data in digital form in order to generate information which includes but is not limited to patterns, trends and correlations'.

[50]Margoni and Kretschmer (2022).

dominance of incumbent players, dooming startups to using cheaper, older datasets and thus being unable to compete, leading to creation of 'second-class' AI applications for those not affluent enough to afford the prime quality products, not to mention the risks of recycling older datasets (or older pre-trained models), proliferation of substandard, opaque AI black boxes, perpetuation of data biases, as well as propagating inequality and algorithmic discrimination.[51]

At the same time, research institutions wishing to benefit from the Article 3 exception would face a number of obstacles, from the possible narrow interpretation of the 'natural and human sciences' qualifier to the lack of remedies against technical protection measures deployed by rightsholders, to the 'legal access' requirement which, as stated, is interpreted in Recital 14 as the data being either freely available, subject to an open access policy or a covered by a contractual arrangement. On the one hand, from a policy perspective, such restrictions are certain to render it less attractive to commercial actors to engage in unethical 'AI data laundering' activities by piggybacking on research institutions who do all the legwork in collecting the data and training the models as a way of shielding themselves from accountability (and, in the U.S., also increasing the likelihood of the training being found to be fair use).[52] On the other hand, this again means that the only realistic means for an AI startup to secure lawful access to data is again to rely on a contract—which, as said earlier, in the case of grassroots experimenters with no financial means is likely to render the whole affair unfeasible before it may even begin.

For a full picture, one more aspect should be noted: while reliance on contract as a policy tool presupposes the existence of contracting power on the part of the innovator, the Copyright Directive is not where the legal troubles of 'poor man's innovation' will end. As mentioned earlier in this chapter, at the time of making the last updates to this text, the European Parliament has just adopted its text for the trilogues on the upcoming AI Act, rendering it mandatory to '*document and make publicly available a sufficiently detailed summary of the use of training data protected under copyright law*' (Article 28b (c)).[53] Arriving on top of other, arguably justified requirements for providers of such models in this Article, if the said documentation requirement makes it to the final Act, it will likely further reinforce the factual monopoly of Big Tech companies who will have considerably less difficulty to allocate resources to this insurmountable task, with considerable consequences to us all.[54] Strengthening further the competitive position of the big players via the 2019 Copyright Directive is perhaps doubly ironic, given that the

[51] For a broader discussion on discrimination in algorithmic processes informing decision-making, see Williams et al. (2018).

[52] On AI data laundering, see Vincent (2022) and Baio (2022).

[53] https://www.europarl.europa.eu/doceo/document/TA-9-2023-0236_EN.html.

[54] On the reinforcement of monopolies, see further Trendacosta and Doctorow (2023). Quintais (2023) argues that the AI Act's transparency provision only serves copyright holders and is not possible to comply with in practice, not least due to factors such as territorial fragmentation of copyright, poor quality of metadata or the lack of a registration requirement for protected works.

Treaty reference in its Recital 1 speaks of the goal to ensure that competition in the internal market is not distorted, the means to this end being EU copyright law.[55]

5.6 Productive Reuse of Data (Not): The Failed Hopes for the Data Act

5.6.1 Fulfilling the Promises of the European Strategy for Data

What if the goals of innovative productive reuse of intangible property could be achieved through access to data instead?[56] In 2022 the European Commission proposed the Regulation on Harmonised Rules on Fair Access to and Use of Data (Data Act): a Union regulation advertised as a remedy for the lock-in effects created by the digital market. Arriving amidst a wave of other Regulation-level legislation aimed at addressing the inefficiencies of the digital economy[57] it was preceded by years of discussions surrounding the inefficiencies of the European data economy and giving a tangible form to ambitions expressed in the European Strategy for Data published by the Commission in 2020.[58]

The Strategy for Data spoke of empowering citizens to make better decisions based on insights from non-personal data. Already in the introduction the stated goal was a bold one: that '*data should be available to all—whether public or private, big or small, start-up or giant. This [would] help society to get the most out of innovation and competition and ensure that everyone benefits from a digital dividend. This digital Europe should reflect the best of Europe—open, fair, diverse, democratic, and confident.*'[59]

From the perspective on enabling innovation, the Strategy was also quite clear (if a bit verbose) on the importance of this data access: it described data as the 'lifeblood of economic development', the 'basis for many new products and services', a driver of 'productivity and resource efficiency gains across all sectors of the economy', an 'essential resource for start-ups and small and medium-sized enterprises' in developing products and services. It noted the essential character of data for training artificial intelligence systems, including the move towards de-centralised

[55] CDSM Recital 1.

[56] According to a 2020 study by Deloitte, SMEs that used data-driven innovation were found to be able to increase their productivity by 8.9%. See Deloitte (2020), p. 15.

[57] In short succession starting between late 2020 and early 2022, the Commission put out a draft Data Governance Act, Digital Services Act, Digital Markets Act, AI Act, with substantive focus respectively on trusted mechanisms for data sharing, online platforms, digital gatekeepers and high-risk artificial intelligence systems.

[58] European Commission (2020a).

[59] European Commission (2020a), section 1.

data processing[60] and away from pattern recognition towards more sophisticated forecasting techniques.[61]

Lastly, it seemed to recognize the core of the underlying problem: the stockpiling of power through monopolizing access to data by 'a small number of Big Tech firms' and noting (if cautiously) that in the U.S. and Chinese data access models are being projected onto the rest of the world—and none of those appears particularly appealing to Europeans, with China using a blend of government and Big Tech- driven measures of control with little room for empowering individuals, while in the U.S., the organisation of the data space was 'left to the private sector, with considerable concentration effects'.

Concentration is an issue given that, as noted in the Strategy, the value of data lies both in its use and reuse.[62] Currently, as the paper states, not enough data is available for innovative re-use, including for the development of artificial intelligence. In the B2B dimension, this is—not surprisingly—linked to the lack of economic incentives and fear of losing the competitive advantage, but also a general lack of trust, imbalances in negotiating power, risks of misappropriation of data, lastly the lack of legal clarity as to the right and obligations, particularly in terms of data generated by IoT devices.[63]

These issues would be addressed via the creation of a Common European industrial data space, aiming at:

- getting key players of the manufacturing sector to agree the conditions for them to share their data and further boosting data generation, including via smart connected products;
- addressing key issues on usage of co-generated industrial data[64] via a separate Data Act.

Here too the Strategy showed high hopes for the harnessing of the creative potential in data, citing Europe's strong industrial base and the difference that data access can make for the performance and competitiveness of European industry, citing a 2018 study by Deloitte which estimated the potential value of use of non-personal data in

[60] This reflects a process that had already made headlines in 2019 when Google first announced its move towards edge computing, where the data would no longer be sent from end devices to data processing centers. As the 2020 Strategy notes, currently 80% of the processing and analysis of data is currently carried out in such centralized facilities in data centres, while only 20% takes place in smart connected objects (the examples given are cars, home appliances or manufacturing robots) or in computing facilities close to the user. It also anticipated these proportions to be inverted by 2025. See European Commission (2020a), section 2.

[61] European Commission (2020a), section 2.

[62] European Commission (2020a), section 4.

[63] European Commission (2020a), section 4.

[64] In the context of connected devices operated by their users, the rights over co-generated data was a grey area due to clashing claims of the user (who bought/leased, paid for and operated the device) and the data holder (who supplied the infrastructure for the data to be created and held). The Commission proposed to clear this uncertainty in favour of data holders in the draft Data Act of 2022.

manufacturing at € 1.4 trillion by 2027.[65] Read jointly with the notion of *data available to all*, the promise held here seemed a great one: to punch a hole in the wall of legal protection around powerful rights holders and enable a greater diversity of innovation.

The following sections will analyze the evidence of bold and forward-looking conceptual reasoning that could be seen in the European Commission's drafting of the Data Act proposal, then toned-down with a conservative mindset that prevailed over the general character of the text. Still, from the perspective of this work, it is interesting to look at the traces of what the Data Act could have been, still visible at the time of the finalized proposal. For this reason, the final compromise version adopted in the trilogues is less relevant to this discussion, although footnotes will be added wherever a substantial change was made to the discussed provisions.

5.6.2 *The Data Act Proposal: A Transformative Use of Data?*

As stated specifically in the recitals, the declared ambition of the Data Act was to '*foster the development of new, innovative products or related services, stimulate innovation on aftermarkets, but also stimulate the development of entirely novel services making use of the data, including based on data from a variety of products or related services*'.[66] This would be achieved by ensuring that users of connected devices could access the data generated by their operation and provide this data to third parties, with considerable latitude as to what it could be used for. The Commission's Impact Assessment Study[67] spoke of *maximising the value of the data in the economy and society by ensuring that a wider range of stakeholders gain control over their data and that more data is available for use* (as a general objective) and then empowering consumers and companies using connected products '*to participate more in the data economy*'. This greater participation would be realized by ensuring that they '*have access to the data their connected product* [s] *collect and be able to choose to give a third-party access to such data for reuse*'.[68]

The proposal indeed addressed a number of issues pertaining to use of data generated by connected devices, including business-to-government data sharing or cloud interoperability to facilitate open innovation in a multi-cloud environment.[69] However, the core of the Act was aimed at regulating the relationships between users of connected devices and data holders (in most cases, device manufacturers). Users were to gain rights to the data generated by their operation of the device, including

[65] Deloitte (2018), p. 7.

[66] Recital 28.

[67] European Commission (2022c), p. 26.

[68] European Commission (2022c), p. 26.

[69] Recital 76.

sharing it with third parties, with big promises made to enable 'productive use' of such data in the presentation speech by Executive Vice-President Vestager.[70] To the reader of this work, the term might have a familiar ring to it; the construct of productive use would lie at the very roots of the transformative use concept as put forward by Pierre Leval.[71] Could it be that the Commission sought to introduce a sui-generis form of transformative use exceptions into the data market ecosystem, weaved elegantly into provisions on use of data? Outrageous though it may perhaps seem, for this possibility to be entertained, two considerations would need to be made: first, is there any evidence in the fabric of the Data Act proposal of there being (or having been, at the drafting stage) such an idea? And secondly, data rights are not copyright—to conduct such thought experiments, one would need to assume that rights to data are already perceived on a policy level as gravitating so much towards intellectual property protection (in the wake of the discussions that followed the Database Directive) that conceptual cross-pollination may not be at all unthinkable.

Although the proposal would only whet the appetite before it ultimately disappointed in that respect, it would seem that on both accounts it might have come quite close, with the possible implications being actually opening the door to a usable principle-based exception in the protection regime, an opportunity that could indeed be seized by non-corporate digital innovators. The clues will now be discussed together with the restrictions that will likely keep this scenario only theoretical.

5.6.2.1 Clue 1: Thou Shalt Not Develop a Competing Product (but Behold What You May Do Instead)

What are the clues in the substance of the Commission's proposal? The first pertains to a classic situation where a repair shop works on connected devices and receives access to their data for this purpose. Were it inclined to use its know-how and plant to work on developing a new product, under Article 6 2) e)[72] and Recital 35[73] it is allowed to do so, as long as:

(a) the product (or related service) developed is new and innovative;
(b) the product developed does not compete against the product from which the accessed data originated.

[70] European Commission (2022b).

[71] See the transformative use discussion in Chap. 4, Sects. 4.2 et seq.

[72] 'The third party shall not [...] (e) use the data it receives to develop a product that competes with the product from which the accessed data originate or share the data with another third party for that purpose'—Article 6 2) e), Proposal for the Data Act.

[73] "[...] The third party may use the data to develop a new and innovative product or related service but not to develop a competing product."—Recital 35, Proposal for the Data Act.

As such, examined in isolation from all the other provisions of the proposal, as long as the new creation is indeed an innovation and does not impact the market for the original work, it can benefit from the provisions allowing access to data generated by a device manufactured by someone else. The criterion of the work being innovative is not explained in the proposal; however, if one were to look for convergence with the productive/transformative use discussion, the meaning of 'innovative' could quite successfully be construed to pertain to embedding 'new information, new aesthetics, new insights and understandings' as per Leval's characterisation of transformative use.[74]

So much for the wording applicable to the third party receiving access to data and wishing to let off some creative steam. What about the actual **user of the device**, whose operation of it has generated the data in the first place—and who, according to the Explanatory Memorandum, is to be placed in a position of 'meaningful control' over their device-generated data?[75] On the surface, it would appear that the user of the device[76] can do even more than this, being:

(a) free to use the data for any lawful purpose;[77]
(b) exempted from the sui generis right protecting databases under Article 7 of Directive 96/9/EC.

The meaning of 'lawful purpose' is not explained and the question of how this impacts the rights of the user to put on the innovator's hat is not tackled in more detail in the Recitals and Articles and entirely left out of the Impact Assessment Report.[78] As such, the proposal gives very little indication as to what the user of the connected device might actually do with the data, and whether and to what extent they may use it to create an innovative (or any, for that matter) product or service. Against this uncertainty, the position of third parties, with the requirements of innovativeness and non-competing nature of their work, is clearer—still, both the users' and third parties' rights suffer from being severely limited in other respects on a more practical level.

5.6.2.2 Data Access Considerations: 'Meaningful' v. Factual Control

The promising picture falls apart under closer examination. From the perspective of users under the proposed Act, although they are intended to enjoy access to the data their use of the device generates '*without undue delay, free of charge and, where*

[74] See Leval (1990), p. 1111.

[75] European Commission (2022a), Explanatory Memorandum, p. 13.

[76] Defined as 'a natural or legal person that owns, rents or leases a product or receives a service'—Article 2 (5) of the Proposal.

[77] Recital 28.

[78] European Commission (2022c).

applicable, continuously and in real-time',[79] nothing in the Act seems to suggest that they may actually exercise **any direct dominion** over the data, including copying it, or transferring it anywhere outside of the technical framework of the data holder. On the contrary, users and third parties are apparently only expected to access data either on the product itself, or through the cloud framework of the data holder.

This interpretation appears to align with the wording used in the applicable recitals, speaking of 'bringing algorithms to the data' (Recital 8) and data holders 'making data available on the product or on their server' (Recital 21). It would suggest that the promising 'meaningful control' language used to describe the rights of the user does not convey the full picture: in reality, this is always to be exercised in the looming shadow of the data holder who remains in *factual control* of the data (and if Recital 8 is to be read literally, also encouraged to *only* enable this type of access).

Interestingly, this emerging vision of user's access to data as being more of a *courtesy by the data holder*—rather than a basic right of the user—is backed by an envisaged restriction against users who might take the promise in the provisions of proposed Article 4 (the access being provided '*free of charge and, where applicable, continuously and in real-time*', on the basis of a *simple request through electronic means where technically feasible*') a little too seriously. Under the Commission's Impact Assessment, the preferred policy option for the Data Act[80] would entail that users who ask (1) **too often** or (2) for **too much** (making '*manifestly excessive, or repetitive requests for the data*') would be simply refused access—or subjected to an additional fee to cover the costs of the data holder.[81]

What does this translate into for potential innovators who want to build on the data produced by a device? On-site data access means that the data holder is also in a position to monitor the interactions of users and third parties with the data generated by the device. The proposed Act takes this into consideration, deploying certain protective measures against data holders generating insights from such monitoring. In the case of users, these amount to a prohibition of deriving insights *about the economic situation, assets and production methods of or the use by the user*, however only to the extent that such insights could *undermine the commercial position of the user in the markets in which the user is active* (Article 4 (6)). In other words, despite the declaratively broad gateway to using data generated by their connected device, users are not only constrained to using the cloud service of the data holder or the device itself; they will also likely be monitored in their interactions with the data as the only protection there is tied to the existing presence of the user in certain markets. Feeble as it may be, for a start-up or a group of nerds experimenting

[79] Article 4(1) of the Proposal. The final compromise version added further qualifiers like *easily, securely and in a comprehensive, structured, commonly used and machine-readable format,* as well as [*where relevant and technically feasible*] *of the same quality as is available to the data holder.*

[80] European Commission (2022c), pp. 66 et seq.

[81] European Commission (2022c), pp. 32, 153.

with AI, the lack of any market presence invalidates this measure of protection entirely.

The same scenario applies to the case of third parties who received access to data (such as the aforementioned repair shop that the user contracts to perform maintenance work on the device). Data holders monitoring their interaction with the data would only be held back by a similar provision in Article 5 (5) prohibiting deriving insights about the *economic situation, assets and production methods of or use by the third party that could undermine the commercial position of the third party on the markets in which the third party is active*. Ironically, one could say that the construct applied in these provisions is specifically aimed against certain types of innovation: as soon as one were to step out of the box and try to develop something new, their interactions will be closely monitored by the data holder who *de facto* controls the data environment.

Lastly, it should be reiterated that, according to the Impact Assessment, the user's access requests must not be 'manifestly unfounded' or too repetitive (the judge of this likely being the data holder), with the sanction being refusal of access or a fee imposed by the data holder. To grassroots innovators that do not have financial means and are hoping to benefit from the Data Act's provisions on fostering innovation as a gateway to new creativity, both scenarios would likely simply mean the end of the line.

5.6.2.3 Clue 2: A Sui Generis Quasi-IP Protection on Data?

As described above, the Act proposal does nothing to undermine the factual control of the data holder over device-generated data. It rests on more pillars than the spatial factor discussed above (i.e. where and under whose control the data is physically stored): there are also matters of the format and interoperability of data or the technical design of the product which may render it near-impossible for any entity save for the manufacturer to derive any utility value from the generated data.

This factual monopoly of the data holder is strengthened further by a number of provisions of the proposed Data Act. Under Article 11(1) they were authorized to deploy '*appropriate technical protection measures, including smart contracts, to prevent unauthorised access to the data and to ensure compliance with Articles 5, 6, 9 and 10, as well as with the agreed contractual terms for making data available*'.[82] This is accompanied by the requirement to both destroy the obtained data and any infringing products built using this data (sic!) under Article 11(2) which also requires them to '*end the production, offering, placing on the market or use of goods, derivative data or services produced on the basis of knowledge obtained through such data, or the importation, export or storage of infringing goods for*

[82] This was then further strengthened in the compromise version, adding encryption, broadening the scope of the compliance protection and adding an anti-circumvention clause for users and third parties to echo the prohibition of Article 5(4).

those purposes'.[83] This should be read together with the prohibition to overcome existing protections to gain access in Article 5(4) which prohibits '*deploy[ing] coercive means or abus*[ing] *evident gaps in the technical infrastructure of the data holder designed to protect the data in order to obtain access to data*'.

These protections might ring familiar bells to an IP lawyer. Moreover, as noted by W. Kerber, they are not just to apply to trade secrets only: they are the default rules on *any* generated IoT data.[84] Such exclusive control over IoT data by data holders resembles to some extent the protection of IP rights.[85] The assumed technological exclusivity, reinforced by the technological protection measures and additional rules like those referenced above, taken together with the contractual framing of the relationships between data holders and third parties which (as will also be discussed below) strongly resembles licensing contracts, on an economic level all amount to creating an IP-like exclusive right on data that is awarded to data holders.[86] Kerber notes that absent these provisions, the rights of data holders to control these datasets would only rest on the *de facto* control discussed above. Granting them a *by default* right to freely access and use this data would equate to a 'very significant political and economic success' for data holders, putting them in a position that has not been acknowledged or discussed by society.[87] From the perspective of fostering competition and innovation based on access to device-generated data, this means that a so-far grey area pertaining to the dominion over data generated by an industry whose value the Impact Assessment Study[88] placed between 5.5 and 12.6 trillion USD by 2030 would be officially handed over to industry incumbents, along with instruments to protect the new status quo. If this was indeed the original intention, it is difficult to reconcile with the innovation-friendly language in the proposal and the communications surrounding it as discussed above.

5.6.2.4 It Is All Down to Contract, Again

Although the proposed Act recognises the imbalance in the bargaining power between the data holder and other entities and seeks to remedy it with unfair contract terms for b2b contracts,[89] it strongly relies on contract as the go-to tool for creating a

[83] In the compromise version, a further qualifier was added to say 'where there is a serious risk that the unlawful use of those data will cause a significant harm to the data holder or the user or where such a measure would not be disproportionate in light of the interests of the data holder or the user'.

[84] Kerber (2022).

[85] Kerber (2022), p. 9.

[86] Kerber (2022), p. 15.

[87] Kerber (2022), p. 15.

[88] European Commission (2022c), p. 2.

[89] Remedying this imbalance in bargaining power was mentioned as one of the 'selling points' of the new Act. See European Commission (2022b).

legal basis for using non-personal data.[90] Following deployment of the product onto the market, the first contract is to be concluded between the user and the data holder upon purchase, rental or lease of the product. Under Recital 24, this contract will form the basis of the non-personal data collection and use by the data holder (as the Act is not to create a basis for the processing of personal data under the General Data Protection Regulation) and be preceded by disclosure outlining, under Article 3(2), inter alia:

- the nature and volume of the data likely to be generated by the use of the product or related service;
- how the user may access those data;
- how the user may request that the data are shared with a third-party.

Notably however, the above items are part of pre-contractual disclosure and not the actual contract (which, as mentioned, is meant to serve as basis for the data holder to process data).

So what expectations can the user have, regarding accessing the data their own use would generate? Article 3(1) stipulates that '*products shall be designed and manufactured [...] in such a manner that data generated by their use are, by default, easily, securely and, where relevant and appropriate* [sic!], *directly accessible to the user.*'[91] In practice, however, there is little room for any negotiations between the prospective user and the data holder; if the user is not comfortable with the terms of accessing the data (for instance, where allowing direct access is not considered 'relevant or appropriate' by the data holder), there will not be a negotiation (even more so, a 'bespoke' one, as the 2013 Commission report would have it). Discontented would-be users will simply be welcome to take their business elsewhere.

Such imbalances between parties are not new. In situations where the weaker party cannot sufficiently control their legal situation when faced with a stronger player, such as in standard terms contract, consumer law responds with both *ex-ante* and *ex-post* protection measures, such as the unfairness test for contract terms or the unfair commercial practices framework. Here, the drafting intention was clearly more nuanced as can be seen from the arrangement of protections proposed for contracts between users and data holders and then users and third parties. Under Recital 26, when contracting with the data holder e.g. upon purchase of a device, users being consumers or micro, small and medium enterprises can enjoy some protection under the Unfair Contract Terms Directive (although some doubts have

---

[90] In theory, the Act is not to create a standalone basis for processing of personal data. However, this may be difficult in practice given how the datasets generated by connected devices will often be mixed by definition; moreover, once a dataset is isolated on request of a user as originating from their device, in some cases it may be difficult to make the argument that it does not contain personal data. See BEUC (2022b), p. 17.

[91] The compromise version employed a revised wording to say '*by default, easily, securely, free of charge, in a comprehensive, structured, commonly used and machine-readable format, and, where relevant and technically feasible, directly accessible to the user.*'

been expressed as to its usefulness in this context[92]). Importantly however, no protection was put in place regarding practices by data holders that would target the user's decision-making autonomy (dark patterns).[93] This was not an accidental omission as such a clause, prohibiting practices that would '*coerce, deceive or manipulate the user in any way, by subverting or impairing the autonomy, decision-making or choices of the user, including by means of a digital interface*'[94] had been put in place for downstream contracts where the user would make the data available to a third party under Article 6(2) (a). As mentioned above, a streamlined version of this clause also applied to the 'quasi-licensing' contracts to be concluded between data holders and third parties; here the deployment of 'deceptive or coercive means' by a third party is a sufficient precondition for the data and all its copies, along with any products developed on this basis, to be destroyed (Article 11 (2)).

Thus the data holder, most often an industry incumbent and already the strongest party in the user-data holder-third party triangle, is yet again given the light treatment while the others are left to exercising their rights by relying on their bargaining power in a contract—which will be, in most cases, insignificant. In dealing with users, they are only limited by applicability of *ex-post* protection under the unfair contract terms framework which requires any party feeling aggrieved to go to court.

Importantly, no provisions are proposed in regard to contracts between users and data holders that would actually protect users' choice autonomy—be it the applicability of the Unfair Commercial Practices Directive (left out of Recital 26) or a 'dark patterns' clause (as in regard to contracts with third parties). When dealing with third parties wishing to obtain access to the data, the data holder is protected both at the level of decision-making autonomy and the possible gaps in their technical infrastructure; they also benefit from an exemption from divulging trade secrets (Article 8 (6)) and is entitled to compensation under such a contract (Article 9). All this puts into question the empowering effect that the Data Act was meant to have on parties wishing to activate the innovative potential in device-generated data.

Lastly, an interesting (and quite unexpected) reversal of the contract-favouring attitude can be seen in regard to contracts regulated in Article 24 (which are generally less relevant to this discussion as they tackle cloud switching). The freedom of contract there is significantly curbed by the inclusion of a minimum set of contractual clauses directly in the provisions of the proposed Act. These provisions can be seen as surprisingly detailed, particularly viewed in context of the reliance on contract that prevails regarding the data access rights.

To give a few examples, these mandatory clauses are to allow the customer:

---

[92] BEUC (2022b), p. 11.

[93] This imbalance did not survive the trilogue negotiations and the compromise version adds protection for users in Article 4.

[94] To align with the anti-circumvention clause of Article 13 of the Digital Markets Act, a further qualifier was added in the compromise version to say '*make the exercise of the rights or choices of users unduly difficult including by offering choices to the users in a non-neutral manner*'. An analogous provision was added to protect users in Article 4.

- upon request, to switch to a cloud (processing) service offered by another provider, or
- to port all data, applications and digital assets generated directly or indirectly by the customer to an on-premise system;
- to establish a mandatory maximum transition period of 30 calendar days, during which the data processing service provider is to assist and (where technically feasible) complete the switching process, as well as to ensure full continuity in the provision of the respective functions or services;
- to exhaustively specify of all data and application categories exportable during the switching process;
- to set a minimum period for data retrieval of at least 30 calendar days including, at minimum, all data imported by the customer at the inception of the service agreement and all data and metadata created by the customer and by the use of the service during the period the service was provided, including configuration parameters, security settings, access rights and access logs.

Some authors proposed to explain this far-reaching change of attitude with the necessity to overcome vendor and data lock-in effects in cloud services markets which are typically dominated by the biggest tech companies (Amazon, Microsoft, Google) and would thus benefit from such a measure to enable innovation by newcomers into the market. The Big Tech companies, the argument goes, would be addressees of the contestability-protecting Digital Markets Act which these provisions would then complement; however, the DMA does not generally introduce any regulatory limits to freedom of contract (and the applicability of the above provisions would be far broader than just the digital gatekeepers).[95]

Nonetheless, if the intention here was indeed to safeguard innovation when faced with overwhelming market power, the mystery remains why the data access and sharing rights (to which the entire premise of the Data Act is pinned as an Act enabling innovation via fair access and use of data) have been left largely dependent on contracting with industry incumbents who, as established, will almost certainly benefit from a significantly greater bargaining power.

5.6.2.5 Clue 3: The 'Balancing Incentives' Language

A recurrent theme in discussions over the goals that intellectual property protection aims to achieve, as cited earlier in this book, is that of balancing incentives between i) safeguarding the position of authors of existing works to allow them to reap the fruit of their intellectual creation, and ii) enabling the creation of new works.[96] This

[95] Drexl et al. (2022), p. 64.

[96] See Chap. 1, Sect. 1.2; also the SCOTUS discussion in Oracle v. Google, pointing out the 1978 National Commission on New Technological Uses of Copyrighted Works end report noting (in the context of software) that copyright should not 'grant anyone more economic power than is necessary to achieve the incentive to create' in Chap. 4. See also a discussion about exclusion of

perspective, although initially more characteristic of the U.S. discussions due to the inherent constitutional weaknesses of EU copyright law, is now just as prominent in European scholarship, not least thanks to the case law of the CJEU.[97]

The proposal for the Data Act used a similar framing in Recital 28, noting that '*[i]t is important to preserve incentives to invest in products with functionalities based on the use of data from sensors built into that product.*' The Recital goes on to elaborate that '*the aim of the proposed Regulation should accordingly be understood as to foster the development of new, innovative products or related services, stimulate innovation on aftermarkets, but also stimulate the development of entirely novel services making use of the data, including based on data from a variety of products or related services.*' However, it also '*aims to avoid undermining the investment incentives for the type of product from which the data are obtained, for instance, by the use of data to develop a competing product*'.

An analogous statement of the Data Act's general aim is found in the Impact Assessment: '*to maximise the value of the data in the economy and society by ensuring that a wider range of stakeholders gain control over their data and that more data is available for use, while maintaining incentives for data generation and collection*'.[98] The preferred policy option under the Impact Assessment speaks explicitly of the aim being to '*balance existing incentives to invest in data-generating activities with legislative measures that strengthen legal certainty on how data can be used and by whom*'.

An interesting question was asked by Wolfgang Kerber about *where* the need to balance incentives actually comes from in the context of the Data Act. On the surface, the proposed Act only applies to products which are bought, leased or rented by the user, thus the incentive has already been fulfilled. The emphasis on balancing incentives would imply that there is a risk of insufficient investment in the manufacture of connected devices (or in the installation of sensors that enable their data collection). However, as Kerber notes, there is currently no evidence of such risks; quite the contrary—there is a broad consensus that use of connected devices will continue to spread quickly in multiple contexts while the amounts of IoT data that is generated and collected can be foreseen to grow exponentially.[99]

At the basic level of incentives for the creation of data as generated by the devices' sensors (which, as will be discussed below, does not include inferred data), Kerber's argument could be summarized as follows:

1. If only raw data is to be within scope, there is no undermining of incentives for data holders to invest in extracting value from data (since inferred or derived data is not shared). However, other market players can attempt their own value

copyrightability of APIs to prevent intellectual property rights from not going beyond creating incentives for creativity and innovation in Drexl et al. (2022). p. 82. An attempt at deconstructing this division of incentives is made in Chap. 6 of this work.

[97] This will be discussed further in Chap. 6.

[98] European Commission (2022c), p. 26.

[99] Kerber (2022), p. 16.

extraction from raw data, assuming the sharing mechanisms proposed under the Act fulfil their purpose.

2. A connected device is of more value to consumers than a plain one; thus, in a well-functioning market, the willingness to pay a higher price should provide sufficient incentives for the manufacturer to continue to invest in providing further devices.[100]

Leaving aside the tempting discussion of whether the 'balancing incentives' goal also includes incentivising manufacturers to invest in some additional data collection that would go beyond the device's marketed functionality, one that is not expected (or even can be detested) by the consumer and thus does not increase the monetary value of the device, the question to ask in regard to the above two points is indeed how—on the basic level—can the proclaimed need to further incentivise manufacturers to continue to invest in the creation of data be justified? Perhaps the hypothetical underlying motive to bring non-personal data protection close to the protection of intellectual property should not be outright rejected.

5.6.2.6 Defining 'Products'[101] and 'Data': Is the Offered Database Directive Exception of Any Use?

We have established that the promises of data access unlocking innovative potential and of 'meaningful control' over the data generated by one's use of a connected device (referred to in the Data Act proposal as a 'product') are actually quite underwhelming at the practical level, where all the data remains with the current market incumbent (not surprisingly called the 'data holder') with very little protection against surveillance of any interactions one might wish to have with it and no statutory guarantees that the data could be as much as copied off the cloud or product—even though on the surface users are to be ensured to access the data '*by default, easily, securely and, where relevant and appropriate, directly*' (Article 3) while enjoyment of the exemption from the *sui generis* right under the Database Directive 96/6/EC is explicitly excluded under Article 35.

Moreover, an interesting (although difficult to explain) restriction on the rights offered by the proposal would lie in the narrowing down of its scope. Under the Act, only such connected devices would qualify as 'products' whose primary function is not the storing and processing of data.[102] Recitals 14 and 15 sought to shed some light on this distinction by noting that '*vehicles, home equipment and consumer goods, medical and health devices, or agricultural and industrial machinery*' would be included, while '*personal computers, servers, tablets and smart phones, cameras,*

[100] Kerber (2022), p. 17.

[101] Following the trilogues, the defined term of the Commission's proposal was changed to 'connected products' in the compromise version, with the carving out of products covered by intellectual property rights in Recital 15.

[102] Article 2 (2).

webcams, sound recording systems and text scanners' and other items '*primarily designed to display or play content*' would not be deemed as products at all. Leaving aside the lack of clarity in this distinction (e.g. when considered in the light of technical differences between today's smart TVs, smartphones and tablets),[103] its effect is removing a massive share of connected devices from the scope of the Act, putting again in doubt the true intention of unlocking the innovative potential in device-generated data.

One more interesting catch awaits those who would still put their trust in the big claims about enabling productive reuse of data and unlocking the innovative potential of immeasurable quantities of data currently remaining unused, yet another reality check arrives with the actual scope of applicability of the proposed Act, delineated by the definition of 'data' itself.

In the case of data, the issue lies not so much in the definition of Article 2 (1) making a reference to '*any digital representation of acts, facts or information and any compilation of such acts, facts or information, including in the form of sound, visual or audio-visual recording*'. The problem is that only raw ('first-level') data, as captured by the device's sensors, would actually qualify as data under the proposal (Recital 28).[104] This is ensured by expressly excluding any data that is 'inferred or derived' from raw data, in particular data *resulting from any software process that calculates derivative data from such data* (Recitals 14 and 17).

This general exclusion was raised in literature as one to 'seriously endanger' the effectiveness of the data access right.[105] The reason for this is the relative inutility of raw data recorded before it is processed in any way.[106] For example, a connected vacuum cleaner will produce data about the temperature of the motors, impact events from the bumpers, battery and waste bin status; however, this information without its context may be largely useless from the perspective of the goals promised in the Act proposal—be it for the enabling of third-party maintenance services or for the development of new innovative products or related services. To make the example even more extreme, the sensors of a connected car will produce numerous types of data. However, the requirement of the data being unprocessed means like pings from speed sensors; however, the vehicle speed calculated on this basis will not be included as it would already constitute derivative data. From this perspective, the exception from the application of the *sui generis* right to databases for users (but not third parties) is likely to end up being largely useless in practice as the only types of data that the user will be able to access will be those same that can be of the least use—while all the other data is not even within scope of the proposed regulation.

[103] BEUC (2022b), p. 7.

[104] Following the trilogues, the compromise text makes only a technical adjustment by allowing 'pre-processed' data to the extent necessary to make it understandable prior to further analysis.

[105] Drexl et al. (2022), p. 10.

[106] As mentioned earlier, the Commission's strict limitation in the proposal was softened in the further legislative process.

5.6.2.7 Reuse of Data: Enter Ye, Who Hath Bargaining Power

The Data Act proposal came announced as a regulatory instrument to turn things around in the connected world. By introducing a meticulously crafted framework of rights and obligations, it would address many uncertainties related to the reuse of data, including such data that does not meet the originality criteria for copyright protection but is covered by the Database Directive under the '*sui generis*' clause based on substantial investment in their creation. Users of connected devices would get broad access by default to data generated by their devices, along with a framework for sharing it with third parties and a regulatory gateway towards enabling development of new and innovative products and services. This unlocked innovation potential, according to the recitals and the communications that accompanied the Act proposal, would unleash the largely dormant value of data generated by Internet-of-Things devices and stimulate competition in the digital markets.

With the data-driven markets gravitating towards creating monopolies[107] and the lack of flexibilities in copyright, the question asked by the U.S. Supreme Court on who gets to hold the keys to digital innovation rings more important than ever. The potential of connected devices to create downstream value through generation of data is undisputed. With the Data Act proposal, the European Commission had seemingly had the ambition to respond to the inequal distribution of opportunities to innovate. Sadly, and perhaps partially due to the affinity between the matters of data access and licencing and the matters of copyright proper, also this effort followed down the path of lesser resistance, leaving everything to the market with only minor adjustments.

On a final note, one more observation should be made from the perspective of this work: the Data Act proposal, following in the footsteps of the EU Intellectual Property Action Plan of 2020 perpetuates at its base the perennial dichotomous view of market agents either as businesses or consumers[108] that leaves no room for grassroots small-time innovators. As a result, it responds to new market developments and technological change by defaulting back to licencing and contracts also in terms of access to data (while actually reinforcing the position of the industry incumbents by resolving some gray areas in their favour). This brings the discussion back to square one, where the solution to everything—in the words of the

---

[107] Prüfer (2020).

[108] The 2020 EU Intellectual property action plan to support the EU's recovery and resilience opens by referencing intangible assets such as inventions, artistic and cultural creations, brands, software, know-how, business process and data as cornerstones of today's economy. The framing it uses, however, reproduces the typical division of market between businesses and individuals: it speaks of a need to 'help companies capitalise on their inventions and creations' while 'ensuring that inventions and creations are serving economy and society at large'. The creator and innovator is thus immediately equated with a business company; individuals and society are passive consumers with needs that must be catered for. Fast forward 2 years, the passive role of the consumer was de facto reiterated in the proposal for the Data Act. See European Commission (2020b).

Commission's earlier reports in regard to potential flexibilising copyright—is 'bespoke negotiations'.

5.7 Thought Experiment: A Potential Licensing Model for Mass-Developed Innovation

With all the models discussed in this chapter pointing towards negotiation and contract as means for enabling innovation building on earlier achievements of others, what remains is to try and conceptualise how this solution could apply to the type of innovation discussed in this work—done after office hours, relying on personal interest rather than commercial motivations, often with no start-up capital other than the time and skills of those willing to give the challenge a try.

To take a hypothesized example, let us assume a large group of enthusiasts worldwide is working on a project which makes use of large quantities of existing intellectual property, taken from a highly distributed network of rightsholders. This could be a situation where a new search engine is being devised to voice-recognize, analyse and catalogue the audio tracks of videos posted online, or even ones not freely available on the Internet; this could also simply be a new type of virtual reality social area going beyond the current Metaverse, e.g. such as the digital continents as offered by Ted Chiang in 2010.[109] It is a large- scale project that by its nature reuses existing protected intellectual property; however, it does so in an entirely new way, the exact nature of which is as of yet uncertain as the project may end up evolving into something far more daring than the initial idea. There is considerable conviction among some participants that the intellectual property infringement should not be an option because the servers are located in the United States, counting on a fair use exoneration; but others are making points that violations are being committed worldwide due to how widespread the project's participation is; moreover, the fate of Java APIs that had long been considered free to reuse is also not a soothing factor. Hence, the legalists among the project team are bent on obtaining the licences for the intellectual property being used.

Going about obtaining licencing would then require the following steps:

(a) *Description of the new type of use*

The project would need to be able to define the type of use of intellectual property it requires. Notably, as the entire project is based upon voluntary participation and must have a slow burn rate, the definition would need to be as narrow as possible to avoid high recurring costs that might easily derail the project. However, as the project is based on mass-participation and the exact path of its development may be difficult to predict, hopes of being able to

[109] Ted Chiang's digital continents were social platforms built as virtual reality worlds with their own landscapes, rules and sometimes even physics laws; each was also a standalone software environment that required pre-existing software to be ported to run. See Chiang (2010).

narrowly define the type of use of intellectual property at an early stage may be overly optimistic.

(b) *Conducting negotiations with rightsholders*

While in an open, mass-developed project the matter of secrecy would not be an issue and thus non-disclosure agreements might not be required prior to commencement of licencing negotiations, rightsholders would still likely have little incentive to devote their time and means to (likely) self-proclaimed representatives of an online community, acting through a freshly established ad-hoc legal entity with no credit history, attempting to secure the broadest possible licences for a project whose course they cannot reasonably predict, the returns from which may come in remote future, with payment of royalties being likely considerably deferred and uncertain in general as the entire project may or may not have a fixed monetization date. The situation would be even more difficult if the project was developed under a shroud of secrecy; under such considerations, the added burden of negotiating NDA's could mean that the transaction costs of obtaining licencing could easily become prohibitive.

(c) *Defining the licencing model*

All of the above impediments related to specifying the type and scope of the use of intellectual property in a project whose shape and direction exhibits a great deal of volatility would strike with all force at the point of defining the licencing model. Setting aside the challenges of getting the rightsholders to negotiate, ultimately, the choice would always be reduced to choosing the scope of licencing. This would be a policy choice; with money being a strong consideration, going for the cheaper, more precisely circumscribed option would leave the innovators locked-in at the current stage of their work. As a result, it would be affecting both their choice of tasks and their perspective on the future development of the project, striving to follow a policy agreed on paper at one point with rightsholders and to ensure that deadlines for monetization are met. Unavoidably, this would mean that the adolescent years are over and the project must begin to focus on supporting itself, forfeiting whatever bold developments could lie ahead.

These tendencies may be illustrated using a simple graph: the more is spent on obtaining licences, the greater the latitude 'bought' by the innovator. At the same time however, the greater the spending, the less incentivized the innovator will be to step outside the initial assumptions of the project.

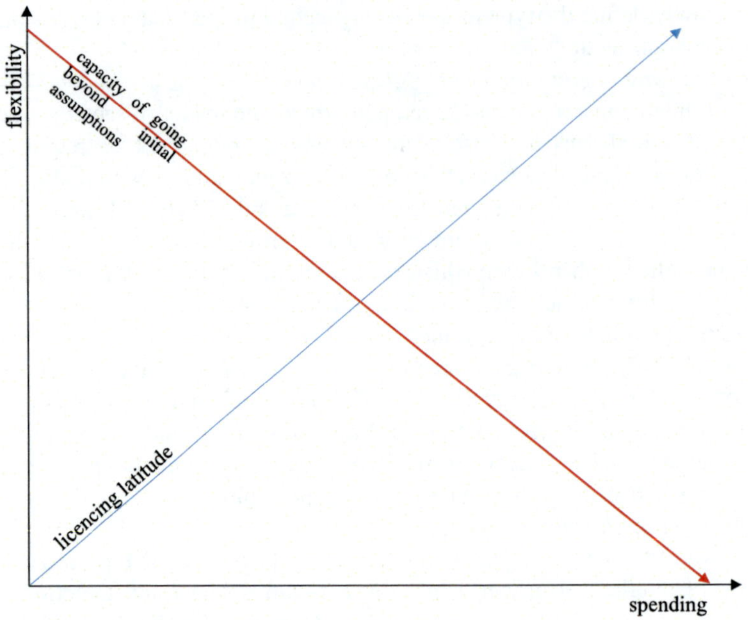

5.8 Conclusions: Contracting with Goliaths and the 'Coffin Corner' for Licencing

5.8.1 The Coffin Corner for Licencing

What are small-time would-be innovators left with in this legal landscape? In subsonic aviation, there is a phenomenon that occurs at high altitudes that is referred to as the 'coffin corner'.[110] It is a situation where, as the air becomes thinner, the minimum airspeed a subsonic aircraft requires for the wings to maintain lift begins to increase towards the maximum safe airspeed which, in turn, becomes lower due to the decreasing speed of sound and the increasing risk of the over-wing airstreams to become supersonic while the aircraft is still moving at subsonic speed, with potentially fatal consequences. As a result, with an increase in altitude, the pilot has an increasingly narrow band of available airspeed, with low-speed stall looming on one side and overspeed stall on the other. In the U2/TR-1 spy plane, at operating altitudes, the reported margin between the two potentially lethal stalls was just 10 knots.

[110] This section contains my non-expert description of the phenomenon. For a more elaborate one, see Claiborne (2022).

In a way, this is analogous to the issues that will be encountered when a Benkler-type, rooted in chaos, semi-organized crowd-sourced project would attempt to obtain licencing for the intellectual property (or, as demonstrated in this chapter, also data) it would be using in a new and unique way that is not entirely definable at a given point, and may never be as the nature of such projects is that they should ideally never cease their development. The greater the desired licencing flexibility, be it crowd-funded or based on profit-sharing, the greater the cost and, in effect, the tighter the attachment to the assumptions made at that given stage as to the shape of the project and the more closed-off it becomes to new opportunities as they could present themselves. In reality, the legalist approach (i.e. making participation in the development project conditional upon its absolute certainty in regard to licencing) would simply disincentivise any such individuals from getting on board in the first place, just as the Google Book Project would have never gotten off the ground if it had not been for the assumption of fair use.

Perhaps the most important takeaway of this chapter is that with the current direction of EU policy there is little hope for new policy measures (like data access rights) to remedy the harms done by non-flexible copyright policy and to foster innovation by non-incumbent agents. Despite the shifts created by the age of data, the core of the issue remains the same: we are still heedlessly applying market rules to mass low-cost innovation, with little regard to creating entry barriers which cannot be evaded by traditional licensing models.

Still, there is considerable reason to believe that online creativity will prevail, if not thrive. The examples presented in earlier chapters seem to point in one direction: to paraphrase the Microsoft Darknet Paper, as long as there are high-speed connections and things remain interesting, we will continue to see creative potential in online communities. This potential may or may not be helped by legislation ensuring adequate flexibility; the ways this could be achieved will be discussed in the following chapter.

5.8.2 Innovating Under Digital Asymmetry

To close off this part of the discussion, it should also be noted that in recent years grassroots innovation, although never likely to receive attention and spotlight even remotely comparable to that gained by the battle over Java APIs, has been gaining one more dimension: that of further increasing asymmetries of knowledge and power between the individual and the data-powered market incumbent, rendering it even more difficult for them to follow the path indicated by legislators and seek to obtain licencing through negotiating a contract.

In 2021, BEUC published a joint research report on structural asymmetries in digital consumer markets.[111] The researchers had made the case that in the modern

[111] Helberger et al. (2021a, b).

day and age, in the digital market the consumer—being the individual acting outside of their professional capacity—is in a weaker position than ever when dealing with digital companies. This report has become the cornerstone of the concept of 'digital asymmetry': a profound, omnipresent, ongoing imbalance of power between individuals and businesses, founded on three pillars:

- architectural/structural, rooted in control of the choice architectures and access to data (and the related difficulty of verifying compliant use of data in the supply chain);
- relational, due to the low bargaining power of the consumer—typically they are faced with 'take it or leave it' contracting situations;
- knowledge-based, as the trader benefits from detailed insights (not rarely mixed with means of behavioural and psychological influence[112]) in regard to the consumer, while the consumer often has a very limited knowledge of the mechanics of the trader's operation.[113]

The joint report, and particularly its framing paper,[114] draws attention to a phenomenon that has changed the balance of power since the early days of digital innovation. One could say it is ironic how the distributed pioneering efforts of computer geeks in the 1970s and the 1980s that had contributed to building the foundations for the digital world of today, have also involuntarily become the engineers of a world where the individual has a weaker position than ever before when facing established players in the digital markets. The structure of the process as examined by the research renders it difficult to envisage that it could ever be fully reversed—due to the very structure of the digitalised market, the sheer extent of data collection by traders and the growing complexity of the online environment, rendering it increasingly impossible for a single individual to grasp, let alone act as an informed contracting party when dealing with a digital trader.

On top of these findings, recent research in the field of competition demonstrates that data-driven markets tend towards monopolisation.[115] The surface of this process is now in plain sight, given the gigantic concentration of market power with only a handful companies operating worldwide, whose services have been becoming of essential nature to modern-day societies.[116] In the context of the *Oracle v. Google* court battle, it might be tempting to consider whether this oligopolisation of cyberspace had not in the meantime become another reason for the U.S. Supreme Court to think twice before allowing companies the level of control that comes with deciding who gets to reimplement their APIs and write compatible software. Discussed through the lens of the fair use test, this could certainly be deemed a creative use

[112] See e.g. Hill (2014) and Dorison et al. (2020).

[113] See also BEUC (2022a), p. 4.

[114] Helberger et al. (2021a, b).

[115] Prüfer (2020).

[116] Lynskey and Rott (2021).

of the last fair use factor (still, it has been repeatedly stated that the statutory list of four factors is by no means an exhaustive one).[117]

In the EU, this unique position of the strongest market players became the reason for regulatory intervention at the level of platforms and digital gatekeepers in the form of the Digital Services Act and the Digital Markets Act. However, the tendency to concentrate technology and innovation in the hands of the powerful few has not yet been met with a regulatory response that would seek to counterbalance the weakness of the individual in this new digitalised world; if anything, the most recent European Commission's effort—the Data Act—that might have been aimed at this has made the initiative turn into its own evil *Doppelgänger*. From the perspective of any would-be grassroots innovators wishing to try their strength in developing a new product or service, the fabulously ambitious goals set for this piece of legislation, the conflicting policy considerations (and the ultimate let-down that the Commission's proposal has been) remain a showcase of both awareness of the problem at the level of policy makers, and a contemporaneous lack of political will to introduce bold solutions to remedy it.

References

Baio A (2022) AI Data Laundering: How Academic and Nonprofit Researchers Shield Tech Companies from Accountability. Waxy.org https://waxy.org/2022/09/ai-data-laundering-how-academic-and-nonprofit-researchers-shield-tech-companies-from-accountability/. Accessed 3 Sept 2023

BEUC (2022a) EU Consumer Protection 2.0: Protecting fairness and consumer choice in a digital economy. BEUC, Brussels. https://www.beuc.eu/sites/default/files/publications/beuc-x-2022-015_protecting_fairness_and_consumer_choice_in_a_digital_economy.pdf, p. 4. Accessed 3 Sept 2023

BEUC (2022b) Giving consumers control of their data. BEUC position on the Data Act proposal, available at https://www.beuc.eu/sites/default/files/publications/BEUC-X-2022-103%20_BEUC_Position_paper_on_the_Data_Act_proposal.pdf. Accessed 3 Sept 2023

Boulanger J, Carbonnel A, De Coninck R, Langus G (2014) Assessing the economic impacts of adapting certain limitations and exceptions to copyright and related rights in the EU. Analysis of specific policy options. A study for DG MARKT by Charles River Associates. https://op.europa.eu/s/u1xZ. Accessed 3 Sept 2023

Chiang T (2010) The lifecycle of software objects. Subterranean Press

Claiborne M (2022) What is the Coffin Corner (pushing the envelope). Aerocorner.com https://aerocorner.com/blog/coffin-corner/. Accessed 3 Sept 2023

Coffman C (2023) Does the Use of Copyrighted Works to Train AI Qualify as a Fair Use? Copyright Alliance 11 April 2023 https://copyrightalliance.org/copyrighted-works-training-ai-fair-use/. Accessed 3 Sept 2023

Cohen JE (2019) Between truth and power. The legal constructions of informational capitalism. Oxford University Press, New York. An open-access copy available at https://fdslive.oup.com/www.oup.com/academic/pdf/openaccess/9780190246693.pdf. Accessed 3 Sept 2023

[117] See Drazewski (2021).

Deloitte (2018) Realising the economic potential of machine-generated, nonpersonal data in the EU. Report for Vodafone Group https://www.vodafone.com/content/dam/vodcom/files/public-policy/Realising_the_potential_of_IoT_data_report_for_Vodafone.pdf. Accessed 3 Sept 2023
Deloitte (2020) SME Digitalisation – charting a course towards resilience and recovery, Vodafone Public Policy Paper, September 2020 https://www.vodafone.com/sites/default/files/2020-10/sme-digitalisation.pdf. Accessed 3 Sept 2023
Dorison K, Wang K, Rees V, Kawachi I, Ericson K, Lerner J (2020) Sadness, but not all negative emotions, heightens addictive substance use, Proc Natl Acad Sci 117 (2) 943-949; https://www.pnas.org/content/117/2/943. Accessed 3 Sept 2023
Drazewski K (2021) Go forth and reimplement your APIs: the April 5th Supreme Court judgment in Google v. Oracle, IP Kat April 28, 2021 https://ipkitten.blogspot.com/2021/04/guest-post-go-forth-and-reimplement.html. Accessed 3 Sept 2023
Drexl J, Banda C, González Otero B, Hoffmann J, Kim D, Kulhari S, Moscon V, Richter H, Wiedemann K (2022) Position Statement of the Max Planck Institute for Innovation and Competition of 25 May 2022 on the Commission's Proposal of 23 February 2022 for a Regulation on harmonised rules on fair access to and use of data (Data Act) https://papers.ssrn.com/sol3/papers.cfm?abstract_id=4136484. Accessed 3 Sept 2023
Ducato R, Strowel AM (2021) Ensuring text and data mining: remaining issues with the EU copyright exceptions and possible ways out (February 1, 2021). Eur Intellect Prop Rev, 2021, https://ssrn.com/abstract=3829858
European Commission (2005) First evaluation of Directive 96/9/EC on the legal protection of databases, DG Internal Market and Services Working Paper, Brussels, 12 December 2005
European Commission (2020a) A European strategy for data, COM(2020) 66 final, Brussels 19.2.2020, https://eur-lex.europa.eu/legal-content/EN/TXT/?uri=CELEX%3A52020DC0066. Accessed 3 Sept 2023
European Commission (2020b) Making the most of the EU's innovative potential: An intellectual property action plan to support the EU's recovery and resilience. COM(2020)760 https://www.eumonitor.eu/9353000/1/j9vvik7m1c3gyxp/vle2l9lr84zw. Accessed 29 Dec 2022
European Commission (2022a) Proposal for a Regulation of the European Parliament and of the Council on harmonised rules on fair access to and use of data (Data Act) https://eur-lex.europa.eu/legal-content/EN/TXT/?uri=COM%3A2022%3A68%3AFIN. Accessed 29 Dec 2022
European Commission (2022b) Speech by Executive Vice-President Vestager on the Data Act. 23 February 2022 Brussels, https://ec.europa.eu/commission/presscorner/detail/en/speech_22_1312. Accessed 3 Sept 2023
European Commission (2022c) Impact Assessment Report accompanying the document Proposal for a Regulation of the European Parliament and of the Council on harmonised rules on fair access to and use of data (Data Act), {COM(2022) 68 final} - {SEC(2022) 81 final} - {SWD (2022) 35 final} 23 February 2022 https://ec.europa.eu/newsroom/dae/redirection/document/83524. Accessed 3 Sept 2023
European Parliament Committee on Industry, Research and Energy and Committee on the Internal Market and Consumer Protection (2015) REPORT on Towards a Digital Single Market Act, A8-0371/2015, https://www.europarl.europa.eu/doceo/document/A-8-2015-0371_EN.html. Accessed 3 Sept 2023
Ezrachi A, Maurice AS (2022) How Big Tech barons smash innovation – and how to strike back. Harper Business June 28, 2022
Geiger C (2021) The missing goal-scorers in the artificial intelligence team: of big data, the fundamental right to research and the failed text and data mining limitations in the CSDM directive. In: Senftleben M et al. Poort J, van Eechoud M, van Gompel S, Helberger N (eds) Intellectual Property and Sports, Essays in Honour of P. Bernt Hugenholtz. Kluwer Law International, Alphen aan den Rijn, pp 383–394., Available at SSRN: https://ssrn.com/abstract=3829768 or https://doi.org/10.2139/ssrn.3829768
Gervais DJ (2022) AI derivatives: the application to the derivative work right to literary and artistic productions of AI Machines (February 8, 2022). Seton Hall Law Review, Vol. 53, 2022,

Vanderbilt Law Research Paper No. 22-12, https://ssrn.com/abstract=402266 5 or https://doi.org/10.2139/ssrn.4022665. Accessed 28 July 2023

Griffiths J, Synodinou T, Xalabarder R (2022) Comment of the European Copyright Society Addressing Selected Aspects of the Implementation of Articles 3 to 7 of Directive (EU) 2019/790 on Copyright in the Digital Single Market. European Copyright Society https://europeancopyrightsocietydotorg.files.wordpress.com/2022/05/ecs_exceptions_final-3.pdf. Accessed 3 Sept 2023

Guadamuz A (2017) Artificial intelligence and copyright. WIPO Magazine 10.2017 https://www.wipo.int/wipo_magazine/en/2017/05/article_0003.html. Accessed 28 July 2023

Guadamuz AA (2023) A scanner darkly: copyright liability and exceptions in artificial intelligence inputs and outputs. February 26, 2023 https://ssrn.com/abstract=4371204 or https://doi.org/10.2139/ssrn.4371204. Accessed 28 July 2023

Helberger N, Diakopoulos N (2023) ChatGPT and the AI Act. Internet Policy Review, 12(1). https://doi.org/10.14763/2023.1.1682. Accessed 26 July 2023

Helberger N, Lynskey O, Micklitz H-W, Rott P, Sax M, Strycharz J (2021a) EU Consumer Protection 2.0: Structural asymmetries in digital consumer markets. BEUC, Brussels. Available online at https://www.beuc.eu/brochure/eu-consumer-protection-20-structural-asymmetries-digital-consumer-markets-0. Accessed 3 Sept 2023

Helberger N, Micklitz H-W, Sax M, Strycharz J (2021b) Surveillance, consent and the vulnerable consumer. Regaining citizen agency in the information economy. In: Helberger N, Lynskey O, Micklitz H-W, Rott P, Sax M, Strycharz J (eds) EU Consumer Protection 2.0: Structural asymmetries in digital consumer markets. BEUC, Brussels, pp 1–79 https://www.beuc.eu/sites/default/files/publications/beuc-x-2021-018_eu_consumer_protection_2.0.pdf. Accessed 3 Sept 2023

Hill K (2014) Facebook Manipulated 689,003 Users' Emotions For Science, https://www.forbes.com/sites/kashmirhill/2014/06/28/facebook-manipulated-689003-users-emotions-forscience/?sh=390b7938197c. Accessed 3 Sept 2023

Joint Institute for Innovation Policy and Technopolis (2018) Study in support of the evaluation of Directive 96/9/EC on the legal protection of databases, Joint Institute for Innovation Policy, by the European Commission, Directorate-General of Communications Networks, Content & Technology, https://op.europa.eu/en/publication-detail/-/publication/5e9c7a51-597c-11e8-ab41-01aa75ed71a1. Accessed 3 Sept 2023

Kerber W (2022) Governance of IoT Data: Why the EU Data Act will not Fulfill Its Objectives (Second Version) (July 18, 2022). GRUR International, ikac107, https://doi.org/10.1093/grurint/ikac107 (open access). https://ssrn.com/abstract=4080436

Kim H (2022) [Paper review] Monolith: TikTok's Real-time Recommender System. Medium.com 19 Nov 2022, https://haneulkim.medium.com/paper-review-monolith-tiktoks-real-time-recommender-system-72b90bece653. Accessed 26 July 2023

Langus G, Neven D, Shier G (2013) Assessing the economic impacts of adapting certain limitations and exceptions to copyright and related rights in the EU. A study for DG MARKT by Charles River Associates. https://op.europa.eu/s/u1xI. Accessed 3 Sept 2023

Lemley MA, Casey B (2021) Fair learning. Texas Law Rev 99(4) https://texaslawreview.org/fair-learning/ Accessed 28 July 2023

Leval PN (1990) Toward a fair use standard. Harv Law Rev 103, 105, 1105

Lynskey O, Rott P (2021) A universal services framework for powerful online platforms. In: Helberger N, Lynskey O, Micklitz HW, Rott P, Sax M, Strycharz J (eds) EU Consumer Protection 2.0. Structural asymmetries in digital consumer markets, pp 145–207 https://www.beuc.eu/sites/default/files/publications/beuc-x-2021-018_eu_consumer_protection_2.0.pdf. Accessed 3 Sept 2023

Mage_AI (2022) How does TikTok use machine learning? Dev.to 16 Feb 2022 https://dev.to/mage_ai/how-does-tiktok-use-machine-learning-5b7i. Accessed 3 Sept 2023

Margoni T, Kretschmer M (2022) A deeper look into the EU text and data mining exceptions: harmonisation, data ownership, and the future of technology. GRUR Int 71(8):685–701. https://doi.org/10.1093/grurint/ikac054

Netherlands Authority for Consumers and Markets (ACM) (2022) Joint European consumer authorities force TikTok to make changes, https://www.acm.nl/en/publications/joint-european-consumer-authorities-force-tiktok-make-changes. Accessed 3 Sept 2023

Polanyi K (1944) The great transformation: the political and economic origins of our time, 2nd edn. Beacon Press (March 28, 2001)

Prüfer J (2020) Competition policy and data sharing on data-driven markets. Tilburg University https://library.fes.de/pdf-files/fes/15999.pdf. Accessed 3 Sept 2023

Quintais JP (2023) Generative AI, Copyright and the AI Act, Kluwer Copyright Blog 9 May 2023, https://copyrightblog.kluweriplaw.com/2023/05/09/generative-ai-copyright-and-the-ai-act/ Accessed 28 July 2023

Rosati E (2020) Copyright as an Obstacle or an Enabler? A European perspective on text and data mining and its role in the development of AI creativity. Asia Pacific Law Rev 27(2):198-217, Available at SSRN: https://ssrn.com/abstract=3452376

Sag M (2019) The new legal landscape for text mining and machine learning. J Copyright Soc USA 66:291. https://ssrn.com/abstract=3331606 or https://doi.org/10.2139/ssrn.3331606 Accessed 28 July 2023

Senftleben M (2022) Study on EU copyright and related rights and access to and reuse of data, Directorate-General for Research and Innovation, European Commission. https://op.europa.eu/s/xmU1. Accessed 3 Sept 2023

Smith B (2021) How TikTok reads your mind. New York Times 5th Dec 2022 https://www.nytimes.com/2021/12/05/business/media/tiktok-algorithm.html Accessed 27 July 2023

Solomon B (2016) Google Just Passed Apple As The World's Most Valuable Company. Forbes.com, https://www.forbes.com/sites/briansolomon/2016/02/01/google-just-passed-apple-as-the-worlds-most-valuable-company/#4beea5de4861. Accessed 3 Sept 2023

Stolton S (2018) MEPs stake claim for the copyright of data in autonomous vehicles, Euractiv, https://www.euractiv.com/section/data-protection/news/meps-stake-claim-for-the-copyright-of-data-in-autonomous-vehicles/. Accessed 3 Sept 2023

Trendacosta K, Doctorow C (2023) AI Art Generators and the Online Image Market. EFF.org 3 April 2023 https://www.eff.org/deeplinks/2023/04/ai-art-generators-and-online-image-market Accessed 27 July 2023

Vercellone C, Brancaccio F, Giuliani A, Puletti F, Rocchi G, Vattimo P (2019) Data-driven disruptive commons-based models. Decentralised Citizens Owned Data Ecosystem, Horizon 2020 project no. 732546 https://ec.europa.eu/research/participants/documents/downloadPublic?documentIds=080166e5bf7dcdd3&appId=PPGMS. Accessed 3 Sept 2023

Vincent J (2022) The scary truth about AI copyright is nobody knows what will happen next. The Verge 15 November 2022, https://www.theverge.com/23444685/generative-ai-copyright-infringement-legal-fair-use-training-data. Accessed 3 Sept 2023

Walsh K (2023) How we think about copyright and AI Art. Electronic Frontier Foundation 3 April 2023 https://www.eff.org/deeplinks/2023/04/how-we-think-about-copyright-and-ai-art-0. Accessed 3 Sept 2023

Wiggers K (2023) The current legal cases against generative AI are just the beginning. TechCrunch 27 January 2023, https://techcrunch.com/2023/01/27/the-current-legal-cases-against-generative-ai-are-just-the-beginning/?guccounter=1. Accessed 3 Sept 2023

Williams BA, Brooks CF, Shmargad Y (2018) How algorithms discriminate based on data they lack: challenges, solutions, and policy implications. J Inf Policy 8:78–115. https://doi.org/10.5325/jinfopoli.8.2018.0078

Worb J (2023) How Does The TikTok Algorithm Work? (+10 Hacks to Go Viral) Later.com 16 February 2023 https://later.com/blog/tiktok-algorithm/ Accessed 27 July 2023

Chapter 6
Courts of Law V. Choke Points for Technological Innovation

Creating new value always rests on existing work, 'borrowing or building on material from a prior body of works, as well as adding original expression to it'[1]—William M. Landes, Richard A. Posner

6.1 Copyright as Means of Balancing Incentives: Is the Division Still Valid?

In the course of our journey, we have seen the 'traditional' approach to innovation becoming challenged by networked individuals involved in grassroots initiatives. It has been discussed at length how the networked innovation culture, which had laid the foundations for the digital reality of today, had operated for years based on sharing and collaborative effort, allowing the coining of quality technological standards and their widespread diffusion. It has also been shown how fragile this type of 'digital evolution' may be when confronted with the licensing schemes for proprietary code. What now merits a closer look is how such innovation models put to the test the very foundations of copyright from the perspective of its purpose of balancing incentives. When the lines between creators and users become blurry, as it happens in the case of a grassroots mass innovation network, the ages-old division into the suppliers and consumers of intellectual property may no longer apply—or apply in an entirely different way.

This leads us back into the broader perspective: the challenge that this will pose to the judges is of a similar variety as when they are faced with a new technology-enabled use of intellectual property that did not seem to fit within the strict interpretation of statutory law. It has been discussed how, in fringe technology-related

[1] Landes and Posner (1989). For a full discussion on the balancing of rights between authors of existing works and creators of new expression, see further in this chapter.

K. Drazewski, *Copyright as a Constraint on Creating Technological Value*, Law, Governance and Technology Series 63,
https://doi.org/10.1007/978-3-031-51276-6_6

copyright cases, judges have found themselves in a position where their decision would likely affect the way a new and beneficial invention can or cannot continue to grow. Particularly in European cases, this has required judges on more than one occasion to rise above the strict interpretation of the letter of the law; now, with the added complexity due to the blurred division between users and creators, their task may become even more taxing.

How valid still is the discourse on copyright as a means of balancing incentives between users and creators? Even a brief glance on the discussions of principles and goals of copyright indicates that, for one, it is certainly quite present in new-technology copyright cases. Despite the EU copyright having been claimed to (initially) lack this balancing capacity due to 'having been born a sterile creature', on account of its original lack of competence in the field and the resulting lack of ability to allow for philosophical considerations of balancing interests,[2] the recent case law of the CJEU, as will now be discussed, also applies the very same utilitarian and balancing optic, whether admitting it openly or not. Similarly, looking back at the European Commission reports on flexibilities in copyright as discussed in the previous chapter, it can be noted that their mention of copyright as means for preventing market failure (a primary one, where the incentive on the part of creators is to be preserved by ensuring exclusivity of distribution)[3] is closely related to the incentive-based take on the aims of copyright.

The incentive-based and utilitarian attitude is easier to observe in the United States case law as such most basic function is enshrined in the U.S. Constitution and its copyright clause;[4] it is that intended to ensure that creators are granted time-limited exclusivity in reaping the fruit of their intellect, for the purpose of promoting progress of science and of useful arts. This main incentive function, both in general terms and in regard to the right to compensation for the 'sweat of the brow' or the 'sacrificial days'[5] invested in the creation of the work, has become somewhat a customary reference used by the courts. At the same time, as mentioned before, courts have also used the 'incentive' function as basis for refusal to protect the original work, seeing that the ultimate goal will be served better by deeming that a derivative use of protected intellectual property is, in fact, fair and serves the 'welfare of the public'.[6] This 'public good' as the ultimate goal has been named as

---

[2]Sganga (2015), p. 6.

[3]In this regard, copyright has been named the 'engine of free expression' supplying an economic incentive to create and disseminate ideas (Harper v. Row Enterprises, quoting Mazer v. Stein, 347 U.S. 201, 209 (1954)).

[4]The Constitutional Clause empowers Congress 'to Promote the Progress of Science and useful Arts, by securing for limited Times to Authors and Inventors the exclusive Right to their respective Writings and Discoveries.' - Article I, section 8, clause 8, United States Constitution.

[5]See e.g. *Mazer v. Stein*, 347 US, opinion by Justice Reed.

[6]See e.g. *Campbell*, 510 U.S. at 575–577114 S.Ct. 1164, quoting Stewart v. Abend, 495 U.S. 207, 236, 110 S.Ct. 1750, 109 L.Ed.2d 184 (1990); see also Sony Corp. of Am. v. Universal City Studios, Inc., 464 U.S. 417, 429 n. 10, 104 S.Ct. 774, 78 L.Ed.2d 574.

an 'ultimate' goal of copyright, superseding even that of the author to secure a fair return on their labour.[7]

This approach, rooted deeply into the theory of copyright,[8] still bears in its DNA a profound and seemingly eternal binary opposition between incentives for creativity and access for dissemination and use.[9] In other words, it reflects a division of the general public into those who create value and those who use it, be it for business or pleasure. Such balancing act is an undertaking of the lawmakers and courts alike.[10] This idea of striking a balance appears to be underlying every major document related to the framework of copyright of today, from TRIPS[11] to the WIPO Copyright Treaty,[12] to the Copyright Directive[13] and the InfoSoc Directive.[14] The 'fair balance of rights and interests' as enshrined in Recital 31 of the latter has been read jointly with Recital 3 [15] and thus construed as one postulated between the rights of copyright holders and, on the other hand, the 'protection of interests and fundamental rights of users', in particular their 'freedom of expression and information' and the public interest' as mentioned in Recital 3 among the aims of the proposed implementation.[16] This puts the interests of users in the context of such fundamental freedoms as freedom of expression, as counterbalance of the interests of publishers on the other end of the scales. In this optic, tipping the balance towards the user reduces the incentive to create, whereas shifting it towards the creator reduces demand and circulation.

---

[7]Twentieth Century Music Corp. v. Aiken 'The immediate effect of our copyright law is to secure a fair return for an 'author's' creative labor. But the ultimate aim is, by this incentive, to stimulate [the creation of useful works] for the general public good.' 422 U.S., at 156. [559].

[8]Fisher (2001).

[9]See generally Mandic (2011).

[10]Spedicato (2015).

[11]TRIPS Art. 7: 'The protection and enforcement of intellectual property rights should contribute to the promotion of technological innovation and to the transfer and dissemination of technology, to the mutual advantage of producers and users of technological knowledge and in a manner conducive to social and economic welfare, and to a balance of rights and obligations.'

[12]'. . .Recognizing the need to maintain a balance between the rights of authors and the larger public interest, particularly education, research and access to information, as reflected in the Berne Convention'.

[13]Copyright Directive, Recital 6: 'The exceptions and limitations provided for in this Directive seek to achieve a fair balance between the rights and interests of authors and other rightholders, on the one hand, and of users on the other. [. . .]'

[14]InfoSoc Directive recital 3: The proposed harmonisation will help to implement the four freedoms of the internal market and relates to compliance with the fundamental principles of law and especially of property, including intellectual property, and freedom of expression and the public interest. Recital 31: 'A fair balance of rights and interests between the different categories of rightholders, as well as between the different categories of rightholders and users of protected subjectmatter must be safeguarded. The existing exceptions and limitations to the rights as set out by the Member States have to be reassessed in the light of the new electronic environment [. . .].'

[15]C-160/15 *GS Media*, para 31.

[16]C-160/15 *GS Media*, para 31.

For a broader perspective on balancing incentives, it has also been noted that excessive protection may also result in stifling supply of new works, as those are always, to some extent, derivative or overlapping with earlier creations of others. This results in a paradox, as offered by Landes and Posner, where it may be in the interest of authors to actually insist on narrowing, instead of broadening, the extent of protection.[17] (Ironically, taking this further we might eventually reach the conclusion that the broadening of protection is, in fact, only in the interest of publishers). As it has been demonstrated earlier, these considerations have increasingly put judges in a position where a flexible application of the statute, be it in Europe or the United States, becomes the 'to be or not to be' for the given case of technological innovation which has stumbled upon a 'legislative choke point' created by inflexible legislation, thus making the role of the judge more important than ever.

6.2 Courts of Law V. Choke Points for Technological Innovation

6.2.1 Market Failure: Where Inflexible Legislation Becomes a Choke Point

As already discussed at length, circumscribed copyright law has been known to create obstacles to human creativity which is always, to some extent, based on—and utilising—already existing ideas and inventions. A handy definition of these obstacles is offered in the aforementioned European Commission reports on flexibilities in EU copyright, in the context of analysing potential for adding more copyright exceptions into European copyright law.[18] As indicated therein, obstacles are created where a market failure occurs and the parties involved cannot satisfy their needs by means of a normal arm's length transaction. This echoes the discussions which rolled over the United States a few decades ago, on the economic rationale of flexible exceptions to copyright law in the context of their codification—on the dawn of their very introduction into the statutes. In her critique of the 9th Circuit Court of Appeals decision in *Betamax*, Wendy Gordon offered an economic analysis of the case that involved a deconstruction of the economic side of the matters involved. As offered by Gordon, fair use is a label courts use when they approve a user's departure from the market;[19] therefore, it occurs whenever 'flaws in the market might make reliance on the judiciary's own analysis of social benefit appropriate'.[20] In other words, fair use is the remedy that a court will come up with where a market failure has occurred—and the prevailing rationale, grounded in case law, suggests in that case

---

[17] Landes and Posner (1989), pp. 332–333.

[18] See the discussion in Chap. 4.

[19] Gordon (1982).

[20] Gordon (1982).

that this departure can be given a free pass and deemed as justified. Conversely, a 'choke point' is reached—where under the existing legislation, a new technology is unable to proceed without means to address the market failure which renders its use impractical or its further development inviable under the existing copyright scheme. A more detailed look into such 'choke points', depending on the scale of the project and the resources available to the innovator, will be discussed below.

6.2.2 Choke Points Affecting Large and Small Innovators

The examples cited earlier may be taken to suggest that the innovation most prone to be affected by a choke point created by inflexible legislation falls into two distinct categories. One, where it is either a large-scale project where the unauthorised reuse involves massive amounts of intellectual property that can be infringed upon by the use of a new household device (*Betamax*) and/or cannot be licensed in a traditional way due to its sheer volume, as was the case of *Google Books*. Second, where it comes from a project that is not a commercial one to begin with, and evolves from a grassroots initiative, a collaboration of individuals that is not focused on the economic aspects and initially disregards entirely such nuisance as third parties' IP—even though it may, at a later stage in the development of the project, become an obstacle for their work to be made available to wider circles of users and/or further developers (as discussed earlier in the context of *Oracle*). The reason why these two categories merit a closer look in opposition to each other is that they represent two ends of a spectrum: on the one hand, we have a big business, seemingly endless funding and a big innovation project, and on the other—its polar opposite, with little to no funding and the only resources at its disposal coming from the (often volatile) allocation of resources by not necessarily economically motivated individuals.

While at first glance, the differences between the two groups could not possibly be greater as they can be defined by pairs of polar opposites (following/disregarding economic principles; maximum/minimum allocated resources; risk-awareness/risk-disregard, potential failure being costly and to be avoided v. cheap and common. However, on closer look, in many cases the structural differences may be far less obvious. As early as 1958, it was observed that large companies with big Research and Development budgets, such as Bell Labs, General Electric or DuPont had decided on a decentralized research structure, leaving effective control of research teams at the level of respective research centres, with big initial budgets but granting 'complete freedom and responsibility' and relying on 'small spontaneous efforts' in the labs, making no effort to control the initial exploration stages on a central level.[21] While it is still hardly the same as the grassroots efforts described here, certain similarities as regards the structuring of initial efforts are quite similar.

[21] Hitch (1958).

Can it then be said, from the perspective of this analysis, that the major difference lay in the allocated resources? Seemingly, a worldwide project like Google Books has an entirely different economic base and enjoys seemingly unlimited funding assuming the willingness to take risks and sufficient dedication to the project on the part of the central management. However, according to a traditional economic view, stemming from the assumed goal to achieve the Pareto optimum, it has been said that, due to the unavoidable uncertainty and limited potential to appropriate the information produced in an innovation project, it will always suffer from being underfunded and thus, in its ideal state, would require state intervention. It will also suffer from underutilization of information, which has been identified as an input just as important as human talent.[22] From that perspective, it could be more vulnerable to yet another choke point that is the failure of the project due to withdrawal of corporate funding that had been propelling the project to-date. Distributed networks of innovators do not seem to share that risk as their budgets will anyway be modest at best—and thus less prone to fluctuations of capital.

Still, what seems to be the differentiating factor between the two types of innovation is the bargaining power to remedy the looming market failure. While the strengths of a distributed network of individuals—its low burn rate, virtually no fixed costs, flexible and distributed management become its weaknesses as soon as the time would come to negotiate the terms of licensing of existing technology—or, as Hitch would call it, simply information[23] – would all become its weaknesses, rendering the bargaining impossible from the upstart. Thus, in the case of small innovators creating informal 'hive minds', market failure would occur much faster and at a greater rate compared to big companies. Similarly, their non-formalised manner of operation and typical lack of a central management will likely derail any bargaining due to the quasi-coffin corner effect as described in the summary to the preceding chapter, where small allocation of means would limit the scope of licensing, but at the same time increasing allocation of means on licensing of information would become counterproductive by tying the structure to whatever initial idea there was for the shape of the project.

To recapitulate, it could be assumed that, in conditions which make the given innovation prone to become affected by market failure due to the nature of its reuse of intellectual property, neither large nor small innovators will emerge unscathed. However, due to the centralised management and economic bargaining power, large corporate innovators are more likely to remedy the situation before (and, to some extent, after)[24] market failure occurs. What happens when it occurs nonetheless will be discussed in the following section.

---

[22] Arrow (1962).

[23] Hitch (1958).

[24] To an extent, such a remedy could be seen in the settlement that was reached for Google Books in France. Still, one cannot overlook that ultimately it was a simple bargain that ended the dispute; thus it could also be claimed that the market ultimately prevailed. However, given the fact that by the time it was reached, the benefits and relatively low risks of Google Books were much better known and the project seemed indeed to be in everybody's interest, one may wonder whether it would be a

6.2.3 Judges and Teleology: Rules and Standards in Service of a Greater Good

6.2.3.1 Hints of Convergence at the Level of Teleological Reasoning

In earlier chapters, considerable attention has been dedicated to the recent history of big tech innovation cases in the EU and the U.S. that went beyond the typical bread and butter of what the judicial system would typically be dealing with. The discussion offered therein was of an analytical nature, going into the details of the cases and the weight they carried in making the final decision in the ruling. In the U.S., such details were those that satisfied the test of the fair use factors as outlined in the 1976 Copyright Act (and its currently prevailing rendition offered in the transformative use doctrine). In the EU, the 'weighing details' were selected in a perhaps less structured manner (from a weak, but undoubtedly creative interpretation of the Berne Convention in the French Google cases to the 'presumed consent' construct in the German court battles over search engine thumbnails); still, alongside the language used by the courts to justify their rulings, the cases offered plenty of material to dissect and analyse.

There is, however, one more angle to these cases that should be explored and that is a reductive one. Disregarding for the moment all of the case details and parameters (value of scanned books, size of thumbnails, location of servers) and leaving only the ultimate result on the table, it may be seen that, ultimately, certain similarities exist in the approach of the courts in the U.S. and the EU. One may wonder whether it is a coincidence that e.g. in the thumbnail cases (*Kelly v. Arriba Soft* and *Perfect 10* in the U.S.,[25] *Vorschaubilder* in the EU) as were discussed here earlier, the innovator ultimately prevailed on appeal—with or without the body of fair use case law behind them, and with or without the benefit of an open-textured norm of law as the underlying legal framework for the dispute. There seems to exist a common tendency, visible particularly among higher courts, to apply a more general view of what will benefit the market and society at large. In other words, it could be said that, in a position of the market having failed to provide a solution, the judge will strive to identify the 'greater good' that can be served better or worse by their ruling, and then substantiate this approach using the tools available at hand, imperfect as they may be. This would mean that, in a situation of a market failure, courts of law (higher courts in particular) are likely to identify the 'spirit and the letter' of the law with the idea of benefiting the unobstructed functioning of the market and the society at

justified conclusion given that it had still taken a presumption of 'getting away with it' to get the project off the ground in the first place (and then considerable time and funding for litigation to allow the world enough time to come to its own conclusions).

[25] Both decided by the U.S. Court of Appeals for the Ninth Circuit: Kelly v. Arriba Soft Corporation, 280 F.3d 934 (9th Cir. 2002); Perfect 10, Inc. v. Amazon.com, Inc., 508 F.3d 1146 (9th Cir. 2007).

large.[26] While evidence of this type of reasoning may be found more easily in U.S. case law, it is interesting to see how a similar paradigm has been applied in continental Europe, despite an entirely different tradition of substantiating decisions and phrasing used in justifying court rulings. This indicates the existence of trans-Atlantic similarities at yet another level than that discussed in Chap. 3 which discussed EU judges seemingly actively looking for flexibilities in the system to avoid shutting the door on innovation: similarities seeming to lie in the application of teleological language in fringe copyright cases. This may take the form of references to ensuring a 'market benefit' or 'social benefit' (as will be demonstrated, this is more likely to be encountered in rulings issued in the U.S.); or it may be a reference to the social context of property itself, or to goals which are to be achieved by legislation, such as fostering substantial investment in creativity and innovation, as well as network infrastructure, or leading to growth and increased competitiveness of the European industry, as offered in plenty in the preamble to the Infosoc Directive (and an honourable mention in the recitals to the Copyright Directive). While never used by the courts as an exclusive or in a decisive manner, use of such language as a supportive measure offers an interesting insight into the reasoning applied by judges to aid a given initiative in passing through a legislative choke point.

6.2.3.2 Social or Market Benefits Language in Fringe Copyright Cases: United States

6.2.3.2.1 Harper & Row v. Nation Enterprises[27]

In the case of *The Nation* engaging in an unlicensed publication quoting to a large extent from a manuscript of President Ford's memoirs, the Supreme Court found against fair use noting that the defence of a 'right to know' of the general public would 'displace normal copyright channels' as, in the words of the Court, any infringer might claim public interest in increasing access to a copyrighted work; therefore, fair use could not be deemed to create any kind of 'compulsory license' to grant access to 'unpublished copyrighted expression' of public figures.

The Court noted, however, that the point of fair use is to remedy situations where the market fails.[28] More interestingly, however, it noted that, in the situation of a 'fully functioning market', fair use would cause a disruption 'without a commensurate public benefit': '[*a*]*s the facts here demonstrate, there is a fully functioning market that encourages the creation and dissemination of memoirs of public figures. In the economists' view, permitting 'fair use' to displace normal copyright channels disrupts the copyright market without a commensurate public benefit*'. Assuming

[26] In a similar vein, on the role of a court in the situation of a market failure see Gordon (1982), p. 1609, 1614.

[27] 471 U.S. 539 - Harper Row Publishers Inc. v. Nation Enterprises (decided May 20, 1985).

[28] *Harper Row*, para. 9.

this observation was not introduced without good reason, it would suggest that the presence of a 'commensurate public benefit' is also a factor to be addressed by the court in the situation of a market failure.[29] This notion seems to be present in later cases citing *Harper & Row*, e.g. *Perfect 10* as will be discussed further below.

6.2.3.2.2 Sony Corporation of America v. Universal City Studios Inc.[30]

The notion of a public benefit that would justify the limiting of an author's copyright also appears in the reasoning of the Supreme Court in the case of Sony v. Universal (Betamax): according to the court, copyright '*gives the author a right to limit or even to cut off access to his work.*[...] *A VTR* [a video tape recorder—K.D.] *recording creates no public benefit sufficient to justify limiting this right.*' Similarly then as in the case of *Harper & Row v. Nation Enterprises*, this reference is made in a context signifying a lack of this condition being fulfilled. This, nonetheless, again suggests that a social benefit criterion would also weigh on whether the original protection could or should be thus limited.

6.2.3.2.3 Campbell v. Acuff-Rose Music Inc.[31]

In the landmark case of 1994, when discussing the reuse of Roy Orbison's '*Oh, Pretty Woman*' by the rap group 2 Live Crew, the Supreme Court showed restraint in judging the artistic value of a parody, noting that '*whether* [...] *parody is in good taste or bad does not and should not matter to fair use*' and that, quoting *Bleistein v. Donaldson Lithographing Co,*[32] '*[i]t would be a dangerous undertaking for persons trained only to the law to constitute themselves final judges of the worth of [a work] [...] works of genius would be sure to miss appreciation. Their very novelty would make them repulsive until the public had learned the new language in which their author spoke*'.

Thus taking a balanced approach and avoiding the discussion on whether that particular time for 2 Live Crew's song is yet to arrive, the Supreme Court has also offered a social benefit justification of showing leniency towards parody in general, noting that '*[l]ike less ostensibly humorous forms of criticism, it can provide social benefit, by shedding light on an earlier work, and, in the process, creating a new one*', at the same time quoting Posner on the social interest laying in the unsuppressed existence of parody: '*There is an obstruction when the parodied*

---

[29] The Court references Wendy Gordon: 'the court generally should engage in balancing costs and benefits only if market failure has left it the only institution able to do so' Gordon (1982), p. 1609, 1614.

[30] 464 U.S. 417.

[31] 510 U.S. 569 - Campbell v. Acuff-Rose Music Inc. (decided March 7, 1994).

[32] Bleistein v. Donaldson Lithographing Co 188 U. S. 239, 251 (1903).

work is a target of the parodist's criticism, for it may be in the private interest of the copyright owner, but not in the social interest, to suppress criticism of the work'.[33]

6.2.3.2.4 Sony Computer Entertainment America Inc. v. Bleem[34]

Decided in 2000 by the U.S. Court of Appeals for the Ninth Circuit, *Sony v. Bleem* pertained to the use of digital screenshots from console games. Bleem was a software company whose products allowed Playstation games to be played on personal computers instead of buying a gaming console; in its advertising, it used screenshots from said games which Sony claimed to be a copyright violation.[35] The Ninth Circuit offered a detailed (and, from today's perspective, mostly outdated) analysis of how console games benefited from being played on a PC, due to the higher quality graphics than those offered [at the time—KD] by a television screen and about the benefits Bleem created for the user, deciding, against the positions of both parties, that they were engaged in competition.

Having established this, the court observed that the use of screenshots in advertising is only fair as long as it benefits the user offering a genuine means of comparing the picture quality between Playstation and the Bleem emulator: '*we must qualify our holding with one caveat. Our conclusions with respect to Bleem's use of screen shots apply only to those screen shots that Bleem has generated by taking the actual images of Sony's games from a television screen. The entire premise of comparative advertising is that the consumer is being made aware of the true choices.* [. . .] *We are persuaded by the need for Bleem to impose minimally upon Sony's copyright with respect to these screen shots because there is no other way to create a truly accurate comparison for the user.* [. . .] *With that limitation in mind, we conclude that Bleem's use of Sony's copyrighted material was fair.*'

In other words, despite the battle being waged over a copyright issue, the weighing factor had been the benefit created to the market by offering comparative advertising, offering a body of case law and ruling by the Federal Trade Commission to confirm the 'social utility' and market benefits of truthful comparative advertising.[36]

---

[33] Posner (1992).

[34] 214 F.3d 1022 (9th Cir.2000).

[35] The original case featured a greater number of copyright violations; however, only the screenshots issue remained at the time of appeal.

[36] 'Comparative advertising, when truthful and non-deceptive, is a source of important information to consumers and assists them in making rational purchase decisions. Comparative advertising encourages product improvement and innovation, and can lead to lower prices in the marketplace.' - 16 C.F.R. S 14.15(c) (1980) https://www.law.cornell.edu/cfr/text/16/14.15. Accessed 03 September 2023.

6.2.3.2.5 Kelly v. Arriba Soft[37]

When discussing Arriba's unauthorized copying of protected images and their reuse as thumbnail images in a search engine, the court offered its remarks on how the use of images as thumbnails is both transformative in nature (without impacting the market for the original work) and beneficial to the public at large. The use in question, it was said, '*promotes the goals of the Copyright Act and the fair use exception*' in that the thumbnails '*do not stifle artistic creativity because they are not used for illustrative or artistic purposes and therefore do not supplant the need for the originals. In addition, they benefit the public by enhancing information-gathering techniques on the internet.*'

Further down, a benefit to the market was outlined more directly below, as the use was likened to that analysed in Sony v Bleem (cited above), by enhancing public awareness of the product, quoting that 'comparative advertising redounds greatly to the purchasing public's benefit with very little corresponding loss to the integrity of Sony's copyrighted material'. The court concluded its 'transformative use' analysis by stating that the first fair use factor—in the words of the court, citing *Campbell*,[38] the most important of the four, if the use is transformative—weighed in favour of the defendant '*due to the public benefit of the search engine and the minimal loss of integrity to Kelly's images.*' Put simply, the public benefit of the use was listed by the court as the first criterion when deciding on the use of thumbnail images being fair.

6.2.3.2.6 Perfect Inc. v. Amazon.com Inc[39]

In *Perfect 10*, as discussed earlier, an operator of a website with adult photographs, sued Google and Amazon in an effort to stop search engines from facilitating access to infringing thumbnail images. When conducting its fair use analysis, the Court of Appeals for the Ninth Circuit noted that, in deciding the nature and character of the use, one must examine Google's '*superseding and commercial*' uses against its '*significant transformative use*' and the extent to which Google 'serves the interest of the public'. While citing the district court in its reference to Google Image Search providing a 'great value to the public' as a truism, it also noted its importance is stressed by the Supreme Court: *'The Supreme Court, however, has directed us to be mindful of the extent to which a use promotes the purposes of copyright and serves*

[37] 336 F. 3d 811 - Kelly v. Arriba Soft Corporation. Online at https://openjurist.org/336/f3d/811. Accessed 03 September 2023.

[38] Campbell v. Acuff-Rose Music, Inc., 510 U.S. 569, 579, 114 S.Ct. 1164, 127 L.Ed.2d 500 (1994).

[39] 487 F. 3d 701 - Perfect Inc. v. Amazon.com Inc.; Perfect 10 v. Google, Inc., 416 F.Supp.2d 828 (C.D.Cal.2006, enjoined).

the interests of the public', citing *Campbell,*[40] *Harper&Row*[41] and *Sony v. Universal.*[42]

6.2.3.2.7 Authors Guild v. Hathitrust

Although more examples of social benefit cited as a factor in copyright rulings could be presented, it may be best to close with perhaps the most noteworthy quote by Judge Baer, ruling in favour of the HathiTrust Digital Library in *Authors Guild v. Hathitrust*. The case was related to the Google Books Project and pertained to digitizing books and offering access to students with disabilities, as discussed in detail in Chap. 2 of this work. In delivering his ruling, Judge Baer admitted that there had indeed been no precedent to rest upon; however, he agreed with the memoranda offered by amici of court: Library Amici Br. ('*the public derives tremendous benefit from HDL, and authors stand to gain very little if the public is deprived*'), Digital Humanities (on metadata and text mining, which '*could actually enhance the market for the underlying work, by causing researchers to revisit the original work and re-examine it in more detail*'). In his final word, Baer famously concluded: *I cannot imagine a definition of fair use that would not encompass the transformative uses made by Defendants' MDP and would require that I terminate this invaluable contribution to the progress of science and cultivation of the arts that at the same time effectuates the ideals espoused by the ADA.*[43]'

6.2.3.3 Teleological Language in European Fringe Cases

The following subsection offers a few examples of teleological reasoning applied in fringe cases by courts in Europe. While the application of a teleological analysis by the CJEU in its jurisprudence is hardly a novelty in many respects, it has also been traditionally limited to areas which lie within its natural area of competence. This needs to be viewed in the light of the origins of EU copyright being sometimes referred to as 'born sterile', given the original lack of competence of the Community in the field and the interventions of the Court being naturally limited to offering remedies to protect the single market and stimulate the competitiveness of the EU economy.[44] However, to some extent mirroring the U.S. courts, the CJEU has also been seen as not shying away from reinforcing its semantic interpretation of the law

---

[40] Campbell, 510 U.S. at 579, 114 S.Ct. 1164.

[41] Harper & Row, 471 U.S. at 556–557, 105 S.Ct. 2218.

[42] Sony, 464 U.S. at 431–432, 104 S.Ct. 774.

[43] Americans with Disabilities Act of 1990.

[44] Sganga (2015), p. 6.; for an outline of different periods of teleological interpretation in view of the harmonization agenda, see also Sganga (2018).

with a teleological analysis.[45] Absent the general indication of a socially desirable purpose that in the U.S. is offered by Constitution, the CJEU turned to another instrument offering similar considerations (albeit with the goal formulated in a slightly different manner[46]): the 2001/29 Information Society Directive. A few further examples of such teleological reasoning from recent European judicial history, all well-known and high-profile cases, have been given below. Interestingly, there is also evidence of a trickle-down effect leading to national courts applying similar considerations in fringe cases.

6.2.3.3.1 Megakini

The Spanish Megakini case, revolving around Google's proxy caching of websites, was already noted earlier for the creativity showed by judges of the Spanish Supreme Court. Yet it deserves another mention in this context, and that is in view of the teleological reasoning used by all courts since the first instance, albeit each time in slightly different manner. The Juzgado de lo Mercantil n° de Barcelona, hearing the case in the first instance, dismissed the claim noting that the use in question was only of 'a small part of the content of the plaintiff's website, under the conditions of temporality, provisionality, respect for the integrity and authorship of the work' (*sólo una pequeña parte del contenido de la página web de la actora, bajo las condiciones de temporalidad, provisionalidad, respeto a la integridad y autoría de la obra*); however, it also added that such use was in conformity with the 'social purpose' of making the works available on the Internet (*la finalidad social para la cual la obra fue divulgada en Internet*).[47] In other words, aside from offering the argument of Google's use of third party protected work being temporary and provisional (and benefitting from the exemption of Art. 31.1 *Texto Refundido de la Ley de Propiedad Intelectual*, ex Art. 5.1 EUCD) the court saw fit to make a reference to the 'social purpose' (*finalidad social*) of the works being published online, and the alignment of Google's actions with that purpose was mentioned as a supporting argument to find the use non-infringing.

---

[45] Favale et al. (2016).

[46] These goals being primarily the 'development of the information society in Europe' and achieving 'a high level of protection of intellectual property, [to] foster substantial investment in creativity and innovation, including network infrastructure, and lead in turn to growth and increased competitiveness of European industry, both in the area of content provision and information technology and more generally across a wide range of industrial and cultural sectors.' - Directive 2001/29/EC of the European Parliament and of the Council of 22 May 2001, rec. 2 and 4.

[47] Sentencia Civil N° 41/2007, Juzgados de lo Mercantil - Barcelona, Sección 5, Rec 92/2006 de 30 de Marzo de 2007. https://www.iberley.es/jurisprudencia/sentencia-civil-n-41-2007-jm-barcelona-sec-5-rec-92-2006-30-03-2007-3618161. Accessed 03 September 2023.

On appeal, the Audiencia Provincial de Barcelona[48] went much further: it noted that the applicability of the exception of Art. 31.1 TRLPI was irrelevant, saying that protection of intellectual property should not be seen as absolute; the restriction on application of copyright exceptions which 'may not interpreted in such a way as to cause unjustified damage to the legitimate interests of the author or to be detrimental to the normal exploitation of the works to which they refer' (art. 40 bis TRLPI, mirroring Directive 96/9/EC and the Berne Convention three-step test) may be read to 'question the limits of these rights beyond the literality of the precepts that regulate them, positively and negatively, in this case the rights of reproduction and making available (*nos cuestionemos los límites de estos derechos más allá de la literalidad de los preceptos que los regulan, positiva y negativamente, en este caso los derechos de reproducción y de puesta a disposición*). Moroeover, protection of intellectual property rights, similarly to the Anglo-Saxon concept of fair use, should be construed in view of a 'natural limit of the property right' (*un límite natural del derecho de propiedad*), as per the concept of *ius usus inoqui*, or the law of harmless use, is in real estate law, as means of avoiding 'absurd overreaching' (*extralimitaciones absurdas*) in this reasoning. In other words, the Audiencia Provincial de Barcelona offered a bold teleological reading of the Berne three-step test as means of avoiding a scenario where, by literal application of the law, the results would be those of overprotection or, as mentioned, constitute 'absurd overreaching' had the analysis not been applied.

Taking purpose-driven analysis of copyright law to an entirely new level, the Spanish Supreme Court issued its ruling in April 2012, putting the exercise of copyright protection into the context of social utility of the construct of property itself. Rejecting the cassation appeal, the court noted that the right to innocuous use of the property of others, brought up by the court of appeal, is a result of the constitutional configuration of property as a right delimited by its social function (*la configuración constitucional de la propiedad como un derecho delimitado por su función social*). Moreover, the Supreme Court observed that doubts raised by the letter of specific laws should be solved by means of rules of a more general nature that, in turn, incorporate principles previously recognized by scientific doctrine and jurisprudence (*las dudas que suscite la letra de la ley especial se resuelvan mediante normas de carácter más general que, a su vez, incorporan principios antes reconocidos por la doctrina científica y la jurisprudencia*). In that context, the court offered that the rules laid down in the LPI (*Ley de Propiedad Intelectual*) referencing the 'unjustified prejudice to legitimate interests' or 'detriment to the normal exploitation of works', incorporating the Berne three-step test, can be read as a 'special manifestation' (*manifestación especial*) in the LPI of the general principle of the exercise of rights according to the requirements of good will ([*el*] *principio general del ejercicio de los derechos conforme a las exigencias de la buena* [*fe*]),

[48] Sentencia Civil Audiencia Provincial de Barcelona, Sección 15, Rec 92/2006 de 17 de Septiembre de 2008. Available at https://www.iberley.es/jurisprudencia/sentencia-civil-ap-barcelona-sec-15-rec-92-2006-17-09-2008-1264761. Accessed 03 September 2023.

Article 7.1 of the Spanish Civil Code), of the general principle of the prohibition of abuse of right or of the anti-social exercise of the same (*la prohibición del abuso del derecho o del ejercicio antisocial del mismo*, Article 7.2) and constitutional configuration of the right of property as a delimited right (*la configuración constitucional del derecho de propiedad como derecho delimitado*). Reductively speaking, taking further AP Barcelona's 'reversed' reading of the Berne three-step test,[49] the Supreme Court has offered that copyright protection needs to be construed in view of the social construct of property and its systemic limitations; this includes its abuse or exercise in an 'anti-social' manner.

6.2.3.3.2 Vorschaubilder III

In the most recent thumbnail case resolved in Germany by the *Bundesgerichtshof*, also deserving attention for the creativity of the legal argument involved,[50] also makes a reference of an underlying goal that needs to be achieved by the application of the law, while discussing the value of neutrality of search engines and its importance in view of the 'objective' of the Infosoc Directive.

In discussing the liability of a search function provider in the case of displaying thumbnail previews of copyrighted images posted online without the author's consent, the court noted that a party supplying a search engine cannot reasonably (*vernünftigerweise*) be expected to verify whether the works had been legally posted online before displaying the thumbnails. Tasking a search function supplier with the duty to assess such legality would contravene the task and functionality of search engines (*Aufgabe und Funktionsweise der Suchmaschinen*) According to the Court, a general monitoring duty would be inappropriate in view of the task of the search engines as they have an 'essential significance for the use of the Internet' (*essentielle Bedeutung für die Nutzung des Internets*) and as such, cannot be burdened with any duties of examination (*Prüfpflichten*) in this regard.

This notion the court explores by conducting an *a contrario* analysis of a hypothetical situation where a general duty for search engine operators to monitor the legitimacy of the content that is being scanned by their automated services. As observed by the court, in view of the 'essential significance' of web search engines to the functioning of the Internet, no duties of care must be imposed that could *'jeopardise or disproportionately hamper'* the operation of search engines. Taking it further, in view of the court, this could lead to an 'impossible-to overlook risk of being sued by a great number of copyright holders' (*'unübersehbare Risiko einer Inanspruchnahme durch eine Vielzahl von Urheberrechtsinhabern'*[51]) a presumption of such a duty could call their very existence into question. This, as concluded

[49]The reasoning offered by the Court around Berne has been described in more detail in Chap. 3.
[50]See Chap. 3 *in fine*.
[51]*Vorschaubilder III*, para. 62.

by the court, would be against the goal of supporting the 'development of the information society' ('*die Entwicklung der Informationsgesellschaft zu fördern*').[52]

Similarly then as in the cases cited before, a teleological argument is used to assist in the main analysis. However, it is noteworthy that the proposed outlook on the matter is of dual nature: aside from citing one of the goals cited in the Information Society Directive, it also builds a justification for an activity that is potentially infringing, which can be read as seeing it as too widespread and socially beneficial to be allowed to face potential litigation, which could potentially be, as admitted by the Court, potentially massive.

6.2.3.3.3 Ulmer

Decided in 2014, *Ulmer* (C-117/13) may serve as another example of references being made to the aims of copyright law protection as enshrined in the preamble to the InfoSoc Directive. The case concerned the practice of the library of Technische Universität Darmstadt which comprised digitization of books and making them available to users of the library at specified terminals. These terminals did not allow for display of more copies of a book than the library owned; however, books could be, in whole or in part, downloaded to a USB stick and carried out of the library. The dispute arose when the library refused an offer to buy e-books from Ulmer KG, a scientific textbook publisher, and opted to digitise its existing paper copies within its system.[53]

In the opinion of the Advocate General of 5 June 2014, a general teleological interpretation was offered alongside a direct reading of the directives and a schematic interpretation in regard to the offer to purchase e-books as not excluding the application of a copyright exception; noting first that '*a simple offer by the copyright holder would allow the application of that exception to be made subject to unilateral decisions, which would* [. . .] *deprive the exception of its effectiveness for the establishments concerned*', then observing that '[a] *teleological interpretation also requires, in view of the general interest objective pursued by the Union legislature, namely to promote learning and culture, that the user is able to rely on that exception.*'[54]

The CJEU judgment of 11 September 2014 offered a teleological reading of a few provisions of the Directive. Analysing the matter of a work being 'subject to purchase or licensing terms', the Court observed that the exception under Article 5(3)n of the Directive '*aims to promote the public interest in promoting research and private study, through the dissemination of knowledge, which constitutes* [. . .] *the core mission of publicly accessible libraries*' and that the interpretation offered by the plaintiff would '*deny the establishment concerned the right to benefit from*

[52] *Vorschaubilder III*, loc. cit.

[53] C-117/13, Opinion of Advocate General Jääskinen of 5 June 2014 (1), para. 12–16.

[54] C-117/13, Opinion of Advocate General Jääskinen of 5 June 2014 (1), para. 24.

that limitation and thereby prevent it from realising its core mission and promoting the public interest'[55] and that it would be '*difficult to reconcile*' with the aim of Article 5(3)n, '*which is to maintain a fair balance between the rights and interests of rightholders*'.[56]

Ulmer was commented on as a case where access to information and cultural promotion were found to prevail over the potential market harm of digitizing books in regard to e-book sales.[57] It should also be noted, however, that a weighing of the two goals is not found in the original judgment. What is offered instead is a consideration of the operation of public libraries in the light of the aim of Article 5(3) of Directive 2001/29 aiming *to promote the public interest in promoting research and private study, through the dissemination of knowledge, which constitutes, moreover, the core mission of publicly accessible libraries.*'[58]

6.2.3.3.4 SAS

Another case containing subsidiary teleological references to the goals of copyright protection is the interoperability case of *SAS Institute Inc. v. World Programming Ltd.* of 2012. World Programming had found itself under fire for offering a low-budget alternative to the SAS data analytics ecosystem that provided a level of cross-compatibility, enabling users of SAS to change their software provider without having to rewrite their applications that were written natively for SAS.

In the dispute that ensued, the Advocate General offered that to allow functionalities of a computer program to be protected '*would amount to making it possible to monopolise ideas, to the detriment of technological progress and industrial development*'.[59] This argument was then repeated by the CJEU in paragraph 40 of the judgment.[60] Furthermore, referencing the explanatory memorandum to the Proposal for Directive 91/250, the Court noted that the 'main advantage' of subjecting computer programs to this type of protection is that this protection only cover '*the individual expression of the work and this leaves other authors the desired latitude to create similar or even identical programs, provided that they refrain from copying*'.[61] Read in the context of the preceding paragraph, it can be observed how the goals of the current framework of copyright protection of software are referenced in regard to both protecting a free flow of ideas, technological progress

---

[55] C-117/13, para. 27–28.

[56] C-117/13, para. 31.

[57] Rendas (2018), p. 18.

[58] C-117/13, para. 27.

[59] C-406/10, Opinion by Advocate General of 29 November 2011.

[60] C-406/10, para. 40.

[61] C-406/10, para. 41, referencing the Proposal for a Council Directive on the legal protection of computer programs COM(88) 816 final — SYN 183, point 3.7.

and development, also by means of allowing competition as enshrined in the quoted explanatory memorandum to the Directive.

6.2.3.3.5 VOB

Vereniging Openbare Bibliotheken v. Stichting Leenrecht[62] C-174/15 is a strong example of extensive teleological reasoning being applied, this time among the main grounds for the recommended interpretation of the law by the Advocate General.

The applicant, an association of public libraries in the Netherlands, attempted to secure a ruling to the effect that the lending exception enshrined in Article 6(1) of the Rental and Lending Rights Directive[63] could also apply to lending of e-books.

The opinion of Advocate General Szpunar set the tone in the first sentence with a reference to libraries being 'one of *civilisation's most ancient institutions*' that predated the invention of paper and print, then the necessary adjustment of the nascent copyright '*it was to the libraries that the law of copyright, which emerged in the 18th century, had to adjust*', ending on an emphatic note: '*the present case undeniably offers the Court a real opportunity to help libraries not only to survive, but also to flourish.*' Teleological references were also made later on, noting e.g. that '*the interpretation of Directive 2006/115 must meet the needs of a contemporary society and make it possible to reconcile the various interests at stake*' (para. 23) and that the omission of digital lending in Directive 92/100 must have occurred due to the technology being too new at the time ('[I]*t is, I think, undeniable that, at that time, the EU legislature did not contemplate the inclusion of the lending of electronic books within the concept of lending of Directive 92/100, if for no other reason than because the technology for commercially viable electronic books was then only in its infancy* (para. 25).

The AG also notes that a broadening interpretation of Article 6(1) of Directive 2006/115 will allow for a greater protection of the interests of authors. Absent an inclusion in said Article 6(1), digital lending will continue under agreements between publishers and libraries, leaving the authors without due remuneration: '*these contractual relationships are principally of benefit to publishers or other intermediaries in the electronic book trade, while no adequate remuneration is received by authors.*' (para. 34). Conversely, if digital lending were to be deemed as falling into the scope of said provisions, '*authors would as a result receive remuneration, in accordance with the requirement laid down in that provision, in addition to that generated by the sale of books and independently of agreements concluded with publishers*'. Consequently, '*it would also make it possible for their*

[62] C-174/15, 16 June 2016.

[63] Directive 2006/115/EC of the European Parliament and of the Council of 12 December 2006 on rental right and lending right and on certain rights related to copyright in the field of intellectual property, http://eur-lex.europa.eu/LexUriServ/LexUriServ.do?uri=OJ:L:2006:376:0028:0035:EN:PDF.

interests to be protected better than they can be in the current climate, which is governed solely by the laws of the market'. The argument is ended on a high note again referencing the historic mission of libraries and the danger they face in today's reality: '[w]*ithout the privileges which flow from a derogation from the exclusive lending right, libraries are therefore in danger of no longer being able to perpetuate, in the digital environment, the role which was always theirs in the era of printed books*' (para. 39).

In its ruling, the CJEU noted that 'rental' as regulated in the WIPO treaty can only apply to tangible objects, i.e. ones fixated in a tangible medium. However, it also observed that 'rental' and 'lending' need not necessarily be deemed as the same concept: '*it* [. . .] *does not follow that the EU legislature necessarily intended to give the same meaning to the concepts of 'objects' and 'copies', whether with regard to the rental system or to the lending system, including public lending within the meaning of Article 6 of that directive'* (para. 36). As such, the concept of 'lending' as included in the Directive, is not precluded from being construed to include digital copies: '*neither that treaty nor that agreed statement preclude the concept of 'lending', within the meaning of that directive, from being interpreted, where appropriate, as also including certain lending carried out digitally*'. Such conclusion, the Court added, is '*borne out by the objective pursued by Directive 2006/115*'. This objective, enshrined in Recital 4, is for copyright to '*adapt to new economic developments such as new forms of exploitation*' given that digital lending '*indisputably forms part of those new forms of exploitation and, accordingly, makes necessary an adaptation of copyright to new economic developments*' (para. 45).

The Court also added that this interpretation is necessary to fulfil the '*general principle*' of requiring a high level of protection for authors (para. 46) and that an exception must be interpreted in a way to ensure its effectiveness and in view of the purpose it is aimed to achieve: '*although Article 6(1)* [. . .] *as a derogation from the exclusive lending right* [. . .] *must, according to the Court's settled case-law, be interpreted strictly, the fact remains that the interpretation given must also enable the effectiveness of the exception thereby established to be safeguarded and its purpose to be observed* [references omitted]'.

Lastly, a teleological argument was also offered regarding the digital lending of e-books obtained from an unlawful source: while not expressly stated in the wording, it can be inferred from the objective of the Directive to counteract piracy: '*although the wording of Article 6(1) of Directive 2006/115 does not expressly set out any requirement that the source of the copy made available by the public library must be lawful, nevertheless one of the objectives of that directive is to combat piracy, as can be seen from recital 2 thereof*; as such, unlawfully sourced copies cannot be accepted as it would '*amount to tolerating, or even encouraging, the circulation of counterfeit or pirated works and would therefore clearly run counter to that objective*'. Similarly, the private copying exception of Article 5(2)(b) of Directive 2001/29 cannot be deemed to include making private copies from unlawful sources due to harm to the market that would ensue: '*if the Member States had the option of adopting legislation which also allowed reproductions for private use to be made from an unlawful source, it would clearly be detrimental to the proper functioning of the internal market*'.

6.2.3.3.6 GS Media

In the case of GS Media (C-160/15), as discussed earlier, revolving around the GeenStijl website's posting of links to infringing content hosted on a third-party website, in para. 44 the Court notably referenced a line of reasoning offered by GS Media itself, as well as the German, Portuguese and Slovak governments, with the support of the European Commission, stating that to interpret all acts of posting links to content hosted by third parties as 'communication to the public' within the meaning of Article 3(1) of Directive 2001/29, '*would have highly restrictive consequences for freedom of expression and of information*' as well as the balancing of interests of the public and the copyright holders that the Directive seeks to establish.[64]

The CJEU agreed with this view, noting that 'the internet is in fact of particular importance to freedom of expression and of information, safeguarded by Article 11 of the Charter, and that hyperlinks contribute to its sound operation as well as to the exchange of opinions and information in that network characterised by the availability of immense amounts of information' (para. 45). In view of these considerations, the Court offered its dualistic view on how the concept of communication to the public must be construed depending on whether or not it is done in the course of a commercial activity. In this attempt to keep the door open for freedom of expression in the case of links posted by private entities where knowledge of illegality cannot be presumed, this imaginative approach earned the case criticism as was described in Chap. 3.

6.2.3.3.7 Bezpečnostní Softwarová Asociace

In the case of *Bezpečnostní softwarová asociace – Svaz softwarové ochrany v. Ministerstvo kultury* (C-393-09), while discussing the copyrightability of a user interface in a computer program, Advocate General Yves Bot offered that such interfaces, while requiring considerable intellectual effort, still needed to meet the criterion of originality as being its author's own intellectual creation.[65] In the case of such interfaces, however, expression is dictated by technical function, and '*the different methods of implementing an idea are so limited that the criterion of originality is not met, since the different methods of implementing an idea are so limited that the idea and the expression become indissociable*'. To deem otherwise, AG Bot noted, could mean to stifle competition, creation and innovation in the

[64] C-160/15, para. 44.

[65] Opinion of AG Bot in C-393-09, para. 74.

software market: '*it would have the consequence of conferring a monopoly on certain companies on the computer program market, thus significantly hampering creation and innovation on that market, which would run contrary to the objective of Directive 2001/29*'.[66]

The CJEU agreed with this view referencing paragraphs 75 and 76 of the AG's opinion and stated that, '*where the expression of such components is dictated by their technical function*'[67] they '*do not permit the author to express his creativity in an original manner and achieve a result which is an intellectual creation of that author*'[68] which rules out the protection of such an interface as a computer program under the Software Directive. However, the 'specific arrangement or configuration' of such components was still able meet the criterion of originality under Directive 2001/29/EC, assuming that it was its author's own creation.[69] Another teleological argument was offered in regard to another aspect of the case, this being the desired manner of interpretation of communication to the public. The Court observed that the concept of 'communication to the public' must be interpreted broadly ('*it follows from the 23rd recital in the preamble to Directive 2001/29 that 'communication to the public' must be interpreted broadly. Such an interpretation is moreover essential to achieve the principal objective of that directive, which, as can be seen from its 9th and 10th recitals, is to establish a high level of protection of, inter alia, authors* [...]'.[70] This broad interpretation was applied in order to fulfil the objective of establishing a 'high level of protection' of authors as enshrined in recitals 9th and 10th of Directive 2001/29.[71]

6.2.3.4 Rules, Standards and Judicial Pragmatism

While not at all surprising in the U.S. context, teleological reasoning as a subsidiary method of solving fringe cases may still raise eyebrows in the realm of the European tradition of copyright, even factoring in the particular origins of copyright at the EU level. The CJEU's use of teleological arguments, while perhaps necessary when navigating the difficult waters of what has been referred to as constitutional pluralism,[72] in the copyright context has certainly attracted criticism as a tool of pushing forward a harmonization agenda extending beyond the Commission's policy framework, creating issues for national courts operating within the continental tradition and being both fragmented and lacking a 'systematic indication'.[73]

[66] Opinion of AG Bot in C-393-09, para. 76.

[67] C-393-09, para. 49.

[68] C-393-09, para. 50.

[69] C-393-09, para. 51.

[70] C-393-09, para. 54.

[71] C-393-09, para. 54.

[72] Maduro (2007).

[73] Sganga (2018), p. 125.

It is unquestionable that attempts at transplanting teleological reasoning into the context of continental copyright are just as easy a target for criticism as are claims of a need to flexibilise the European copyright framework. The arguments against are widely known; chief among those, the lack of a body of case law to support and guide courts in the challenges they encounter. However, as it has already been discussed earlier in this work, on the U.S. side, this body of case law does not necessarily contribute to a greater level of legal certainty, particularly in cases testing the boundaries of the system; when faced with a new and challenging case, judges have been noted to approach flexible standards themselves in a flexible manner while new case law is being coined, instead of sticking to the already established doctrine (see e.g. comments on *AP v. Meltwater*, *Dr Seuss* and *Castle Rock* in Chap. 3). In that sense, a feeble convergence appears to emerge on both sides of the Atlantic, with rules and standards being applied flexibly by courts seeking to serve a higher purpose, be it the progress of useful arts, or, in the EU, harmonization or the development of an information society. In that regard, further rulings of the variety of *GS Media* and, at a national level, *Megakini* should not come as a surprise, perhaps even more so given the attempts at tightening copyright protection rules at the EU level. Adopting this optic, such moves should no longer be labelled as judicial activism; in a world changing too quickly for any legislator to be able to keep up, such an approach can only be seen as an example of an approach characterised more likely by profound pragmatism, powered by the ethos of the judicial profession. While a due examination of the chances of the CJEU's newfound flexible approach of effecting a shift in judicial culture may require a separate monograph, it cannot be ruled out that such a tendency—along with a 'trickle-down effect' to national courts will actually manifest itself, if cases such as *Megakini* or *Vorschaubilder III* can be any indication.

Taking a broader look, however, on what the above samples of case law seem to suggest—notably, comprising exclusively high-profile cases heard either by a national supreme court or the CJEU—is the very particular nature of the role of a judge in a fringe copyright case, this being one which extends beyond simple application of statutory law. The nature of this role merits attention as, by the very nature of such cases, it is likely to continue to come into play as new inventions will put existing copyright frameworks to the test and will continue to affect the manner in which such cases are resolved, in turn ultimately affecting the competitive advantage of the industry.

Looking at the very real struggle of judges in Europe since such cases as the 2005 *SAIF v. Google* or the first *Vorschaubilder* of 2010, with their sometimes surprising oversimplification of some matters and a clear goal-orientated reasoning,[74] and then taking account of the growing body of case law applying a teleological analysis and making straight references of the 'goals' of copyright protection as enshrined in directive recitals, it is tempting to hypothesize that ultimately, the role of the judges is in fact to see the bigger picture and rise above the mere application of the letter of

[74] See Chap. 3.

the law in service of the greater good, or plain common sense. Seeing as the CJEU does not shy away from a similar line of thinking (as e.g. in *VOB*, commenting on the state of technology when the applicable law was being written) and, notably, does so in an area where for a long time it has shown restraint and attachment to narrow application of exceptions, one may reasonably expect that courts in Member States would, over time, also increasingly gravitate towards the temptation of using copyright law, as in the case of *Megakini*, as a framework whose flexible interpretation can allow for justifying a solution that was deemed to be the least harmful in the realm of an information society. The extent of such a 'trickle-down effect' from the heights of the CJEU to national courts is a matter that would certainly merit further study. However, even by analysing the cases discussed above, it would seem that the relationship is more complex and multi-dimensional than with national courts simply offering a weakened reflection of the jurisprudence of the CJEU. As observed by Tito Rendas in a reference to the Spanish court in *Megakini* (noting the 'absurd overreaching' that direct application of the statute would have led to), '*a candid statement acknowledging that such constraints would lead to 'absurd' conclusions [...] is extremely unlikely at the CJEU level. In most cases where the Court departs from the constraints of the EU framework, the departure is not made explicit in the text of ruling.*'[75]

While only time can tell whether the flexible approach of a national supreme court to an insufficiently flexible copyright law as proposed in *Megakini* will serve as precedent (and encouragement) for future rulings, it is certainly true that, armed with the teleological considerations in the directives on the one hand side, and a growing body of CJEU case law applying teleological analysis in copyright law, despite it being seemingly impossible at first, national judges are obtaining a useful toolkit for navigating the circumscribed waters of EU copyright protection.

When first discussing earlier cases like *Vorschaubilder* or *SAIF v. Google*, where European judges went to great lengths to avoid shutting the door on innovation that was socially useful and beneficial for the market, in view of the strict manner in which the applicable law was written, the first instinct seemed to be to discuss them from the perspective of judicial activism. However, having reviewed the gradual shift occurring, albeit at glacial pace, in the European jurisprudence regarding strict application of copyright (and likely reinforced, albeit certainly illustrated in the CJEU's obvious departure from its own doctrine about exceptions needing to be interpreted narrowly), one may conclude that the true nature of the process is simply judicial pragmatism. It is that pragmatism that prompts judges to flexibly switch between applying rules or standards, in the service of a greater good; be it 'to promote the progress of science and useful arts' as enshrined in the U.S. constitution, or to ensure development of the information society and European competitive advantage. As it has been discussed, however, this process is forced to operate on a legal basis in Europe that still relies, particularly in the national context, on individual characteristics of the judge in question, lacking the statutory basis for

[75] Rendas (2018), loc. cit.

judicial flexibility in innovation cases which will likely continue to create such challenges. The possible manner of improving this is discussed below.

6.3 Innovative Reuse in Europe?

6.3.1 To Legislate or Not to Legislate? The Case of Betamax Falling Back on Flexibility

This subchapter will address the big question lurking from underneath all the case law, the history of personal computing, the nerd culture of distributed innovation and a certain convergence on the level of the reasoning of courts of law when faced with a valuable technological development that stumbles upon unfavourable legislation, earlier referred to as a legislative choke point: how can the situation be remedied in the European copyright reality, in a way that would ensure that the ultimate goals of ensuring a 'high level of protection' of authors and the 'fair balance' of rights and incentives do not suffer in the process.

Before moving on to discussing the legislative room for introducing a solution, one more case needs to be referenced that has already been discussed earlier. Notably, this time is not exclusively for its ultimate manner of resolution, which divided the bench and resulted in a famous majority opinion-turned-dissent of a Judges Blackmun, Marshall, Powell and Rehnquist of the United States Supreme Court; the case of *Sony Corp. of America v. Universal City Studios, Inc.*, also known as the *Betamax* case is unique because of the circumstances of its origin and the strategic political decision to let the matter of timeshifting be decided by a court of law, instead of going through the political process of adding a specific exemption into the statute. On may wonder why—carried by the tidal waves created by the *Williams & Wilkins* photocopying case[76] which led to the copyright exceptions regarding copying by archives and libraries finding their way into Section 108 of the 1976 Copyright Act—the legislators never chose to legislate for another novelty that was, at the time, already becoming widespread: the consumer-grade VCR. A possible explanation is offered by Paul Goldstein in his *Copyright's Highway*: that it was a matter of not upsetting the frail balance of political compromises that needed to be struck for the statute to be passed and introducing another controversial matter into the bill would risk upsetting the entire revision, prepared with great effort over the course of 15 years.[77]

Note that this was before the 1976 Act and its fair use provisions. Despite its obvious risks, a politically safer route was to simply wait, in the face of the growing

[76] *Williams & Wilkins Company v. The United States*; 487 F.2d 1345, United States Court of Claims, 1973; 203 Ct. Cl. 74, 487 F.2d 1345, affirmed by an equally divided Supreme Court on February 25, 1975.

[77] Goldstein (2003), Chap. 4 – Private copies.

popularity of home videocassette recorders, for a case that would set a due precedent. And a precedent was indeed set, after a stormy legal battle ending up in a very divided Supreme Court and an opinion that—due to the obvious lack of applicable legislation—had to be built upon the somewhat shaky grounds of fair use (but, at the same time, faced criticism for taking the easy way out).[78] This carries a certain irony: when discussing the struggle over *Betamax*, Goldstein points out that, while laws passed by Congress can be 'delicately crafted' to account for various interests and fine details of a particular matter, a precedent-setting case is a 'winner-take-all' event.[79] In other words, a deliberately open-ended and imprecise legal construct leads to the creation of case law which, by its nature and however weak a majority will end up supporting it, can only lead to a binary outcome.

Applying this optic to innovation, it would mean that, instead of a precision legal framework that could be applied to a new product, we are met with a ruling that results in either greenlighting the given conduct or product, or in an injunction wiping it off the face of the planet. On the other hand, however, *Betamax* inadvertently points out another issue with the 'precision framework' scenario: the time, effort and dedication, as well as the amount of political manoeuvring and compromises it takes for a new law to be passed (of which, from the recent European perspective, the lengthy legislative process surrounding the 2019 Copyright Directive is a fine example). Secondly, once the bill has been passed into law, the result of all this effort may become useless on the very next day, due to a new technological development which will lay bare its obsolescence (that it may likely die in the process makes for a poor consolation).

From the perspective of this analysis, however, *Sony v. Universal* remains a real-life example of the lawmakers consciously choosing not to get involved into a lengthy legal process to retroactively create a legal space for a nascent technology that defied the existing legal status quo. Instead, they chose to leave the matter to be resolved under the flexibility considerations coined in case law—and ended up prompting the birth of a landmark fair use ruling that has since become one of the pillars of the U.S. copyright system.

6.3.2 Back to Leval: The General Criteria for Creative Reuse

6.3.2.1 Overview

In 1982, before the battle of Hollywood against Sony over the Betamax VCR and fair use could find its ultimate solution, the hard-line ruling of the 9th Circuit had already sparked comments from representatives of the scholarship due to the

[78] See Chap. 3, Sect. 3.2.1.; see also See *Sony v. Universal*, dissenting opinion by Justice Blackmun, with Justice Marshall, Justice Powell, and Justice Rehnquist.

[79] Goldstein (2003), loc. cit.

questions it was asking. When offering her critique of the *Sony* case, Wendy Gordon made a mention of three general concerns nearly always underlying questions touching upon the fair use doctrine, despite it being otherwise considered an 'equitable rule of reason' and as such, eluding any attempt at coining a straightforward definition. These three considerations are:

(1) whether the defendant could appropriately purchase the desired use through the market;
(2) whether transferring control over the use to the defendant would serve public interest;
(3) whether the copyright's owner's incentives would not be substantially impaired.

During that time, the courts commonly approached the fair use analysis through the lens of what was then referred to as 'productive use', that being one appropriating the original work but being, in itself, creative (historically, this would involve reportage, biographies, criticism, parodies) and serve a function different than the work being appropriated.[80] The social benefits involved would incentivise the courts to pay less attention to such aspects as the value of the work or the productive use engaging into competition with the original.[81] Another optic was that of the test of reasonableness, which, due to its focusing on purely the factor of the 'amount taken' was criticised for its deviation from the utilitarian rationale of copyright law and its dubious value in terms of incentivising creativity.[82]

In 1990, when Pierre N. Leval published his landmark article *Toward a fair use standard*, he made note of the courts having failed to coin 'a set of governing principles or values' that would guide the interpretation of such cases, instead offering 'intuitive reactions to individual fact patterns'.[83] Importantly however, he also noted that such a set of governing principles does indeed exist within the very objectives of copyright law; one that is not a 'disorderly basket of exceptions to the rules of copyright' but a rational and integral part of copyright, essential for the achievement of its objectives.[84] These objectives, as he pointed out, have historically pertained to the stimulation of activity and progress in the arts, as well as the intellectual enrichment of the public. Ensuring that authors are duly remunerated for their work is merely means of achieving this goal, rather than the primary objective itself.[85] This, he points out, is not at all at odds with the notions offered by the British Statute of Anne of 1709 and the famous 'Encouragement of Learning'

[80]The Harvard Law Review Association (1984), p. 1399.

[81]The Harvard Law Review Association (1984), p. 1400.

[82]The Harvard Law Review Association (1984) citing Quinto v. Legal Times of Washington, Inc., So6 F. Supp. 554, 56o (D.D.C.1981) and Consumers Union of United States, Inc. v. General Signal Corp., 724 F.2d I044, I05I (2d Cir. 1983); 'The theory behind the copyright laws is that creation will be discouraged if demand can be undercut by copiers. Where the copy does not compete in any way with the original, this concern is absent.'; See Lillis (1983), p. 356.

[83]Leval (1990), p. 1107.

[84]Leval (1990), loc. cit.

[85]Leval (1990), loc. cit.

and 'Encouragement of Learned Men to compose and write useful Books'.[86] In other words, it could be said that the common root of copyright that is the Statute of Anne, however utilitarian its origin, had already formulated an objective to safeguard the creative process. This, Leval claims, in turn requires safeguards against overprotection as the creative activity is all in part derivative of already existing work.[87] In that sense, copyright exceptions—and in this case, the fair use doctrine—play an important role in protecting 'secondary creativity as a legitimate concern of copyright' and one that is not a 'bizarre, occasionally tolerated departure' from the rules of copyright.[88] On this basis, Leval offers his view of the type of use that should pass the fair use test: that of the particular use being, by its nature and purpose, transformative.

Transformative use, according to Leval, means that the secondary use must not repackage, or 'supersede the objects' of the original. Employing the reused work in a new manner, or for a new purpose, adding value to it by using it as raw material for the creation of 'new information, new aesthetics, new insights and understandings' is indeed the type of use which the fair use is meant to protect, and one that ensures that secondary creativity receives due protection. Notably, satisfying these criteria was not offered to be sufficient by itself; the court would still need to examine the remaining fair use factors and weigh them against the transformative analysis. In other words, where the amount taken, the nature of the copyrighted work and the effect on the market suggest against a finding of a use being fair, the court would still need to factor them in its analysis.

6.3.2.2 Benefits to Technological Innovation

As described in detail in Chap. 3, transformative use (commonly referred to as a doctrine in itself, despite its subsidiary character to the fair use doctrine) first applied by Leval in *Texaco*, was picked up by the Supreme Court in *Pretty Woman* and soon became the prevailing optic for examining fair use cases.[89] Its application in practice has given rise to as much benefit in resolving cases as it has caused controversy, leaving in its wake such infamous rulings as *Righthaven v. Jama*, where the transformative use approach was put on its head just to punish a copyright troll and was never reversed due to the winding up of the plaintiff.[90]

---

[86] See the Preamble to the Act for the Encouragement of Learning (Statute of Anne), 1709.

[87] Leval offers citations from Chafee (1945): 'The world goes ahead because each of us builds on the work of our predecessors.' 'A dwarf standing on the shoulders of a giant can see farther than the giant himself.' 'Progress would be stifled if the author had a complete monopoly of everything in his book.' Leval (1990).

[88] Leval (1990), p. 1109.

[89] For more details and a broad critique of this approach, see Chap. 3.

[90] See Chap. 3.

However, setting aside its popularity in the U.S. judicial reality, it is important to note that, when applying transformative use considerations to the realm of technological innovation, it is difficult not to see immediately the universal benefits that they offer. As much as they have been indirectly discussed throughout this work, it is important to recapitulate them in the summary below.

6.3.2.2.1 Existence of a Flexible Framework Able to Adapt to New Circumstances

The first major advantage lies in the very fact of the existence of a Hugenholtz-Senftleben 'escape valve'[91] within the system of copyright proper, to be used by courts when the need arises, without the need for creative interpretation of the facts of the case or of the law, sometimes seeking justification in an application of a teleological framework. The greater predictability of such a system, as postulated by some scholars[92] may take some time to arise, particularly in view of the struggles of the transformative use doctrine in the U.S. and the hell that was *Oracle v. Google*. Nonetheless, it can be said with reasonable certainty, on the basis of the *Betamax* political considerations but also the political process of updating the EU Copyright Directive, that it offers a type of efficiency in the adaptation of law of intellectual property to the changing circumstances that the continental system tied to circumscribed exceptions cannot hope to match even with the efforts of the CJEU and its departure from narrow interpretation of exceptions.

6.3.2.2.2 Protection of Creators: Transformative Use Does Not Equal Free Use

It could be argued that the chaotic application of the transformative use doctrine in the U.S. as well as its inherent means of bypassing the traditional continental system of intellectual property would mean that the introduction of a legal solution inspired by transformative use would result in the loosening of protection of intellectual property, thus stifling creativity instead of fostering it. However, no data exists that would support this view. Instead, the strong international position of the United States in the field of digital innovation seems to suggest that it is nothing if not a jurisdiction that protects the original authors against unauthorized reuse of their works.

---

[91] Hugenholtz and Senftleben (2011), p. 12.

[92] Rendas (2018).

6.3.2.2.3 Incentivising Small Innovators

It is also important to reiterate that the existence of this type of a 'safety valve' is most crucial to small innovators in the electronic tinkering subculture. Users banding together to code have no bargaining power; their power lies in their numbers and the statistical probability of coming up with something useful. However, as discussed earlier, this is also the type of creators who are the most fickle and easiest to disincentivise: working largely for non-economic motivations, an individual user with some ideas and coding abilities will not even attempt to overcome choke points such as licencing requirements; they will likely just abandon the idea and move on to a more promising perspectives, such as simply looking at another project or an evening with Fortnite.

Conversely, from the perspective of incentivising creativity, the existence of such a sui generis flexibility solution within the copyright system also unavoidably sends a signal to innovators who may count on getting a free pass for building upon the works of others, on condition that their reuse is creative enough and creates new useful value, without unreasonably harming the market for the original work, in short—when it is sufficiently transformative.

6.3.3 Room for Flexibilities in EU Law

In regard to introducing a measure of flexibility into the EU copyright framework, a number of arguments are usually raised against such a solution. A summary of those most often encountered will be offered below. It must be noted that they are all valid points and deserving of far more attention than the following summary. However, the purpose here is to point out that, in every case, the said arguments are not without flaws and have left plenty room for discussion in the literature (also, at times, had been simply abandoned by the CJEU as in the case of broad interpretation of rights and narrow interpretation of exceptions).

6.3.3.1 Exceptions to Be Interpreted Narrowly

An oft-cited rule of copyright is that rights of rightsholders are to be interpreted broadly, while copyright exceptions and limitations require a narrow interpretation. This approach is found in the recitals to Directive 2001/29/EC, noting that a 'high level of protection' of authors is required, along with case law stressing the need for a narrow construal of any exceptions and limitations to copyright, stated expressly in *Infopaq*.[93] As observed by M. Senftleben, this is a direct result of the author-centric civil law system which seeks to safeguard rights broad enough to ensure authors may

---

[93] See, e.g., C-5/08 *Infopaq*; C-325/14 *SBS Belgium*.

profit from the use of their self-expression, while barring obstacles to such exploitation. Consequently, '*civil law copyright systems recognize flexible, broad exclusive rights. Exceptions, by contrast, are defined narrowly and often interpreted restrictively*'.[94]

However, it is also true that the narrow interpretation of exceptions is a canon of legal reasoning that the CJEU has departed from on more than one occasion when faced with a prevailing rationale, such as 'ensuring the effectiveness of the exception' and permitting 'observance of the exception's purpose' (C-403/08 and C-429/08, *Premier League*).[95] In a 2016 study by Marcella Favale, Martin Kretschmer and Paul C. Torremans, undertaking an empirical analysis of CJEU case law, it was found that only around half of all examined judgments relating to copyright protection offered a broad interpretation of the rights of the owner, suggesting that the broad/narrow interpretation approach does not guide the CJEU jurisprudence at all.[96] A similar task was also undertaken in 2017 by Tito Rendas, leading to similar conclusions in regard to CJEU case law relating to technology-enabled uses.[97]

6.3.3.2 Compatibility of Fair Use with the Berne Three-Step Test

The Berne Convention three-step test, requiring that exceptions apply only in certain special cases, without affecting normal exploitation of the work and without unreasonably prejudicing the interests of the author. Traditionally, the rigidity of the test—despite its formulation in a standard-like manner—has been raised as an argument against compatibility with fair use[98] and with any means of flexibilising European copyright. This attitude was already visible in the text of the Directive 2001/29/EC which used the test as a further limitation on the already circumscribed catalogue of exceptions and is again present in Directive (EU) 2019/790, with the formulation of Recital 6.[99] However, this approach has not been left undisputed from the scholarly circles. It has been noted that the international law test should be used to 'open up'

---

[94] Senftleben (2010).

[95] For a critique of strict application of exceptions putting at risk their effective application, see Xalabarder (2012).

[96] Favale et al. (2016).

[97] Rendas (2018).

[98] On how a future WTO panel could conclude that the 'free-wheeling' fair use doctrine applied by US courts--the Supreme Court's decision in *Campbell* violates Article 9 of the Berne Convention, see Nimmer and Nimmer (1996).

[99] 'The exceptions and limitations provided for in this Directive seek to achieve a fair balance between the rights and interests of authors and other rightholders, on the one hand, and of users on the other. They can be applied only in certain special cases that do not conflict with the normal exploitation of the works or other subject matter and do not unreasonably prejudice the legitimate interests of the rightholders.' – Recital 6, Directive (EU) 2019/790 on copyright and related rights in the Digital Single Market.

the available exceptions, offering 'sufficient breathing space' for social, cultural and economic needs.[100]

As regards the alleged incompatibility of fair use with the Berne three-step test (more particularly the 'certain special cases' requirement), it should be noted that this particular issue has been analysed by the WTO Panel on United States—Section 110(5) of the US Copyright Act in 2000. Analysing the meaning of the term 'certain', the Panel noted the following:

> 6.108 The ordinary meaning of 'certain' is 'known and particularised, but not explicitly identified', 'determined, fixed, not variable; definitive, precise, exact'.111 In other words, this term means that, under the first condition, an exception or limitation in national legislation must be clearly defined. However, there is no need to identify explicitly each and every possible situation to which the exception could apply, provided that the scope of the exception is known and particularised. This guarantees a sufficient degree of legal certainty[101]

Similar considerations were also offered by the Australian Law Reform Commission in its 2014 Report on Copyright and Digital Economy[102] quoting the Munich Declaration on a Balanced Interpretation of the 'Three-Step Test' in Copyright Law, noting that:

> The Three-Step Test's restriction of limitations and exceptions to exclusive rights to certain special cases does not prevent
>
> (a) legislatures from introducing open ended limitations and exceptions, so long as the scope of such limitations and exceptions is reasonably foreseeable . . .[103]

and making the introduction of fair use its recommendation for the 1968 Copyright Act. Interestingly, some scholars have noted that the Berne framework is, in fact, more flexible than the U.S. fair use system in that it offers for more tailored analysis, rather than the 'all-or-nothing' result of a fair use case.[104]

6.3.3.3 Different Legal Traditions of Copyright (and Lack of a Reference Base in Case Law)

The origins of fair use, as coming from a legal tradition alien to continental Europe, where the rights of authors require positive legal enactment rather than stem from the bond that connects the author and their work, have long been raised as a major point of incompatibility between fair use and the continental copyright system.[105] In view

---

[100] For a broader analysis and examples of this type of application of the three-step test by national courts, see Senftleben (2010).

[101] World Trade Organization (2000). For comments on the report, see Senftleben (2006), p. 407.

[102] Australian Law Reform Commission (2013), p. 113.

[103] Geiger et al. (2010).

[104] Dworkin (2000).

[105] Senftleben (2010), p. 68.

of that, the EU approach has been criticised as an unfortunate compilation bringing together the 'worst of both worlds': using an enumerated list of allowed exceptions and then applying the by its nature open-ended fabric of the three-step test to further cap any attempts at a broadening interpretation of the closed list.[106]

In response to this, however, it should be noted that, on the basis of the jurisprudence cited earlier in this work, the practical attitudes of European national courts, but most visibly the CJEU, have been for a long time—and most certainly since *Premier League*—extending beyond the tight interpretation regime in view of other rationales, such as striking a 'fair balance', ensuring effective application of an exemption or the development of the information society.

Adopting this perspective, one could also claim that the concerns of the lack of a body of case law in the European context as raised by opponents of fair use[107] are somewhat overexaggerated. Empirical studies[108] have shown the CJEU as quite successful in shaping its own jurisprudence in the absence of a legislatively-endorsed 'safety valve' of the variety under discussion. As demonstrated earlier, in the U.S. judicial reality the manner of application of transformative use considerations, starting from the most oft-cited *Campbell*, has also been largely limited to relatively recent precedent and treated by courts of law in a highly flexible manner, keeping some of the language of the landmark fair use judgments but at the same time seeking to adjust the analysis to the circumstances of the particular case, not unlike the CJEU in some cases cited earlier.

Consequently, no valid evidence appears to remain that the incompatibility of legal traditions or the perceived lack of a body of case law would indeed lead to a loosening of copyright protection, were a flexible exception to be established; particularly given that the legislative safeguards such as the required 'high level of protection' for authors would still remain in place.

References

Arrow KJ (1962) Economic welfare and the allocation of resources to invention. In: Nelson RR (ed) The rate and direction of inventive activities. Princeton University Press, pp 609–626

Australian Law Reform Commission (2013) Copyright and the Digital Economy (ALRC Report 122). Commonwealth of Australia 2013. Available at https://www.alrc.gov.au/wp-content/uploads/2019/08/final_report_alrc_122_2nd_december_2013_.pdf. Accessed 3 Sept 2023

Chafee Z (1945) Reflections on the law of copyright. Colum Law Rev 45:503, 5011

Dworkin G (2000) Exceptions to copyright exclusivity: is fair use consistent with Article 9.2 Berne and the new international order. Int Intellect Prop Law Policy 4:66-1-66-22

Favale M, Kretschmer M, Torremans PLC (2016) Is there a EU Copyright Jurisprudence? An empirical analysis of the workings of the European Court of Justice. Mod Law Rev 79(1):31–75

[106] Senftleben (2010), p. 69.

[107] See e.g. Federation of European Publishers (2011).

[108] See Favale et al. (2016), Rendas (2018).

Federation of European Publishers (2011) FEP Position Paper on a Transposition of Fair Use at EU Level – DBEI, https://dbei.gov.ie/en/Consultations/Consultations-files/Publishing-Ireland-FEP-Paper-on-Fair-Use.pdf. Accessed 3 Sept 2023

Fisher WW (2001) Theories of Intellectual Property. In: Munzer S (ed) New Essays in the legal and political theory of property. Cambridge University Press, Cambridge

Geiger C, Hilty R, Griffiths J, Suthersanen U (2010) Declaration a balanced interpretation of the "Three-Step Test" in copyright law. JIPITEC 1:119 para 1

Goldstein P (2003) Copyright's highway: from Gutenberg to the Celestial Jukebox. Stanford Law and Politics, Stanford

Gordon WJ (1982) Fair use as market failure: a structural and economic analysis of the Betamax case and its predecessors. Colum Law Rev 82:1600. Archived in OpenBU at https://hdl.handle.net/2144/22971. Accessed 5 Nov 2021

Hitch CJ (1958) The Character of Research and Development in a Competitive Economy, The RAND Corporation, May 1958

Hugenholtz PB, Senftleben M (2011) Fair use in Europe: In Search of Flexibilities. SSRN Electronic Journal. https://doi.org/10.2139/ssrn.1959554

Landes WM, Posner RA (1989) An economic analysis of copyright law. J Legal Stud 18:325

Leval PN (1990) Toward a fair use standard. Harv Law Rev 103, 105, 1105

Lillis MA (ed) (1983) Decisions of the United States courts involving copyright. Copyright Office Bulletin No. 47. Library of Congress, Washington

Maduro MP (2007) Interpreting European law - judicial adjudication in a context of constitutional pluralism. Eur J Legal Stud, 2007, 1, 2, Florence, Italy

Mandic D (2011) Resolving the conundrum between copyright and technology. WIPO working paper, http://www.wipo.int/edocs/mdocs/mdocs/en/wipo_ipr_ge_11/wipo_ipr_ge_11_topic2-related2.pdf. Accessed 3 Sept 2023

Nimmer MB, Nimmer D (1996) Nimmer on Copyright. Matthew Bender Elite Products, LexisNexis

Posner RA (1992) When Is Parody Fair Use? J Legal Stud 21, 67, 73

Rendas T (2018) Copyright, Technology and the CJEU: An Empirical Study. International Review of Intellectual Property and Competition Law 153. Available at SSRN: https://ssrn.com/abstract=3051197

Senftleben M (2006) Towards a horizontal standard for limiting intellectual property rights? – WTO panel reports shed light on the three-step test in copyright law and related tests in patent and trademark law. Int Rev Intellect Prop Compet Law 37

Senftleben M (2010) The international three-step test. A model provision for EC fair use legislation JIPITEC 1:67(1)

Sganga C (2015) EU copyright law between property and fundamental rights: a proposal to connect the dots. In: Caso R, Giovanella F (eds) Balancing copyright law in the digital age. Springer, Berlin, Heidelberg

Sganga C (2018) Propertizing European Copyright. History, challenges and opportunities. Edward Elgar Publishing, Cheltenham-Northampton MA

Spedicato G (2015) Online exhaustion and the boundaries of interpretation. In: Caso R, Giovanella F (eds) Balancing copyright law in the digital age – comparative perspectives. Springer, Heidelberg

The Harvard Law Review Association (1984) The Parody defense to copyright infringement: productive fair use after "Betamax". Harv Law Rev 97(6)

World Trade Organization (2000) United States – Section 110(5) of the US Copyright Act. Report of the Panel. WT/DS160/R, available at https://www.wto.org/english/tratop_e/dispu_e/1234da.pdf. Accessed 3 Sept 2023

Xalabarder R (2012) Spanish Supreme Court Rules in favour of Google search engine... and a flexible reading of copyright statutes? JIPITEC 3:162. https://www.jipitec.eu/issues/jipitec-3-2-2012/3445/xalabarder.pdf. Accessed 3 Sept 2023

Chapter 7
Conclusions

7.1 Calculating Returns or Paving the Way?

When discussing legislative choke points to digital innovation, it is important to note that there is one more level of convergence between those potentially affecting corporate innovation and grassroots collaborative projects involving networked individuals: in both cases, the benefit from eliminating such obstacles is not quantifiable. Just as one cannot, with any certainty at least, make predictions on the quantity (or quality) of innovative projects to be developed within the coming year, how many of them will be commercialised[1] and to what extent this will affect future developments,[2] it appears similarly impossible to try and quantify the potential increase in GDP, the well-being of society or the behaviour of the stock market due to anticipated technological innovation in the wake of any given legislative change. In consequence, it cannot be said with any certainty how big an improvement Europe would see in the area of technological innovation should it choose to add a measure of flexibility to its copyright law. Applying this framing to innovation is misleading given the nature of the problem under discussion; for want of a better comparison, the situation can be likened to that of the government in a country that is

[1]Despite its risks, commercialization of results some cannot be ruled out nor should it be precluded; as discussed in Chaps. 5 and 6, just as digital innovation can transition towards proprietisation that would hinder further development, a privately developed project may also be rendered unable to go public for reasons of copyright. In an ideal scenario, both types of risks should be addressed by flexible legislation.

[2]Particularly given that the involvement of large business investment may also come with the arrival of questionable ethics (as seen in the 'AI data laundering' examples in Chap. 5). If unethical behaviors lead to regulatory or enforcement action resulting in shutting down the initiative altogether, this might add to the list of perils that the commercialization of results can bring on board, aside from such risks as evidenced by the *Oracle* case.

K. Drazewski, *Copyright as a Constraint on Creating Technological Value*, Law, Governance and Technology Series 63,
https://doi.org/10.1007/978-3-031-51276-6_7

hungry for quality road infrastructure pinning the decision to build roads on whether it can be guaranteed how much money will toll fees bring into the treasury.

Human creativity tends to evade precise measurements, even though it can be statistically (and reasonably) expected to occur, given the right circumstances. Still, these will merely be predictions based on a general predilection of lazy individuals to create solutions which make life easier, or of creative ones to try and develop their ideas into projects, or of tech companies constantly looking for ways to create new technological value and gain a competitive edge. In this sense, one should differentiate between saying (with no knowledge of any such project already being under way): *A new type of social media platform will definitely premiere within the next two years,* and saying *I reasonably expect someone should soon come up with a new idea for social media platforms.* Technically speaking, both predictions may be true, but while the first can make a great newspaper heading, only the latter can be voiced with any degree of certainty.

Similarly, no quantifiable predictions can be made regarding how the availability of a fair use defence in copyright cases would affect the competitiveness of the European economy. However, there is a difference between expecting a certain volume of innovative projects to arise, and the removal of that unnecessary obstacles to their operation and growth; those legislative choke points where, save for a creative intervention of the judge (as seen e.g. in the *Vorschaubilder* cases), the door would become shut on a useful solution that does not unreasonably prejudice anyone's interests and does not affect normal exploitation of the original work. In other words, just as few predicted the rapid explosion of generative AI models in the early 2020s, I cannot predict that within one or two years someone will come up with the idea e.g. of a database bringing together voice-recognized dialogue lists of all movies and documentaries in history and offering an indexing and search function; I can, however, say that I would count on projects of such magnitude having a fighting chance of being developed also in the European copyright environment. After all, rather than resting on a justification on the expected returns from tolls, building motorways should be thought of in the context of strategic development of the entire country.

7.2 Flexibility Has Many Faces, But Fair Use Addresses the Particular Nature of Software

It is important to note that adding a measure of flexibility to European Union copyright *acquis* can take other forms than simply involving a generic 'fair use transplant'[3] where an open norm would be added to supplement the catalogue of

[3] Yu (2017).

existing exceptions, or perhaps replace some of them due to a systemic overlap[4] with the proposed open-ended norm. A particularly cautious approach has been offered by Hugenholtz and Senftleben since their landmark paper *Fair use in Europe: in search for flexibilities*.[5] The authors noted that a considerable level of flexibility could be achieved by literal transposition of the entire catalogue of exceptions of the Infosoc Directive into national law, together with the Berne three-step test, thus setting up a semi-open framework that would be nearly as flexible as the U.S. fair use system. It should perhaps be noted here that Senftleben has been involved in historic analysis of the first Berne pre-requisite (the 'certain special cases') and has advocated for not interpreting the 'certain' parameter as if disallowing open-ended exception systems, such as that of fair use.[6] In the 2017 paper *Flexible Copyright: Can EU Author's Right Accommodate Fair Use?*, Hugenholtz rephrased his cautious position on the matter, noting that there were risks involved in introducing an open norm into the EU's copyright system which has traditionally been based on circumscribed norms and exceptions. Instead, a different path could be considered and that is to introduce '*a measure of flexibility alongside the existing structure of well-defined limitations and exceptions*' as means to achieve a '*better fit the European tradition of author's right, combining the advantages of legal certainty and technological neutrality.*'[7] Still, assuming for a moment the luxury of disregarding the different copyright traditions (for instance, on grounds of the last two decades of U.S. tech-related copyright cases seeming indeed as a 'learning-by-doing phase', as demonstrated earlier in this work) from the perspective of software innovation, there are aspects to its nature that seem to render fair use (and transformative use, for that matter) the seemingly best fitting option. These will be considered below.

As it was again brought to the attention of the public at the time of Oracle's fight with Google over the protection of APIs, there is a functional dimension to the protection of copyright that renders the matter of its protection less straightforward than that of a typical literary work. The CJEU tried to navigate around these matters in *SAS v. WPI*, stating that '*neither the functionality of a computer program nor the programming language and the format of data files used in a computer program in order to exploit certain of its functions constitute a form of expression of that program and, as such, are not protected by copyright* [...]'; still, if such elements were included in a program manual, their reproduction would constitute '*an infringement of that right in the latter manual*' if the criterion of originality has

[4]Australian Law Reform Commission (2014) Ch. 5. The Fair Exception, p. 159, https://www.alrc.gov.au/publication/copyright-and-the-digital-economy-alrc-report-122/5-the-fair-use-exception/. Accessed 03 September 2023.

[5]Hugenholtz and Senftleben (2011).

[6]See Senftleben (2010). For an analysis of the open-endedness of the Berne test itself, see Geiger et al. (2014).

[7]Hugenholtz (2017).

been met. This has been criticized as puzzling and short on policy;[8] still, the conundrum appears to be a mere consequence of the fact that the court needed to combine fire with water: to respect both the protection of software as a literary work,[9] yet still leave some leeway for the unprotectable functional aspects of software, and, lastly, look again at those functional aspects where they were embodied in yet another literary work (the manual) assuming the criterion of originality had been met.

In the *Oracle* proceedings, a similar clash of conflicting interpretations has ultimately led to the United States Court of Appeals for the Federal Circuit ruling, in 2014, that APIs were, indeed, copyrightable. In doing so, the Court still left open the window for Google's partial reuse of the 37 interfaces to be defensible as fair use, a matter eventually resolved by the Supreme Court in 2021.[10]

It is a commonly encountered fear that the introduction of a fair use defence would inherently weaken the fabric of EU copyright. If anything, the *Oracle* case should be seen as proof that this is not the case: by analysing the first and second fair use factors, this being the character of the use and the nature of the copyrighted work, the court is granted considerable leeway to both:

(1) account for the fact that software is indeed different from other creations of intellect, and as such examining a case of reuse of code will require a different approach than i.e. a musical, visual work or one of literature;
(2) examine whether the character of the use is deserving of passing the test of relying on the source material to create new meanings, aesthetics or understandings; simply put, whether it is indeed transformative.

Were *Oracle v. Google* to be reduced to one major takeaway, it would be fair use's capability of a 'context check' as proposed by SCOTUS in the 2021 ruling, and that the very nature of fair use appears to match well the nature of judicial considerations over partial replication of certain characteristics of software—in this case even without tackling the interoperability-based justifications as proposed earlier in the case. From this perspective, the unease about a general loosening of copyright protection in the wake of introducing an open-ended exception should be seen as overly cautious; given the long continental tradition, national courts of the EU can hardly be expected to jump at the new opportunity and start exonerating derivative works *en masse*. What is more likely, they would see it as a welcome simplification of a work they had already been engaging in while looking for flexibilities where the nature of the case and the applicable legislation suggested they were necessary.

[8] Sookman (2012).

[9] See Article 4 of the WIPO Copyright Treaty, Article 10 of the WTO TRIPS Agreement and Article 1 of the European Council Directive 91/250/EEC on the Legal Protection of Computer Programs for a consistent qualification of software as literary work subject to copyright protection.

[10] See the discussion in Chap. 4.

7.3 Will a Network of Coders Benefit from Proportionality?

It has been noted that, over the recent years, the CJEU has achieved considerable flexibility where copyright law was lacking in this respect. This has been commented upon as finding an 'expressed route' for harmonization of the EU copyright acquis, which had so far been suffering fragmentation and inconsistencies due to the having been led by the subsidiarity principle.[11] An argument can certainly be made that, by doing this, the CJEU has been laying foundation for a new goal-oriented understanding of copyright law in the EU; perhaps even with some potential for inspiring national courts into applying a similar rationale. It is therefore tempting to ask—could this be seen as a viable alternative to introducing a statutory open-ended flexible exception?

In the context of tackling this particular question, the present analysis benefits from having its perspective narrowed to that of clearing the way for innovation, particularly of the non-corporate origin as described earlier. Looking from the perspective of a group of willing coders working on a project, what matters—aside from their blatant disregard towards any copyright considerations, which is the most likely—is that solution which can be applied at as early a stage as possible. In other words, from a very practical perspective, the fair use defence benefits from being available immediately; the principle of proportionality will likely be applied no earlier than by the Court of Justice of the European Union, which can be reasonably expected to take a long enough time to make sure there is nothing left both of the project and of its participants. In other words, as long as we are looking at the matter of providing incentives to innovators, the perspective of a fair use defence can be reasonably expected to have a much stronger impact than the faint hope of the CJEU continuing to carve out its policy amidst inflexible legislation.

This approach could be criticised for being overly skewed towards the agenda of supporting grassroots initiatives run by individuals whose productivity cannot be quantified or even reasonably predicted within a specific timeframe. To this one could respond in a way that summarises the entire argument: both the history of personal computing and the still-present grassroots efforts at creating new technological value seem to be evidence enough that non-corporate, non-commercial projects have a considerable power, even if it is spread among countless forums, discussion groups with often no clearly visible decision-making center.

Still, one more aspect should be noted. In a world where Big Tech tends to grow even bigger and more concentrated, such online communities may be end up as the only line of defence against the world of digital creation and innovation market becoming dominated by Silicon Valley giants who can always afford to litigate and more importantly, can also claim fair use with a growing body of case law behind it—and if everything else fails, settle out of court as Google did in France, behind closed doors. Ultimately then it is as the Supreme Court put it in the 2021 *Oracle* ruling: it is about making a choice on who should hold the key to future creativity.

[11] Xalabarder (2016).

References

Geiger C, Gervais DJ and Senftleben M (2014) The three-step-test revisited: how to use the test's flexibility in national copyright law. Am Univ Int Law Rev, 29, 3, 581–626. Available at SSRN: https://ssrn.com/abstract=2356619 or https://doi.org/10.2139/ssrn.2356619

Hugenholtz PB (2017) Flexible copyright: can EU author's right accommodate fair use? In: Okediji RL (ed) Copyright law in an age of limitations and exceptions. Cambridge University Press, New York, pp 275–291

Hugenholtz PB, Senftleben M (2011) Fair use in Europe: In Search of Flexibilities. SSRN Electronic Journal. https://doi.org/10.2139/ssrn.1959554

Senftleben M (2010) The international three-step test. A model provision for EC fair use legislation JIPITEC 1:67(1)

Sookman B (2012) So yo EU copyright acquis, which had so far been suffering fragmentation and inconsistencies u want to protect computer programs by copyright, the Oracle v Google and SAS v WPL cases (Updated). Via Barrysookman.com, http://www.barrysookman.com/2012/06/03/so-you-want-to-protect-computer-programs-by-copyright-oracle-v-google-and-the-sas-v-wpl-cases/. Accessed 3 Sept 2023

Xalabarder R (2016) The Role of the CJEU in Harmonizing EU Copyright Law. IIC 47: 635. https://doi.org/10.1007/s40319-016-0509-2. Online at https://link.springer.com/content/pdf/10.1007/s40319-016-0509-2.pdf. Accessed 3 Sept 2023

Yu PK (2017) Customizing fair use transplants. Laws, Vol. 7, Issue 1, Article 9, 2018; Texas A&M University School of Law Legal Studies Research Paper No. 17-78. Available at SSRN: https://ssrn.com/abstract=3052158. Accessed 11 Dec 2021